THIRD

REALIZING WESTWARD

AMERICAN CHARACTER AND COWBOY MYTHOLOGY

⚞ STEPHEN P. COOK ⚟

Custom Publishing

New York   Boston   San Francisco
London   Toronto   Sydney   Tokyo   Singapore   Madrid
Mexico City   Munich   Paris   Cape Town   Hong Kong   Montreal

Pearson
Custom Publishing
is a division of

www.pearsonhighered.com

ISBN 10: 0-558-22475-X
ISBN 13: 978-0-558-22475-2

Copyright Acknowledgements

CONTENTS

Introduction   vii
Why This Book Matters (Especially Now)

THE SEEDBED   1

From "What Is an American?"   3
Hector St. John de Crèvecoeur

The Significance of the Frontier in American History   7
Frederick Jackson Turner

Introduction to *Looking Far West: The Search for
the American West in History, Myth, and Literature*   11
Frank Bergon and Zeese Papanikolas

Open Space and American Culture   23
Stephen Cook

Study Questions and Suggested Essay Topics   31

AMERICAN HEROIC MYTHOLOGY   37

The Altruistic Hero   39
Stephen Cook

Individualism   45
Robert Bellah

Savior in the Saddle: The Sagebrush Testament   51
Michael T. Marsden

Wade in the Water: Wyatt Earp's Transformation in *Tombstone*   59
Stephen Cook

The Matrix   65
Stephen Cook

Study Questions and Suggested Essay Topics   67

THE REEL WEST   71

The Western   73
Thomas Schatz

West of Everything: The Inner Life of Westerns   97
Jane Tompkins

Gunsmoke and Mirrors   109
Richard Slotkin

Material and Metaphorical—Horse and Rider in *Lonely Are the Brave*   115
Stephen Cook

Study Questions and Suggested Essay Topics   121

THE POST-WESTERN WESTERN   125

Variations on a Theme by Crèvecoeur   129
W. Stegner

The American West and the Burden of Belief   141
N. Scott Momaday

The New West in John Sayles' *Lone Star*   155
Stephen Cook

West of the Western   161
Stephen Cook

Study Questions and Suggested Essay Topics   165

The 21st Century Cowboy: From Owen Wister and Teddy Roosevelt to Barack Obama and a Contemporary Progressive Movement   169
Stephen Cook

The Cowboy as Symbol of the American Middle Class   173
Heather Cox Richardson

American Exceptionalism   179
Stephen Cook

Study Questions and Suggested Essay Topics   185

INTRODUCTION TO
REALIZING WESTWARD: AMERICAN CHARACTER AND COWBOY MYTHOLOGY
OR
WHY THIS BOOK MATTERS (ESPECIALLY NOW)

> The American mentality is a cowboy mentality—if you confront them . . . they will react in an extreme manner. In other words, America with all its resources and establishments will shrink into a cowboy when irritated successfully. They will then elevate you, and this will satisfy the Muslim longing for a leader who can successfully challenge the West. (al-Faqih qtd by Fallows 71)

In the September 2006 issue of *The Atlantic*, James Fallows references an interview with Saad al-Faqih, a Saudi exile and reformist, who has long observed Osama bin Laden and his key strategist Ayman al-Zawahiri. According to al-Faqih, "Zawahiri impressed upon bin Laden the importance of understanding the American mentality" (Fallows 71), likely using words close to the ones paraphrased by al-faqih in the quote above. The Fallows article followed on the heels of the July 17th issue of *Time* which had as its cover story "The End to Cowboy Diplomacy." The article by Mike Allen and Romesh Ratnesar details the way in which George W. Bush was forced by circumstances to alter a unilateral pursuit of an unprecedented realignment of power in the Middle East as well as to abandon the Wild West rhetoric (Osama bin-Laden Wanted Dead or Alive) and iconography (photos of the bullet-riddled corpses of desperadoes) accompanying that quest.

Any aware observer of the current geopolitical scene has to wonder if our avowed enemies know Americans better than we know ourselves. Certainly, the question must arise whether al-Qaeda set a trap calculated to take advantage of the American penchant for overreaction. At a minimum, it is an odd coincidence that Bush and bin-Laden collided and on such a grand stage.

In Bush, we see a president who gained the White House by following the Karl Rove strategy of moving to Crawford, Texas—a place perfectly suited to his laconic, "yep" and "nope" way of speaking—and buying a ranch and pick up truck, thereby taking on the Populist trappings of our most heroic figure, the cowboy. Rove's brilliant strategy allowed Bush to so effectively shed his Eastern, prep school, Yale, elitist origins that conventional wisdom says he is a native Texan.

In bin-Laden, we have a Saudi who grew up watching American Westerns, a man who forsook a moneyed and privileged life for a cowboy existence of traveling on horses in a vast wilderness, sleeping on the ground, and pursuing a highly mobile fight on behalf of everyday people whom he sees as oppressed. Except for the clothing he wears, bin-Laden could be a character from *The Magnificent Seven*.

Pundits are fond of discussing the American conflict with radical Islamists as a war of ideologies, and while that is true to some degree, it may very well be even more accurate that we are involved in a collision between two competing interpretations of the same mythology.

The purpose of this slender anthology is to provide an overview of the development of the American mentality to which al-Zawahiri referred in the analysis he presented to bin-Laden (and it was probably an argument well received by a man already quite familiar with American Heroic Mythology as presented by one of America's few organic art forms, the Western). Most likely, al-Zawahiri had an easier time of it than I do at the beginning of each semester. For over ten years, I have taught a composition class with this theme: "American Character and Cowboy Mythology," and at the start of each semester when I explain the ideas and symbols that will be a focus for the class, I see many confused and disappointed faces. Students have muttered, "I can't believe this—a class in cowboys and Indians" as well as other words and phrases I can't print. It's true that while we do look at cowboys and Indians (although not in the clichéd ways students expect), the class is so much more, for the controlling principle is to examine American Culture through the microscope of the mythological West.

Thus, I establish a connection, and even the most reluctant student becomes receptive to the material. Let's face it: most of us have a fascination with ourselves and how we came to be who we are. Culture is a huge factor in shaping us—very few people question this. Nobody lives in a vacuum, not even a hermit on the highest hill because it is culture he is rejecting. Surely, advertisers believe in the formative power of culture since they spend billions shaping attitudes, creating needs and desires, and convincing us to adopt a "look" or a "style."

However, this text moves beyond the temporary fashions of popular culture into a discussion of many of the values we Americans live by, sometimes admirable, sometimes not, but certainly ones that define us. The ethos of the cowboy, especially as it is presented in film, exemplifies so many quintessentially American values, for example, courage, physical prowess, independence, commitment to democratic ideals, and an innate sense of justice expressed in commonly-accepted codes of conduct and applied against those who contravene these codes. The prototypical American is often seen as an outdoorsman/frontiersman/cowboy. Presidents like Andrew Jackson, Abraham Lincoln, Teddy Roosevelt, Ronald Reagan, and of course, George W. Bush come to mind as representative of this archetype. If presidential history is not your thing, think of an action hero from popular culture, and you have a heroic figure modeled after the mythological cowboy. For example, Clint Eastwood and Viggo Mortensen are actors who move comfortably between westerns and action movies, for they portray essentially the same character regardless of the genre, a figure many Americans embrace but one that others regard with distaste or horror. There is certainly a downside to the myth, and the critics of the iconic cowboy see him as violent, arrogant, racist, and misogynistic, in short, embodying all of the qualities of the Eurocentric male colonialist who stole this land from its rightful owners. However, as is so often the case in a hybrid culture, a rational, even-handed analysis of this American symbol will reveal that the cowboy figure exemplifies, to some extent, the negative qualities above as well as the heroic qualities I list.

In *Realizing Westward: American Character and Cowboy Mythology* are analytical essays to give undergraduates an overview of how the American experience allowed for the creation of an American "type" and to reveal the ways in which the Western refines and gives expression to this figure, codifying an American mythology, one that continues to influence us deeply 130 years after the heyday of the drovers who took part in real cattle drives.

Especially today, an understanding of Cowboy Mythology is critical, for it is rooted in premises, conscious and unconscious, that guide our decisions. Certainly, the 2008 elections presented Americans with some groundbreaking options. The direction we overwhelmingly chose will determine how the American character will express itself nationally and globally in upcoming years, and it is my hope that students who encounter this text will be prepared to enter the debate over those choices at hand.

A Word about *Realizing Westward* and Writing across the Curriculum

Many universities increasingly emphasize writing across the curriculum, and *Realizing Westward* lies squarely within that movement. For example, one may examine the essays within this text through the microscope of many disciplines: American Studies, History, Cultural Studies, Religion, Women's Studies, Public Policy, Anthropology, Film Studies, Geography, Native American Studies, Economics, Biology and Humanities, for example.

Furthermore, the study questions at the end of each chapter invite students to approach topics employing the rhetorical approaches of the disciplines listed above and others. However, since many of the undergraduates for whom I have written and edited *Realizing Westward* are not yet fully immersed in the conventions of their majors, some of the study questions will simply ask students to *begin* learning ways of presenting ideas as practiced within each discipline.

And in all cases, including that of undeclared students, the questions and assignments will ask writers to practice the basic skills of argumentation: thesis, support, evidence, coordination, and making sense on a sentence-level. Practice and discipline in these elements of composition can only make students better writers, more prepared for whatever specialty they choose, and more likely to be hired, retained, and promoted in the private sector.

THE SEEDBED

> . . . Such as we were we gave ourselves outright . . .
> To the Land vaguely realizing westward,
> But still unstoried, artless, unenhanced,
> Such as she was, such as she would become.

Robert Frost—"The Gift Outright"

In this section are four essays intended to give readers historical background on the early development of our hybrid American culture and how it began to evolve from encounters with geography and indigenous people by a loose confederation of outsiders possessing dreams, ambition, energy, and an overarching greed. Students will see how Native and European cultures initially combined to create the frontiersman, the predecessor to the cowboy, in "What is an American?" by Hector St. John de Crèvecoeur, a Frenchman who observed and wrote about early American society.

The following essay, "The Significance of the Frontier in American History," an address in 1893 at the World's Fair by historian Frederick Jackson Turner, had little impact initially. However, many contemporary historians consider it a seminal document in what has become the field of American Studies. Turner's thesis is that the census report of 1890 marked the end of the frontier and that our journey from East to West (as well as away from Europe) created certain distinctive qualities in Americans. Other scholars argue that Turner's thesis is too reductive and too simplistic for such a large and diverse country, but to some degree, their objections are moot. The fact that Turner's ideas are still debated more than one hundred years after his speech confirms the power of his observations.

In the introduction to *Looking Far West: The Search for the American West in History, Myth, and Literature*, Frank Bergon and Zeese Papanikolas provide an extraordinary analysis of the mythology of the American West, its historical roots, and the ways in which it has been (and continues to be) expressed in a variety of American art forms. The last essay, "Open Space and American Culture," examines the legacy of physical space and distance Americans enjoy and how we continue to interact with it today. Finally, study questions for Michael Mann's film *The Last of the Mohicans* aid students in creating an artistic interpretation of the early American frontier and the people who inhabited it.

Certainly, it is true that our movement west (and into its vast terrain) was one of the most important events in American history. There are others—the Revolution, the codifying of rights in our Constitution, the Civil War, the Great Depression, two World Wars, and the Civil Rights Movement—but there can be no disputing the reality of how the Western diaspora focused the brawling energy of a vigorous people, giving that dynamic force room to move, to destroy, and to create again.

And in that movement are the roots of a national character, the values of a people unafraid to challenge a frontier or to cross borders, and the heroic mythology of a restless, powerful culture.

From *Letters from an American Farmer*

From "What Is an American?"

Hector St. John de Crèvecoeur

Men are like plants; the goodness and flavour of the fruit proceeds from the peculiar soil and exposition in which they grow. We are nothing but what we derive from the air we breathe, the climate we inhabit, the government we obey, the system of religion we profess, and the nature of our employment. Here you will find but few crimes; these have acquired as yet no root among us. I wish I were able to trace all my ideas; if my ignorance prevents me from describing them properly, I hope I shall be able to delineate a few of the outlines, which are all I propose.

Those who live near the sea, feed more on fish than on flesh, and often encounter that boisterous element. This renders them more bold and enterprising; this leads them to neglect the confined occupations of the land. They see and converse with a variety of people; their intercourse with mankind becomes extensive. The sea inspires them with a love of traffic, a desire of transporting produce from one place to another; and leads them to a variety of resources which supply the place of labour. Those who inhabit the middle settlements, by far the most numerous, must be very different; the simple cultivation of the earth purifies them, but the indulgences of the government, the soft remonstrances of religion, the rank of independent freeholders, must necessarily inspire them with sentiments, very little known in Europe among people of the same class. What do I say? Europe has no such class of men; the early knowledge they acquire, the early bargains they make, give them a great degree of sagacity. As freemen they will be litigious; pride and obstinacy are often the cause of law suits; the nature of our laws and governments may be another. As citizens it is easy to imagine, that they will carefully read the newspapers, enter into every political disquisition, freely blame or censure governors and others. As farmers they will be careful and anxious to get as much as they can, because what they get is their own. As northern men they will love the chearful cup. As Christians, religion curbs them not in their opinions; the general indulgence leaves every one to think for themselves in spiritual matters; the laws inspect our actions, our thoughts are left to God. Industry, good living, selfishness, litigiousness, country politics, the pride of free-men, religious indifference, are their characteristics. If you recede still farther from the sea, you will come into more modern settlements; they exhibit the same strong lineaments, in a ruder appearance. Religion seems to have still less influence, and their manners are less improved.

Now we arrive near the great woods, near the last inhabited districts; there men seem to be placed still farther beyond the reach of government, which in some measure leaves them to themselves. How can it pervade every corner; as they were driven there by misfortunes, necessity of beginnings, desire of acquiring large tracks of land, idleness, frequent want of oeconomy, ancient debts; the re-union of such people does not afford a very pleasing spectacle. When discord, want of unity and friendship; when either drunkenness or idleness prevail in such remote districts; contention, inactivity, and wretchedness must ensue. There are not the same remedies to these evils as in a long established community. The few magistrates they have, are in general little better than the rest; they are often in a perfect state of war; that of man against man, sometimes decided by blows, sometimes by means of the law; that of man against every wild inhabitant of these venerable woods, of which they are come to dispossess them. There men appear to be no better than carnivorous animals of a superior rank, living on the flesh of wild animals when they can catch them, and when they are not able, they subsist on grain. He who would wish to see America in its proper light, and have a true idea of its feeble beginnings and barbarous rudiments, must visit our extended line of frontiers where the last settlers dwell, and where he may see the first labours of settlement, the mode of clearing the earth, in all their different appearances; where men are wholly left dependent on their native tempers, and on the spur of uncertain industry, which often fails when not sanctified by the efficacy of a few moral rules. There, remote from the power of example, and check of shame, many families exhibit the most hideous parts of our society. They are a kind of forlorn hope, preceding by ten or twelve years the most respectable army of veterans which come after them. In that space, prosperity will polish some, vice and the law will drive off the rest, who uniting again with others like themselves will recede still farther; making room for more industrious people, who will finish their improvements, convert the loghouse into a convenient habitation, and rejoicing that the first heavy labours are finished, will change in a few years that hitherto barbarous country into a fine fertile, well regulated district. Such is our progress, such is the march of the Europeans toward the interior parts of this continent. In all societies there are off-casts; this impure part serves as our precursors or pioneers; my father himself was one of that class, but he came upon honest principles, and was therefore one of the few who held fast; by good conduct and temperance, he transmitted to me his fair inheritance, when not above one in fourteen of his contemporaries had the same good fortune.

———

But to return to our back settlers. I must tell you, that there is something in the proximity of the woods, which is very singular. It is with men as it is with the plants and animals that grow and live in the forests; they are entirely different from those that live in the plains. I will candidly tell you all my thoughts but you are not to expect that I shall advance any reasons. By living in or near the woods, their actions are regulated by the wildness of the neighbourhood. The deer often come to eat their grain, the wolves to destroy their sheep, the bears to kill their hogs, the foxes to catch their poultry. This surrounding hostility, immediately puts the gun into their hands; they watch these animals, they kill some; and thus by defending their property, they soon become professed hunters; this is the progress; once hunters, farewell to the plough. The chase renders them ferocious, gloomy, and unsociable; a hunter wants no neighbour, he rather hates them, because he dreads the competition. In a little time their success in the woods makes them neglect their tillage. They trust to the natural fecundity of the earth, and therefore do little; carelessness in fencing, often exposes what little they sow to destruction; they are not at home to watch; in order therefore to make up the deficiency, they go oftener to the woods. That new mode of life brings along with it a new set of manners, which I cannot easily describe. These new manners being grafted on the old stock, produce a strange sort of lawless profligacy, the impressions of which are indelible. The manners of the Indian natives are respectable, compared with this European medley. Their wives and children live in sloth and inactivity; and having no proper pursuits, you may judge what education the latter receive. Their tender minds have nothing else to contemplate but the example of their parents; like them they grow up a mongrel breed, half civilized, half savage, except nature stamps on them some constitutional propensities. That rich, that voluptuous sentiment is gone that struck them so forcibly; the possession of their freeholds no longer conveys to their minds the same pleasure and pride. To all these reasons you must add, their lonely situation, and you cannot imagine what an effect on manners the great distances they live from each other has. . . !

The Significance of the Frontier in American History

Frederick Jackson Turner

In a recent bulletin of the Superintendent of the Census for 1890 appear these significant words: "Up to and including 1880 the country had a frontier of settlement, but at present the unsettled area has been so broken into by isolated bodies of settlement that there can hardly be said to be a frontier line, in the discussion of its extent, its westward movement, etc., it can not therefore, any longer have a place in the census reports." This brief official statement marks the closing of a great historic movement. Up to our own day American history has been in a large degree the history of the colonization of the Great West. The existence of an area of free land, its continuous recession, and the advance of American settlement westward, explain American development.

Behind institutions, behind constitutional forms and modifications, lie the vital forces that call these organs into life and shape them to meet changing conditions. The peculiarity of American institutions is, the fact that they have been compelled to adapt themselves to the changes of an expanding people—to the changes involved in crossing a continent, in winning a wilderness, and in developing at each area of this progress out of the primitive economic and political conditions of the frontier into the complexity of city life. Said Calhoun in 1817, "We are great, and rapidly—I was about to say fearfully—growing!" So saying, he touched the distinguishing feature of American life. All peoples show development. . . . In the case of most nations, however, the development has occurred in a limited area; and if the nation has expanded, it has met other growing peoples whom it has conquered. But in the case of the United States we have a different phenomenon. Limiting our attention to the Atlantic coast, we have the familiar phenomenon of the evolution of institutions in a limited area, such as the rise of representative government; the differentiation of simple colonial governments into complex organs; the progress from primitive industrial society, without division of labor, up to manufacturing civilization. But we have in addition to this a recurrence of the process of evolution in each western area reached in the process of expansion. Thus American development has exhibited not merely advance along a single line, but a return to primitive conditions on a continually advancing frontier line, and a new development for that area. American social development has been continually beginning over again on the frontier. This perennial rebirth, this fluidity of American life, this expansion westward with its new opportunities, its continuous touch with the simplicity of primitive society, furnish the forces dominating American character. The true point of view in the history of this nation is not the Atlantic coast, it is the great West. Even the slavery struggle, which is made so exclusive an object of attention by writers like Prof. von Hoist, occupies its important place in American history because of its relation to westward expansion.

In this advance, the frontier is the outer edge of the wave—the meeting point between savagery and civilization. Much has been written about the frontier from the point of view of border warfare and the chase, but as a field for the serious study of the economist and the historian it has been neglected.

The American frontier is sharply distinguished from the European frontier—a fortified boundary line running through dense populations. The most significant thing about the American frontier is, that it lies at the hither edge of free land. In the census reports it is treated as the margin of that settlement which has a density of two or more to the square mile. The term is an elastic one, and for our purposes does not need sharp definition. We shall consider the whole frontier belt, including the Indian country and the outer margin of the "settled area" of the census reports. This paper will make no attempt to treat the subject exhaustively; its aim is simply to call attention to the frontier as a fertile field for investigation, and to suggest some of the problems which arise in connection with it.

In the settlement of America we have to observe how European life entered the continent, and how America modified and developed that life and reacted on Europe. Our early history is the study of European germs developing in an American environment. Too exclusive attention has been paid by institutional students to the Germanic origins, too little to the American factors. The frontier is the line of most rapid and effective Americanization. The wilderness masters the colonist. It finds him a European in dress, industries, tools, modes of travel, and thought. It takes him from the railroad car and puts him in the birch canoe. It strips off the garments of civilization and arrays him in the hunting shirt and the moccasin. It puts him in the log cabin of the Cherokee and Iroquois and runs an Indian palisade around him. Before long he has gone to planting Indian corn and plowing with a sharp stick; he shouts the war cry and takes the scalp in orthodox Indian fashion. In short, at the frontier the environment is at first too strong for the man. He must accept the conditions which it furnishes, or perish, and so he fits himself into the Indian clearings and follows the Indian trails. Little by little he transforms the wilderness, but the outcome is not the old Europe, not simply the development of Germanic germs, any more than the first phenomenon was a case of reversion to the Germanic mark. The fact is, that here is a new product that is American. At first, the frontier was the Atlantic coast. It was the frontier of Europe in a very real sense. Moving westward, the frontier became more and more American. As successive terminal moraines result from successive glaciations, so each frontier leaves its traces behind it, and when it becomes a settled area the region still partakes of the frontier characteristics. Thus the advance of the frontier has meant a steady movement away from the influence of Europe, a steady growth of independence on American lines. And to study this advance, the men who grew up under these conditions, and the political, economic, and social results of it, is to study the really American part of our history.

COMPOSITE NATIONALITY

First, we note that the frontier promoted the formation of a composite nationality for the American people. The coast was preponderantly English, but the later tides of continental immigration flowed across to the free lands. This was the case from the early colonial days. The Scotch-Irish and the Palatine Germans, or "Pennsylvania Dutch," furnished the dominant element in the stock of the colonial frontier. With these peoples were also the freed indented servants, or redemptioners, who at the expiration of their time of service passed to the frontier. Governor Spottswood of Virginia writes in 1717, "The inhabitants of our frontiers are composed generally of such as have been transported hither as servants, and, being out of their time, settle themselves where land is to be taken up and that will produce the necessarys of life with little labour." Very generally these redemptioners were of non-English stock. In the crucible of the frontier the immigrants were Americanized, liberated, and fused into a mixed race, English in neither nationality nor characteristics. The process has gone on from the early days to our own. Burke and other writers in the middle of the eighteenth century believed that Pennsylvania was "threatened with the danger of being wholly foreign in language, manners, and perhaps even inclinations." The German and Scotch-Irish elements in the frontier of the South were only less great. In the middle of the present century the German element in Wisconsin was already so considerable that leading publicists looked to the creation of a German state out of the commonwealth by concentrating their colonization. Such examples teach us to beware of misinterpreting the fact that there is a common English speech in America into a belief that the stock is also English.

INTELLECTUAL TRAITS

From the conditions of frontier life came intellectual traits of profound importance. The works of travelers along each frontier from colonial days onward describe certain common traits, and these traits have, while softening down, still persisted as survivals in the place of their origin, even when a higher social organization succeeded. The result is that to the frontier the American intellect owes its striking characteristics. That coarseness and strength combined with acuteness and inquisitiveness, that practical, inventive turn of mind, quick to find expedients; that masterful grasp of material things, lacking in the artistic but powerful to effect great ends; that restless, nervous energy; that dominant individualism, working for good and for evil, and withal that buoyancy and exuberance which comes with freedom—these are traits of the frontier, or traits called out elsewhere because of the existence of the frontier. Since the days when the fleet of Columbus sailed into the waters of the New World, America has been another name for opportunity, and the people of the United States have taken their tone from the incessant expansion which has not only been open but has even been forced upon them. He would be a rash prophet who should assert that the expansive character of American life has now entirely ceased. Movement has been its dominant fact, and, unless this training has no effect upon a people, the American energy will continually demand a wider field for its exercise. But never again will such gifts of free land offer themselves. For a moment, at the frontier, the bonds of custom are broken and unrestraint is triumphant. There is not tabula rasa. The stubborn American environment is there with its imperious summons to accept its conditions; the inherited ways of doing things are also there; and yet, in spite of environment, and in spite of custom, each frontier did indeed furnish a new field of opportunity, a gate of escape from the bondage of the past; and freshness, and confidence, and scorn of older society, impatience of its restraints and its ideas, and indifference to its lessons, have accompanied the frontier. What the Mediterranean Sea was to the Greeks, breaking the bond of custom, offering new experiences, calling out new institutions and activities, that, and more, the ever retreating frontier has been to the United States directly, and to the nations of Europe more remotely. And now, four centuries from the discovery of America, at the end of a hundred years of life under the Constitution, the frontier has gone, and with its going has closed the first period of American history.

Introduction to
Looking Far West: The Search for the American West in History, Myth, and Literature

Frank Bergon and Zeese Papanikolas

General Introduction

> "Oh, I don't know, but it seems to me this man has been reading dime-novels, and he thinks he's right out in the middle of it—the shootin' and stabbin' and all."
>
> "But," said the cowboy, deeply scandalized, "this ain't Wyoming, ner none of them places. This is Nebrasker."
>
> "Yes," added Johnnie, "an' why don't he wait till he gits out West?"
>
> The traveled Easterner laughed. "It isn't different there even—not in these days. But he thinks he's right in the middle of hell."
>
> —Stephen Crane, "The Blue Hotel"

America has always had a West. To the new republics along the eastern seaboard, the West was an unexplored territory somewhere beyond the Appalachian mountains "inhabited by savage nations . . . almost unknown and without a name." To Daniel Boone, immortalized by Lord Byron as the "happiest amongst mortals anywhere," Kentucky was the West. To many Americans—whether in Pennsylvania or Tennessee or Ohio—the West was a virgin land that was always retreating just beyond the edge of settlement. With the Louisiana Purchase and the Lewis and Clark expedition of 1804–1806, the West became more than merely a direction or receding line of wilderness. It became a region, a vast country extending across the North American continent from the Mississippi River to the Pacific Ocean. A natural division between East and West seemed to fall roughly along the 98th meridian where annual rainfall dropped below 20 inches and the eastern hills and forests leveled into flat, treeless plains inhabited by Indians. But even that boundary was vague. The trans-Mississippi West was not a wilderness inhabited only by Indians, nor was it settled by a gradual pioneering advance westward. Spaniards were already living in Santa Fe before Puritans even reached the Atlantic coastline, and in the same year that colonies in the East were declaring their independence from England, settlement in the West had advanced to San Francisco. What, then, as George Catlin asked in the 1840s, is the true definition of the term "West"? And where is its location?

More than other American regions, the West eludes definition because it is as much a dream as a fact, and its locale was never solely geographical. Before it was a place, it was a conception. Its characteristics were invented as well as discovered, and its history cannot be separated from its myths. Because the West has become so overlaid with legend, it is popularly assumed that a stripping of its mythic veneer would reveal the "real" West. Nothing could be less true. The American West was an intricate combination of both myth and reality. The West surely created myths, but myths themselves just as surely created the West. Listen to the voices of nineteenth-century Westerners, and you hear how the Western dream, though often debunked, still played a role in shaping the lives of those who were mocking the dream. The West and the Westerner were creations of the total American Imagination, and it is for this reason that the real West can be seen as what Archibald MacLeish called "a country in the mind." As dream, such a country extends from the early Spanish Image of the West as El Dorado to the contemporary vision of Marlboro Country. As fact, it exists in the jumble of assumptions, ideas, expectations, prejudices, and values that characterize Western speech and shape Western experience. Both as fact and as dream, the West is more than a history of westward movement, and the pioneering frontier is only one aspect of that combination of land, people, experience, and culture we broadly call the American West.

Before there was a West, the Indians who lived in the land usually called themselves The People. They lived in a self-contained visionary world where the distant landscape, far from being the great unknown that would give impetus to the white dream of the West as a "yonder," was to them a spiritual and literal home. The whole impulse behind their stories, their poems, even their economy was to erase the line between what was mythical and what was real. The Coyote of Indian myth attempts to find his place in the universe so that its wholeness will not be violated, and a Yuma medicine song reveals: "The water-bug is drawing the shadows of evening toward him across the water." Here, in the Indian scheme, the ephemeral bug "weighs" as much in the scale of nature as the entire evening. Andrew Garcia, the young Mexican trader in the Montana country of the 1870s, came across the hooves of many deer hanging from the trees along the trail. The Indians had left them there to let the deer people know they had used everything they could of the deer but the unusable hooves. Still, Indians saw no need to be conservationists in our contemporary sense. They caught salmon during the spring spawning season or drove buffalo over a cliff, because as long as respect was shown and the proper ceremonies observed, the animal people would be appeased, harmony would be maintained, and the supply of salmon or buffalo would be inexhaustible. If animals were killed needlessly, or, as the Washo believed, if animal remains, particularly bones, were treated callously, the animals would go away and no longer allow themselves to be killed for the benefit of man. The arrival of the whites would violate this closed Indian world, and the Indian response, after defeat, would be an attempt to replace the old world and the old myths with new ones: the myth of the Ghost Dance and its messianic message.

Since the white newcomers, unlike the Indians, had to make themselves into natives of the West, what most distinctly defines them as Westerners, it has been argued, are those adaptations, habits, and attitudes that evolved out of their encounter with the raw land and the Indians. As a group, the mountain men were the first of these Westerners to find occupations in the trans-Mississippi West and to adopt Indian crafts and skills necessary for survival in the region. "The wilderness masters the colonist," Frederick Jackson Turner claimed in his provocative essay about the significance of the frontier in American history. Walter Prescott Webb pursues the argument in *The Great Plains*, maintaining that the semi-arid plains shaped a distinct character and mode of life, most evident in the world of the open cattle range, where the cowboy, borrowing methods largely from the *vaquero*, became "the first permanent white occupant of the Plains." What must be remembered, to keep the creation of the Westerner in balance, is that newcomers brought with them expectations and preconceptions that molded their reactions to the country. They shaped the West as much as it shaped them. Webb comments that the "memoirs and journals of the Spanish explorers in America reveal few expressions of surprise and astonishment at the nature of the country [or] the aridity or lack of water or the unfitness of the country for human habitation" because the landscape and climate of the West were much like those of the Spaniards' homeland. In contrast, Americans from homes in the wet, timbered East labeled the same area the "Great American Desert," unfit for habitation and comparable to the "sandy deserts of Africa."

The tradition of the "Great American Desert" shows that while the West was being discovered, it was also being invented. Perception of the West was bent to fit various cultural images. The comparison of the Great Plains to the Sahara shows that men like Zebulon M. Pike and Stephen H. Long, who created the image, were products of a time that actively sought what was grand and exotic and romantic. No doubt the Southwest was more like Spain than like Virginia or Pennsylvania, but this similarity does not totally explain the placidity of Pedro de Castaneda's description of the Grand Canyon. He, too, was a man of his times, the early 1600s, when natural scenery was less astonishing to a Catholic European than were events that smacked of the uncanny. When thousands of men and animals could cross the plains without leaving a trace of their passage, this was an event to Castaneda that bordered on the miraculous. But to the Spaniards the rim of the Grand Canyon was merely a "bank of a river [that] was impossible to descend," and there was small surprise in Castaneda's dry report that some of the rocks on the sides of the canyon were "bigger than the great tower of Seville." The Western landscape we have come to know as astonishingly beautiful and sublime was largely a creation of a sensibility that emerged 250 years after Castaneda. It was not until the early nineteenth century that so sober an explorer as Meriwether Lewis could sit in wonderment before two Western waterfalls and comment that one "was *pleasingly beautiful,* while the other was *sublimely grand.*" Captain Lewis, like Castaneda, created his own mythical topography.

This creation of a mythological West included people along with the landscape. A good example is California, that island of the West and of the mind. It was named after a mythical island in a popular sixteenth-century romance, an island supposedly near the Terrestrial Paradise and ruled by women. The only metal on the island was said to be gold. The Spanish never found the gold that really was in California, but by the 1800s they did establish communities, presidial towns, and ranchos that many outsiders viewed with disdain. With the exception of some mountain men, most visitors described the early Californians as "lazy" or "idle" or—a favorite word—"indolent." Unable to accept Spanish methods of letting thousands of cattle graze freely through fertile hills, observers condemned *Californios* for not putting the land to efficient and productive agricultural use. Sir George Simpson summed up most reactions in 1841. "Here, on the very threshold of the country was California in a nutshell, Nature doing everything and man doing nothing."

This habit of imposing values on others was typical of the young American nation without an identity of its own. Defining Californians as "lazy" and "wasteful" was of course a way for others to call themselves "industrious" and "virtuous" and later to rationalize seizure of the coveted lands for themselves. Likewise, if Indians could be defined as "barbaric savages," whites could define themselves as "civilized." The other way to avoid taking the Indian on his own terms was to romanticize him out of existence. In the 1820s and 1830s, as Constance Rourke has shown in *American Humor*, a favorite figure of popular theater was the noble and tragic Indian of lofty vision and enviable kinship with nature. Recent sensitivity to the sickening record of the Indians' destruction has brought the stereotype of the superior Indian back into prominence, but stereotypes only obscure our vision of Indians as people, with the virtues and faults of people, and the differences of culture. Today's goal still remains much as Robinson Jeffers expressed it: to be able to look at the rock paintings of Tassajara and hear their makers' message from the past: "Look: we also were human."

Partly because of Indians and partly because of the harsh terrain, the West was seen as forbidding, and we are mistaken in our contemporary tendency to imagine the trans-Mississippi West as a natural magnet, or as a virgin land that inevitably stirred up spontaneous movements of expansion and settlement. The story is told of a Borgian heiress in the 1700s who offered a large sum for the establishment of missions in the most outlandish place in the world. The Jesuits consulted their atlases and announced, "The most outlandish place in all the world is California." To promote missionary work, Father Euseblo Kino had to plead with his superiors and cajole his benefactors to see that the West was not worthless in its apparent lack of gold, but valuable in its rich abundance of souls to be saved. The idea of the West as a wasteland was still prevalent in the 1830s, and this speech, attributed to Daniel Webster, is an example of what was commonly heard in and out of Congress:

> What do we want with this vast, worthless area? This region of savages and wild beasts, of deserts, shifting sands, and whirlwinds of dust, of cactus and prairie dogs? To what use could we ever hope to put these great deserts, or those endless mountain ranges, impregnable and covered to their very base with eternal snow? What can we ever hope to do with the western coast, a coast of three thousand miles, rockbound, cheerless, uninviting, and not a harbor on it? What use have we for such a country? Mr. President, I will never vote one cent from the public treasury to place the Pacific coast one inch nearer to Boston than it now is.

One of the West's first promoters was probably the first European to visit its interior, Cabeza de Vaca, who wandered through the Southwest between 1528 and 1536 and brought back an image of a land that "lacks nothing to be regarded as blest." The stated purpose of the nineteenth-century government-funded expedition of Lewis and Clark was to promote the fur trade; and their reports of fish, timber, minerals, furbearing animals, and other natural riches helped fix the West as a bonanza open to raid and rape. By the time the West was largely stripped of beaver, men were rushing to gold fields where most Forty-niners, as Prentice Mulford said at the time, expected to stay no more than a couple of years. "Five years at most was to be given to rifling California of her treasures, and then that country was to be thrown aside like a used-up newspaper and the rich adventurers would spend the remainder of their days in wealth, peace, and prosperity at their Eastern homes." John C. Frémont's description of vegetation and rainstorms on the plains was his attempt to undermine the myth of the Great American Desert and to portray the interior West as a place ripe for settlement. Initially only the edge of the West, like the lush Northwest, seemed attractive, but that trek far West was still prohibitive; at first only those with money, like the Donners and Reeds, could afford the oxen, wagons, and supplies needed by early settlers. Even after 1862, when land was free, it took elaborate advertising campaigns by railroads and land speculators to spur migration West.

Many who came to exploit the West found themselves exploited. Working cattlemen found themselves dependent on Eastern railroads and markets, and cowboys soon found themselves working for absentee owners in Edinburgh and London as well as in the East. Chinese who built railroads and logging flumes, Scandinavians who cut timber, Basques who raised sheep, and Greeks, Cornishmen, Finns, Italians, Slavs, and others from Europe and Asia who mined the West's wealth too often labored to make other men wealthy, and aspiring homesteaders too often found themselves busted by land deals or in hock to banks. These new Westerners, along with Latins, Indians, and blacks, did not melt into a homogeneous American society, but they did stamp the West, and by extension America, as a pluralistic society. What brought many of the early pioneers West was not a dream of adapting to the land and creating a new, distinct society of equals, but rather the desire to transfer to the West society as they had known it in the East, with one difference: they would be at the top of the heap. The vision railroads and steamship companies later offered to peasant immigrants was that of proprietorship, but even as railroads promoted a dream of the West as the home of free, independent, classless, self-sufficient tillers of the soil, their presence in the West made that dream impossible. Industrialization transformed the West. Soon individual efforts were subsumed by corporate ones, and the Wild West and the Industrial West interpenetrated, each giving shape to the other. In 1890, the Superintendent of the Census officially announced that the frontier had "closed," and Frederick Jackson Turner added that "with its going was closed the first period of American history."

What is perhaps most remarkable about this period of America's history is its brevity. No doubt the announcement of the frontier's demise was a bit early, and parts of the West ignored it. But even if we extend the date from 1890 to the end of the century, or to 1915, not many more than a hundred years had passed since Lewis and Clark ventured into what was just a vast wilderness. The West of the mountain men and their rendezvous formed a fleeting twenty years of that period, the Forty-niners took up about ten, and the cowboy—that most prominent figure of the Old West—found his world in decline after just twenty years of riding the Chisholm and Western trails. This brief history was also discontinuous. Parts of the Southwest may look back 300 years to when the Spanish first entered the region, but rapid change, not continuity, characterizes the many Wests that followed the Spanish West. The history of the West consists of a history of transitions, and fleeting figures of these brief, broken moments, could not have hardened into legend and endured as myth if there had not been such a longing and a need for mythic sustenance in America. At the time of the Louisiana Purchase, the United States was barely ten years old. There had been no time to develop a mythical center to the nation, no mystique of the Race or of the State or Empire, no national poem, *Iliad* or *Chanson de Roland* or *Kalevala*, to fall back upon. The Constitution and Declaration, too rational in their underpinnings, were dry substitutes for an epic, and although hundreds of patriotic plays about the Revolution were written, few were staged, and even fewer were popular except as farces. Revolutionary heroes on stage were not taken seriously as legendary figures and were popular only as comic ones. Noble Indians, though, were taken seriously. The country had no past, but it did have a West, a faraway, romantic place that could serve as a basis for myth. And the West did become an epic, an epic that did not exist in one poem or in several, or in one historical moment or another, but in a consciousness and a yonder. Americans became a people looking far West.

The nostalgia and regret that color much literature about the West no doubt spring from a true lament for what was actually passing with such quickness, but the West was being mourned as a lost past almost before it began. In 1853, before the era of the cowboys and cattle towns and homesteaders, Edward P. Mitchell wrote an elegy for the West: "In 1820, Missouri was the 'far West,' and Independence the boundary of civilization. Now, in 1854. there is no 'far West' . . . Pioneer life and pioneer progress must soon pass away for ever, to be remembered only in story." This elegiac tone was firmly established as early as 1827 when James Fenimore Cooper published *The Prairie*. As Kevin Starr points out in *Americans and the California Dream*, one of the appeals of Bret Harte's stories was that they imposed on recent events the charm of antiquity and transformed the Gold Rush, while it was still warm, into a thing of the distant past. In all of these instances, the spatial distance of the West was being translated into the temporal distance of the mythic.

The heroes of this national epic were often the conscious creations of Eastern dudes and Western promoters. Kit Carson made a brief appearance in the Reverend Samuel Parker's popular report of a journey across the Rockies in the 1830s, but in the 1840s Carson's reputation was still negligible, and John C. Frémont went to the trouble of checking out the man's credentials before accepting him as a scout. Through Frémont's subsequent reports and memoirs, Carson gained national attention, and his heroic status rapidly rose to mythic dimensions until, in a biography by Charles Burdett, Carson's exploits were linked to those of the old Danish sea-kings in the age of Canute. A more stunning transformation saw the cowboy change from lout to knight. In *Virgin Land*, Henry Nash Smith charts how the image of the rowdy, dirty cattle drover, denounced by President Chester A. Arthur in a message to Congress in 1881, was replaced by a chivalric hero. Buck Taylor, the first "King of the Cowboys," became a six-foot-five matinee idol of Buffalo Bill's Wild West Show and a dime-novel hero glorified by Prentiss Ingraham. Taylor was largely the creation of William F. Cody, who was himself largely the "Buffalo Bill" creation of Ned Buntline and the Beadle Half-Dime Library. The later literary and film stereotype of the cowboy stems largely from the demigod cooked up between Owen Wister and Frederic Remington. The cowboy emerged as the taciturn gunfighting hero of Wister's *The Virginian* and won the praise of no less respectable an Easterner than Henry James. Letting friendship dictate the tone, James wrote to Wister, "I very heartily congratulate you; you have made [the Virginian] live, with a high, but lucid complexity, from head to foot & from beginning to end; you have not only intensely seen & conceived him, but you have reached with him an admirable objectivity, & I find the whole thing a rare & remarkable feat. . . . Bravo, bravo."

The East wanted the West wild, but not too wild, and Western heroes, like the Virginian, often became embodiments of Victorian virtue. When Henry M. Stanley, of later Dr. Livingstone fame, met Wild Bill Hickok in 1867, he presented him to readers as a handsome man with "wavy, silken curls" who had no "swaggering gait" or "barbaric jargon"; he spoke well, would not perform a "mean action," was "more inclined to be sociable than otherwise," and was "generous, even to extravagance." The only thing Stanley seems to have forgotten were Wild Bill's fondness for children and kindness to dogs. The reverse of such images was also possible, and the West then became the dark side of the East's soul: knives flashed, bullets and arrows flew, and William H. Bonney or William McCarty or Bill Harrigan—whoever he was—became Billy the Kid, and blood flowed like rivers across the plains.

The obvious distortion of this mythic West is not so interesting as is its nearness to the surface of history. Legendary Westerners were not drawn from figures already eternalized by Arthurian mists of a dim past, they were real men who confronted their own myths and often helped shape them. Kit Carson faced himself as a melodramatic hero in 1849 when he found a sensationalized paperback novel about himself among the Indian spoils plundered from a wagon train. In his own autobiography Carson significantly recounts this incident with Western reticence: he doesn't say whether he is embarrassed or flattered by this sensationalized version of himself. As the man of the West he simply looks at himself as myth before he is cold, and he doesn't flinch. Twenty-four years later, Wild Bill Hickok was appearing on stage playing the popular role of "Wild Bill Hickok" during an Eastern theater tour he made in 1873, three years before he was murdered in Deadwood. With Buffalo Bill, who signed his name to no fewer than fifteen ghost-written autobiographies and Buffalo Bill dime novels, we reach that example of Western history and subsequent American life where fact and publicity blur, and myth completely overtakes reality. In the West itself, this overlapping of the mythic and the real gave rise to Westerners' self-conscious tendency to play (or play down) the role of the Westerner. In 1867 a Kansas newspaper reported that "the story of 'Wild Bill,' as told in Harper's for February is not easily credited hereabouts . . . it sounds mythical." Five years later, the *Kansas Daily Commonwealth* presented the border-state view of Hickok as "nothing more than a drunken, restless, murderous coward, who is treated with contempt by true border men, and who should have been hung years ago for the murder of innocent men." Years earlier, Charles Preuss, the reluctant cartographer of the Frémont expeditions, found Kit Carson's "butchery" similarly "disgusting," while Frémont found it noble.

The other side of this coin is that these mythic figures offered Westerners something to live up to. When Kit Carson happened to join a party on the Taos Trail, young Lewis Garrard, who was there, described him as the "renowned Kit Carson, so celebrated as the companion and guide of Colonel Frémont." But Garrard makes no attempt "to detract from Carson's well-earned fame." He merely comments that "there are numbers of mountainmen as fearless and expert as he, though to the reading world little known, whose prowess in scalptaking and beaver trapping is the theme of many campfires, and the highest admiration of younger mountaineers." It is easy to understand how the West became a state of mind for those boys sitting around campfires end aspiring to live up to the reputations of Jim Bridger and Joe Walker and Tom Fitzpatrick. The later cowboy's pride and sense of self is reflected in his quickness to put on his "woollies" or fancy chaps, draw his pistol, hang a cigarette from his lips, and pose for photographs of himself as a tough swashbuckler of the plains. It is instructive to imagine the state of mind of three bandits who were captured in the Dakotas in the 1880s. Theodore Roosevelt, who was a member of the capturing party, tells us that the outlaws' saddlebags were crammed with dime novels about daring desperadoes. Again and again, the West shows that when a state of mind finds expression in action, myth becomes history, just as history is always aspiring to become myth.

No one was more aware of this phenomenon of Western experience than Stephen Crane, who was twenty-three and already the author of *The Red Badge of Courage* when he came West in 1895. Crane was not alone in his impulse to look at the reality under the Western myth, for unlike the never-never land of Arthurian England, the myth of the West was a myth that *could* be tested: all a homesteader or dime-novel addict had to do was take the train out to where he thought the West began. Even before there were railroads, every season brought some bookish young Easterner or traveling grand duke or painter out to where *he* thought the West began. But unlike many chroniclers who simply spotlighted the tension between their own mythical expectations and the actuality of the West, Crane was quick to recognize the extent to which a mythology was recognized and lived out self-consciously by Westerners themselves. He wrote stories that used the stuff of pulp fiction such as lynchings, gunfights, and last-minute rescues by troopers, but he made them uncharacteristic Westerns in his refusal to follow dime-novel formulas. In a Crane story, a lynching in the name of justice and morality might be seen for what it really was: a "speculation in real estate."

It was the death of a gunfighting hero in another Crane story that caused an offended Teddy Roosevelt to write Crane a letter urging him to stick to the proper myths: "Some day I want you to write another story of the frontiersman and the Mexican greaser in which the frontiersman shall come out on top; it is more normal that way!" In one of the great short stories of American literature, "The Blue Hotel," Crane shows how the mythical Wild West, as a place in the mind, could become a deadly reality in an unlikely town in Nebraska. To the citizens of Fort Romper, their town is on the edge of becoming a metropolis with a second railroad line, a factory, four churches, electric streetcars, a big brick schoolhouse—all the institutions representing the law and civility of the East. To them the Wild West still exists, but it is yonder, *out West*, in Wyoming. When violence erupts in this town, the scene could be in New York or Nebraska or Nevada; geography no longer matters. "The Blue Hotel" reveals a truth that both East and West knew about their churches and theaters and hotels. Culture is a thin and perilous veneer and beneath it lie Crazy Horse and Liver-Eating Johnson and Hangtown and Dodge City.

In the twentieth century, the recent, brief history of the West remains near the skin of the present, and weighted with legend, it remains burdensome, prompting Westerners to spurn it or honor it. The surface of life in the West has changed in the last seventy years, but scattered remnants of an older West survive in corners of the Southwest and Great Basin deserts and in back towns of the Northwest and in stretches of the high plateau cattle-grazing country; John Gregory Dunne in *Delano: The Story of the California Grape Strike* portrays pockets of the agricultural Central Valley of the early 1960s as "largely insulated from what industrial America thinks and does and worries about. . . . The prevailing ethic is that of the nineteenth century frontier."

The heritage of the West most often invoked is that of its code. Often attributed mistakenly to the solitary gunslinger, the real code of the West was communal, a set of unspoken assumptions and unwritten social rules. At the heart of the code was the prescription that when in doubt, one minds his own business and keeps his mouth shut. Pain, for instance, was simply something to be endured, not talked about. The most condemned violators of the code were self-pitiers, braggarts, complainers, shirkers, and horsethieves. The ethic of fair play commanded that you did not deprive a man of what was most necessary for his survival or livelihood. To a cowboy it was his horse, but to a Basque sheepherder like Robert Laxalt's father in *Sweet Promised Land*, it was his dog. You were expected to be hospitable to a stranger's need, but respectful of his privacy; a man's past was his own business. "Oh, what was your name in the States?" an early song wryly asks, "Was it Thompson or Johnson or Bates?/Did you murder your wife/And fly for your life?/Say, what was your name in the States?"

There are certain things, according to J. B. Priestley, that a cowboy "must be able to do well, or it is all up with him, and they cannot be faked, as politicians and professional men and directors of companies so often fake things. He cannot pretend to be able to ride and rope, and get away with it." As a result, the code graced the necessity of competence with the virtue of pride, but roughhouse practical joking, an important strain of Western humor, was allowed to keep that pride within limits. The prohibition against prejudging a person did not disallow testing or "putting the leggins on" him and whoever was the object of laughter was also expected to laugh at himself. The immensity of the West's terrain was the great equalizer, and the code encouraged assertions of individuality in dress or style, but like the response of the impersonal landscape itself, the code admonished anyone from taking himself too seriously. Speech was similarly affected. It could be reckless and extravagant and ebulliant on one hand, but indirect and laconic on the other. Since a man's word was binding, words were to be respected, but no restraint was called for when "puttin the leggins on" someone. As a result, humor was extreme or understated, often grotesque and even brutal, but usually oblique. In *Wolf Willow*, Wallace Stegner points out that cowboys "honored courage, competence, self-reliance, and they honored them tacitly. They took them for granted. It was their absence, not their presence, that was cause for remark. Practicing comradeship in a rough and dangerous job, they lived a life calculated to make a man careless of everything except the few things he really valued."

Like everything else about the West, romanticizing the code has prettified its vices. Too often invoked to justify impulsive violence and overpraise toughness, the code was crude in its standards of judgment and narrow in its range of virtues. While much of it might still be valued, much of it is too limited and callous to meet the complexities of most people's lives. As Stegner has shown, the code of the West was primarily a response to conditions that were particular to a "nearly womanless culture, nomadic, harsh, dangerous, essentially romantic." Perhaps the West's most valuable heritage still stems from what gave rise to the code in the first place, to what shaped the Indian vision of his world, and to what in the West remains from its beginning: the land and the sky. Although diminishing, the immense spaces and lonely terrain of the West might still let us experience a recovered sense of what Robinson Jeffers says we have lost and of what, even today, is perhaps the West's richest legacy: the dignity of room, the value of rareness.

Open Space
and American Culture

Stephen Cook

Any extensive study of the American West must start with the physical reality of geography, which then gives rise to the contemplation of certain abstracts. Certainly, culture, history, and the environment are inseparable; more specifically, in the case of the United States, the vastness flung out before us at our beginnings provided a stage upon which to work out a national story, heroic and inestimably sad, a narrative comprised of truth and mythology. Further, successive western frontiers allowed for multiple recreations of American society, as Frederick Jackson Turner told us a long time ago, and this process gave the basic human nature of the participants a distinctly American cast.

The boosterism of Turner is plainly evident: "Since the days when the fleet of Columbus sailed into the waters of the New World, America has been another name for opportunity, and the people of the United States have taken their tone from the incessant expansion which has not only been open but has ever been forced upon them" (154).

Revisionists would not disagree with Turner's analysis but would choose instead to emphasize the damage done by a people who took the *Old Testament* literally, seeing in it an exact parallel. Surely, the Promised Land was just across the Mississippi River, the only barriers some scattered heathen tribes. Go ye forth; rain follows the plow. Seemingly inexhaustible, sheer space seduced us, the idea of limits dropping away. However, the land was not as generous as the rhetoric, and the plains broke many a heart and mind with sheer distance and relentless wind. The physical frontier has been largely gone for quite some time now—Turner eulogized it in the same long-ago speech—yet the social frontier remains before us, and a linkage between them is our legacy of open space, which still embodies mythology and reality. The open space of the American West is the primary context in which our national story takes place. Certainly, it is the stage upon which the protagonist of the Western, one of America's few organic art forms, engages in his or her heroics. Further, the vastness of the American West is often the setting for another genre: the open-road epic. *Route 66*, *Vanishing Point*, *Thelma and Louise*, and even the recent animated feature *Cars* are rooted in a celebration of mobility and the promise of transformation inherent in the American experience with open space. These works of art exemplify what Merle Haggard calls "white line fever" in the song of that name. Only in the West could *Thelma and Louise* have taken place, for the reach of the landscape and the relative absence of the controlling institutions of society provide the room in which to create a transcendent narrative.

The fact is that openness enthralls the imagination, yet a conundrum is that it simultaneously offends and terrifies. William Least Heat Moon describes this disjunctive relationship in *Blue Highways*:

> The true West differs from the East in one great, pervasive, influential, and awe-some way: space. The vast openness changes the roads, towns, houses, farms, crops, machinery, politics, economics, and, naturally, ways of thinking. How could it do otherwise? Space west of the line is perceptible and often palpable, especially when it appears empty, and it's that apparent emptiness which makes matter look alone, exiled, and unconnected. Those spaces diminish man and reduce his blind-ness to the immensity of the universe; they push him toward a greater reliance upon himself. . . . No one, not even the sojourner, escapes the expanses. You can't get away from them by rolling up the safety-glass and speeding through, because the terrible distances eat up speed. Even dawn takes nearly an hour just to cross Texas. Still, drivers race along; but when you get down to it, they are people uneasy about space. (136)

The American love affair with mobility and the promise of transformation that move-ment offers also has its downside, debilitating attitudes created during our Westward expansion. Wallace Stegner writes of the American obsession with mobility:

> Insofar as the West was a civilization at all between Lewis and Clark's explo-rations and about 1870, it was largely a civilization in motion, driven by dreams. . . . The dreams are not dead even today, and the habit of mobility has only been reinforced by time. . . . But the rootlessness that expresses energy and a thirst for the new and an aspiration toward freedom and personal fulfillment has just as often been a curse. . . . American individualism, much celebrated and cherished, has developed without its essential corrective, which is belonging. Freedom, when found, can turn out to be airless and unsustaining. Especially in the West, what we have instead of place is space. (71–72)

A third source of tension concerns land usage in the West. California particularly exemplifies the dichotomy between development and preservation. Expected to grow by fifteen million in the next twenty years, the state must balance economics and a need for open space. The task for preservationists is to engender on a large scale the idea that openness has intrinsic value, a hard row to hoe in a place where land is at a premium. More enlightened developers have come to understand the esthetic and economic value of parks, greenbelts, trails, riparian habitat, and preserves within communities, but others have had to be forced by laws, codes, and assessments to meet the need for open space within housing tracts. Why such recalcitrance? One aspect of this reluctance comes from a desire to maximize profit, but another aspect may very well be a deeper psychic need to conquer distance.

Gretel Ehrlich comments on the latter notion in *The Solace of Open Spaces*:

> We Americans are great on fillers, as if what we have, what we are is not enough. We have a cultural tendency toward denial, but, being affluent, we strangle ourselves with what we can buy. We have only to look at the houses we build to see how we build *against* space, the way we drink against pain and loneliness. We fill up space as if it were a pie shell, with things whose opacity further obstructs our ability to see what is already there. (15)

Ehrlich knows whereof she speaks, for after the death of her fiancé, Ehrlich's grief is such that she wishes to disappear into the emptiness of Wyoming while eradicating memory through stretches of heavy drinking. However, she strikes a different sort of bargain in time. Ehrlich explains:

> I suspect that my original motive for coming here was to lose myself in new and unpopulated territory. Instead of producing the numbness I thought I wanted, life on the sheep ranch woke me up. The vitality of the people I was working with flushed out what had become a hallucinatory rawness inside me. I threw away my clothes and bought new ones; I cut my hair. The arid country was a clean slate. Its absolute indifference steadied me. (3–4)

Ultimately, she tells us—*witnesses* is a word that rings true here—that "space has a spiritual equivalent and can heal what is divided and burdensome in us" (14).

To feel her itty-bitty place in the universe is a relief for Ehrlich and puts her troubles into perspective, but for homesteaders and others, the immensity of the Great Plains was chilling, and the newcomers made peace with it, went away, or stayed and were broken by it. This is a reality unmentioned by Turner and unacknowledged by the mythmakers. Today the effrontery of openness is still with Americans, many of whom pay lip service to the heroic mythology of a national narrative taking place in the vastness of the West but who still seek to diminish its reach and power.

Ehrlich's experiences are instructive in finding a rational and balanced relationship with open space. I am certain that pain and not some glorious sense of purpose was her prevailing emotion for a long time. The humility engendered by Wyoming is a good place to start the healing she refers to—after all, one is not so unique in grieving.

In Ehrlich's case, the physical space is matched by the emotional space provided by strangers. It *seems* true that one would wish to grieve among friends and family, and yet one is on a kind of display where the quality or duration of one's grief is being measured.

In Wyoming, there is tenderness, but it is tempered by the reality of tending to the daily needs of sheep. One must stay grounded in order to work. One will also have the company of objective people who are in the process of learning to know you as you become someone new, and, without a doubt, there are many private places in which to pour out one's rage, to shake a tiny fist at an enormous and brooding sky. As an open wound needs oxygen to heal, so does the human psyche require room to wonder and to contemplate, to rebuild what has been shattered or to construct anew. Ehrlich speaks of this tenuous process of tempering the old with the new: "One morning a full moon was setting in the west just as the sun was rising. I felt precariously balanced between the two as I loped across a meadow. For a moment, I could believe that the stars, which were still visible, work like cooper's bands, holding together everything above Wyoming" (14).

Barry Lopez echoes Ehrlich in his essay "Out of a Desert Landscape: Open Spaces and the Human Spirit":

> [I]mmersed in the relationships [of the natural world], we regain our spiritual senses. Landscape, in other words, can heal. Urban psychologists have stated that one of the dangers of a highly industrialized society (like ours) is the reduction in demands on the individual imagination. Resourcefulness, self-motivation, and invention, we are told, are dulled—by television, by chemicals in our food, by an array of goods and services which are too readily available. [Being in the natural world] can be seen as a kind of therapy against . . . depression. . . . [O]pen space, where one can see clearly, releases the imagination. (55)

Ehrlich and Lopez speak of open space in spiritual terms, thereby linking geography and the private space within, and while spirituality is a nebulous concept, for our purposes, let us define it as the presence of an inner terrain and let readers decide whether they will think of this place inside of us as the mind or the soul or both. Let us further consider openness to be a social lubricant, one decidedly necessary in urban areas. Thus, it follows that preservation of open space is necessary for social welfare. The reasoning behind this truth lies in an idea Carlos Castaneda presents in *Journey to Ixtlan*. In this dissertation/memoir/novel (who knows?), doctoral candidate Castaneda leaves Los Angeles and journeys into the Sonora Desert, where the University Man encounters the Medicine Man, a Yaqui sorcerer named don Juan.

While the authenticity of Castaneda's research is still questioned, the chapter "Being Inaccessible" offers a bedrock truth don Juan alludes to cryptically when he says,

"'Therein lies the secret of great hunters. To be available and unavailable at the precise turn of the road'" (66). Castaneda is confused, just as the reader is likely to be, asking, "Wherein lies *what?*" because we are all encountering for the first time the paired ideas of "availability" and "unavailability" or as don Juan later calls them, "accessibility" and "inaccessibility." Up until then, the chapter is a rather odd story about hunting, first quail to eat, then the wind as don Juan takes Castaneda to a hilltop where don Juan alternately hides Castaneda from the wind, then exposes him to it. The wind becomes more than a meteorological force, taking on volition of its own. Earlier, don Juan and Castaneda had been the hunters, but now, the wind hunts them. When don Juan covers Castaneda with branches, the wind ceases to blow, yet when he stands, the wind begins to buffet him. Castaneda thus becomes accessible and inaccessible to the wind.

Castaneda finds the notion of a "'willful wind'" (65) laughable and condescendingly explains the science of wind movement, but don Juan believes he has made his point, offering a sarcastic rebuttal:

> "Your opinions are final opinions. . . . They are the last word, aren't they? For a hunter, however, your opinions are pure crap. It makes no difference whether the pressure is one or two or ten; if you would live out here in the wilderness you would know that during the twilight, the wind becomes power. A hunter that is worth his salt knows that, and acts accordingly." (65)

Here in the text is where don Juan introduces his idea that we must regulate our exposure to other human beings. "At one time in my life I . . . made myself available over and over again until there was nothing of me left for anything except perhaps crying. . . . You must take yourself away. . . . You must retrieve yourself from the middle of a trafficked way'" (67).

Castaneda is not persuaded, so don Juan plays his trump card by bringing up, seemingly without any previous knowledge, a former girlfriend of Castaneda's, a move that engenders deep animosity on Castaneda's part, but the sorcerer sees through the bluster, reminding Castaneda that he is no one special, just a man. Castaneda desperately rationalizes that he must have spoken of this relationship previously and momentarily feels better. However, don Juan is relentless, insisting that the "very important blonde girl" (68) had left because Castaneda had been too accessible to her. Castaneda feels another surge of anger that is quickly supplanted by sadness as his mentor summons more memories. At that point in the narrative, don Juan accuses Castaneda of "'indulging in sentimentality'" (22) and with his pupil reeling, begins the lesson again:

> "The art of the hunter is to become inaccessible. . . . In the case of that blond girl, it would've meant that you had to become a hunter and meet her sparingly.

Not the way you did. You stayed with her day after day, until the only feeling that remained was boredom. . . . To be inaccessible means that you touch the world sparingly. . . . You don't expose yourself to the power of the wind unless it is mandatory. You don't use and squeeze people until they have shriveled to nothing, especially the people you love." (69)

Now Castaneda is offended, protesting that he has never used anyone, but don Juan bluntly tells him that he is wrong and that he becomes easily bored with people:

"To be unavailable means that you deliberately avoid exhausting yourself and others. . . . A hunter uses his world sparingly and with tenderness, regardless of whether the world might be things, or plants, or animal, or people, or power. . . . [The hunter] is inaccessible because he's not squeezing the world out of shape. He taps it lightly, stays for as long as he needs to, and then swiftly moves away leaving hardly a mark." (69–70)

Castaneda is ultimately defeated, for even if he cannot see the world in anthropomorphic terms, he still must acknowledge the truth of healthy human relationships— it is a balancing act in which one nourishes the individual while sustaining the other, and it is no easy task. One must consciously regulate physical and psychic space, the ebb and flow of engagement and detachment. Otherwise, the scale tips to either boredom from too much contact or neglect from too little. The truth of this principle seems obvious within intimate relationships and even professional ones, in particular the ones concerned with helping others. Co-dependency, the dissolution of boundaries, the loss of emotional or physical space that one may call one's own, are death blows to personal sovereignty. Just as the loss of a land base and room to maintain a culture decimated the Native Americans, so the loss of personhood will destroy a life.

The Book of Isaiah issues a warning: "Woe unto them that join house to house, that lay field to field, till there be no place that they may be alone in the midst of the earth." "Woe" is truly an *Old Testament* word, but it is appropriate. We cannot live chock-a-block on top of each other. Most of us will live in cities by necessity, but we can design urban areas with parks, preserves, and greenbelts, thus augmenting the internal tolerance we must cultivate, an ideal comparable to the maintenance of room within our minds for divergent views and diverse peoples.

Outside the cities, we must continue to pursue the ideal of preservation, even if we disagree over how it is accomplished. Open tracts of land should be regarded as reservoirs, not only for the protection of wildlife but also as areas where we may go to cultivate our imaginations, seek humility, and even worship if one accepts the notion of God as a force inhabiting all the works of nature.

In my own mid-sized suburb, I see the "divided mind" in our long-running disputes over zoning. The planning commission, as it continues to work out the master plan for our city, genuflects appropriately when quality of life, riparian habitat, and the need to preserve open space are mentioned. However, after the gestures are made, we residents are reminded that, as a bedroom community, our city must build houses, the more the better.

Works Cited

Ehrlich, Gretel. *The Solace of Open Spaces*. New York: Penguin, 1985.

Castaneda, Carlos. *Journey to Ixtlan*. New York: Pocket Books, 1972.

Least Heat Moon, William. *Blue Highways: A Journey into America*. New York: Fawcett, 1982.

Lopez, Barry. "Out of a Desert Landscape: Open Spaces and the Human Spirit." *America West* March–April 1982: 50–55.

Stegner, Wallace. *Where the Bluebird Sings to the Lemonade Springs*. New York; Penguin, 1992.

Turner, Frederick Jackson. "The Significance of the Frontier in American History." *Revisiting America: Readings in Race, Culture, and Conflict*. Ed. Susan Wyle. New Jersey: Pearson, 2004. 147–155.

The Seedbed

Study Questions

1. How does Hector St. John de Crevecoeur regard those who lived on the American frontier prior to 1793, the year *Letters from an American Farmer* was published in the United States? How does he describe the people he refers to as "back settlers"? What is Crevecoeur's attitude toward farmers?
2. Do some research on Crevecoeur's life. Do you think his experiences in America created any bias in his analysis of the farmer and the frontier settler?

Suggested Essay Topics

1. After reading Crevecoeur's descriptions of the farmer and the hunters who live on the frontier, turn to "Reflections on a Theme by Crevecoeur" by Wallace Stegner, and read pages 114 to 118 in *Realizing Westward*. Stegner points out that the frontiersman is a precursor to the mythological figure of the cowboy. Stegner further draws a contrast between the dirt-farmer who stays on the land and builds a community in the process and the romantic lone rider constantly on the move. After reflecting on the qualities of each American archetype, write a paper in which you identify the character you most identify with, and explain why. Are you a farmer or are you a cowboy? Can a person be both?
2. Watch the classic Western *Shane* in light of what you know about the farmer and the cowboy. In particular, compare the characters of Shane and Joe Starrett. How does the movie reveal their differences and similarities? Which character is more romantic? Which character is more necessary for society to be livable and safe? How does *Shane* reveal the tension between a societal need for community-builders and warriors?
3. For a study in aloneness set in the American West, watch *Jeremiah Johnson*. What sort of man is Jeremiah Johnson? Why does living in the Rocky Mountains appeal to him? Why does he refuse to leave even when he is in great danger? What attitude do he and other mountain men have toward farmers and townspeople?
4. Watch *The Right Stuff*. Do the original Mercury 7 astronauts of the film resemble America's mythological frontiersmen? Are they squarely in the tradition

of Lewis and Clark? What qualities do the Mercury 7 reveal? How do they handle danger and the unknown?

Study Questions

1. How did westward expansion and the frontier shape Americans, according to Frederick Jackson Turner in "The Significance of the Frontier in American History"?

2. Turner argues that western expansion created certain intellectual qualities in Americans. The qualities he mentions are positive, except for a reference to individualism sometimes working for evil. Do you largely agree or disagree with his assessment? Why? What less than admirable qualities do we as a country and as a people possess? Do an honest evaluation.

3. In the Introduction to *Looking Far West: The Search for the American West in History, Myth, and Literature,* Frank Bergon and Zeese Papanikolas assert that history and myth are intertwined in the American West. What is the nature of the interplay between the two?

4. How did American experience in the West create a national epic? What is the appeal of a national story?

5. What does Robinson Jeffers mean by the phrase "the dignity of room, the value of rareness"?

Suggested Essay Topic

1. What are the elements of a Western code of behavior as discussed by Bergon and Papanikolas? Is the code simply a part of folklore—"a man's gotta do what a man's gotta do"—or does it still govern behavior in the West? If a politician wants to get votes in the West, does she or he need to tailor her or his message to take into account this code? For more discussion of the specifics of political campaigning in the American West, read "The Code of the West," by Ryan Lizza, in the 9/1/08 issue of *The New Yorker.*

Study Questions

1. What are the contradictions in American experience with open space, according to the author of "Open Space and American Culture"?

2. What are the benefits of the American legacy of open space? What are the negatives?

3. Is there a connection between space and mobility? Is there a connection between mobility and the promise of transformation? Does an American myth exist concerning social mobility?

4. How does open space in urban areas facilitate peaceful human interactions?

5. What does Carlos Castaneda mean by "availability" and "unavailability"? Do these concepts have applications to your life as a college student?

6. Is Barry Lopez correct in his belief that open spaces are an antidote to the stresses placed on people by urban life? Can the quiet and natural darkness of open areas truly counter effects of over-stimulation from city life?

7. Because of the rising cost of fuel, many futurists predict that cities will flourish as consumers seek to minimize costs involved in commuting. Write a report in which you offer ways to design urban centers balancing competing needs for offices, living areas, and open space.

SUGGESTED ESSAY TOPICS

1. What is the proper balance between physical and psychic space? How do they interrelate in your life? Do you actively seek physical space as a means of refreshing your mind and spirit? Is Gretel Ehrlich right in her assertion that open space and sanity are linked?

2. How do physical and psychic space correlate to the concepts of "availability" and "unavailability" articulated by Castaneda? When should we make ourselves "available" to the troubles generated by friends and family members, and when should we detach in order to preserve ourselves?

2. Consider the American love affair with the automobile. How does American car culture reflect our desire for mobility? For example, research the ways in which American cars reflected our new found national fascination with outer space during the early 1960s. Further, and more currently, how do pick up trucks and SUVs reflect our frontier mythology?

3. Watch the movie *City Slickers*. Even though it is a comedy, the movie delivers a very serious message about the promise of transformation inherent in the American West. Trace the ways in which *City Slickers* explores this theme.

4. Watch the movie *Avalon*. Explore the ways in which social mobility in America is both a boon and a curse to the immigrant family featured in the film.

STUDY QUESTIONS—THE LAST OF THE MOHICANS (1992)

1. How does the character of Hawkeye represent the kind of man de Crevecouer looks at with distaste and Turner regards with admiration?

2. "I do not call myself subject to much at all," Hawkeye says. Does he speak for many/most/all Americans? What is Hawkeye subject to?

3. List the ways in which Hawkeye is a hybrid, a man who combines European and Native American characteristics. (By the way, check out the lacrosse game.)

4. The image of the carriage crossing the bridge over a tranquil river also represents hybridity, a blending of Europe and America. How?

5. What connotations does the name "Hawkeye" bring up?

6. Hector St. John de Crevecoeur points out two types of individuals, ones we will refer to as "the farmer" and "the frontiersman." What principal characters represent these two archetypes?

7. Early in the film, Cora sees a mountain lion in the brush. How does she react? What does her reaction mean? What does the scene represent? Why would Michael Mann (the director) include such a scene? How does the scene reveal Cora's inner nature? What sort of woman is she?

8. Why is Hawkeye such a romantic figure? What qualities make a hero romantic? Does a successful culture require some degree of romance, even glory in its national mythology?

9. In the October, 2006 issue of *The Atlantic*, Virginia Postrel writes, "Glamour is an imaginative process that creates a specific emotional response: a sharp mixture of projection, longing, admiration, and aspiration. It evokes an audience's hopes and dreams and makes them seem attainable, all the while maintaining enough distance to sustain the fantasy" (140). Analyze *The Last of the Mohicans* in the light of Postrel's ideas.

10. Postrel also writes that heroes (and superheroes as well) "are masters of their bodies and their physical environment. They often work in teams, providing an ideal of friendship based on competence, shared goals, and complementary talents. They're special, and they know it" (142-143). How does *The Last of the Mohicans* reflect Postrel's analysis?

11. Consider the Native characters, especially Magua, Chingachgook, Uncas. What are their qualities as human beings? What conclusions should we draw about them and their tribes after watching the movie?

12. Does the character of Magua offend you? Should Native Americans always be portrayed in a positive light after all the discrimination they've suffered?

13. How do Europeans and Natives conduct war? How does each method reflect the disparate cultures?

14. What is the difference between confidence and arrogance? To answer this question, compare the characters of Hawkeye and Duncan.

SUGGESTED ESSAY TOPICS

1. How does *The Last of the Mohicans* tie heroism to altruism? How does the movie link heroism and the ability to fight? Why in America are heroism and altruism rarely or never seen as being expressed passively?

2. Watch *The Last of the Mohicans*, *Heat*, *Collateral*, and *Miami Vice*, all Michael Mann movies. What messages about individualism and heroism do these movies offer? How do these movies tell stories about conflict between good and evil? What is the line between the good and evil characters, and do they often share many of the same characteristics?

3. Read Edmund Burke's "Speech on Conciliation with the Colonies," and analyze Burke's attempt to explain the American mentality to his fellow English citizens prior to the American Revolution. What American qualities does Burke mention, and how does he account for their development? How does *The Last of the Mohicans* validate or refute Burke's assessment?

AMERICAN HEROIC MYTHOLOGY

Every culture that endures has its defenders and protectors, altruistic men and women who are called upon to sustain their cultures, sometimes sacrificing their lives in exchange for the continued existence of their respective societies. The first essay in this section, "The Altruistic Hero," analyzes this universal human phenomenon and coins the terms "secular hero" and "selected hero" to differentiate between the two principal expressions of this cultural icon. "The Altruistic Hero" also explains how the cowboy came to represent the quintessential American hero.

This theme of the secular hero is amplified in Robert Bellah's essay "Individualism." We see how secular heroes are in positions of service to communities that they can never join. Secular heroes occupy roles like soldiers, lawmen, ranchers, and trusted friends or "sidekicks." In "Savior in the Saddle: The Sagebrush Testament," Michael Marsden shows how Westerns from the beginning of the genre intertwined Christian symbolism and its theological principal of altruistic sacrifice with American Heroic Mythology to create a selected hero, a cowboy-figure who carries out a task ordained by God in defense of the community.

Essays on *The Matrix* and *Tombstone* provide examples of how Westerns from the beginning of American Cinema to very recent times have made the distinction between secular and selected heroes, yet have shown how both are critical figures in this most organic of American art forms. The two films above have selected heroes at their cores, but these figures are assisted at every turn by secular heroes. In fact, selected heroes cannot realize their ordained destinies without the help of secular heroes. Included in this section are study questions for *Tombstone*, which offers viewers a visual representation of key themes in American Heroic Mythology, especially the way in which *Tombstone* is firmly rooted in the tradition of cowboy as redeemer, first established in American cinema by *Hell's Hinges*, the Thomas H. Ince classic.

THE ALTRUISTIC HERO

Stephen Cook

Any society worth defending will have its defenders. This sense of duty is a biological imperative cultivated and directed by the mythologies of society and called out in those individuals who hear—and answer—the summons to take on and to complete a task on society's behalf. These heroes take two forms: the "secular" and the "selected." The first term refers to people within society who do jobs that serve the community, often in occupations involving danger and potential loss of life, for example, firefighters or police officers. The second term refers to a much rarer individual, one picked by God or by Fate to fulfill a role of leader or savior or principal figure in a liberation drama.

The ubiquity of this phenomenon of a cultural need for heroes has given rise to what Joseph Campbell calls the "monomyth" in *The Hero with a Thousand Faces.* At the center of the monomyth is a "man of self-achieved submission" (16). However, what is it that the hero (and in coming generations as the parameters of heroic mythology expand, the heroine) submits to? Campbell calls it a "riddle" (16) yet proffers a very workable explanation:

> Only birth can conquer death—the birth, not of the old thing again, but of something new. Within the soul, within the body social, there must be—if we are to experience long survival—a continuous "recurrence of birth" (palingenesia) to nullify the unremitting recurrences of death. For it is by means of our own victories, if we are not regenerated, that the work of Nemesis is wrought; doom breaks from the shell of our very virtue. Peace then is a snare; war is a snare; change is a snare; permanence a snare. When our day is come for the victory of death, death closes in; there is nothing we can do, except be crucified—and resurrected; dismembered totally, and then reborn. (16–17)

What Campbell suggests is that the hero comes to terms with his mortality. The hero also comes to understand how death and birth are inextricably linked and, as a corollary, that his death may allow for social rebirth. Thus it is that over deep time and through the influence of ancient mythologies, the need for heroic individualism became ingrained in humans, most likely encoded in the arithmetic of our genes. The group must remain, and this imperative calls for sacrifice by altruistic individuals.

However, their moments on the altar also posit a kind of personal gain as Edward O. Wilson explains: ". . . when individuals subordinate themselves and risk death in a common cause, their genes are more likely to be transmitted to the next generation than are those of competing groups who lack comparable resolve. . . . To put it as concisely as possible: the individual pays, his genes and tribe gain, altruism spreads" (65). The seed dies that nourishing fruit be born, so it is not surprising that societies create celebratory mythologies around the figure of the hero, who may physically vanish, yet whose name and memory go on as compensation. Societies will sing songs of remembrance and have the assurance that they come from heroic stock. Mythology has at its root the pragmatic considerations that the group's survival needs the sacrifice of the individual and that those called in the future need the examples of the past to guide them. For any group to achieve longevity, it must have at its core men and women of goodness, or at least that is the ideal. The definition of "goodness" is key to the understanding of the mythology of the hero, and one should not necessarily see this quality as upright conduct or socially acceptable behavior. Certainly, in the 1993 Western *Tombstone*, Doc Holliday is one who has spent much of his life operating outside law and social convention. However, if "goodness" is selflessness under extreme stress and the ability to contend with conditions that require the possible sacrifice of one's life for an altruistic goal—be it saving a town or protecting the life of a friend—then Holliday is a "good" man.

In America, the prototypical hero has been a man heading into whatever adventures and trials the open spaces of the West will bring. The hero goes to:

> an environment inimical to human beings, where a person is exposed, the sun beats down, and there is no place to hide. But the negations of the physical setting— no shelter, no water, no rest, no comfort—are also its siren song. Be brave, be strong enough to endure this, and you will become like this—hard, austere, sublime. This code of asceticism founds our experience of Western stories. The landscape challenges the body to endure hardship—that is its fundamental message at the physical level. It says, This is a hard place to be; you will have to do without here. Its spiritual message is the same: come, and suffer. (Tompkins 71)

This denial of self is the essence of the Western, a uniquely American form of the hero-quest, yet again we see that this search for the transcendence of self is ubiquitous throughout history. Campbell writes:

> The hero, whether god or goddess, man or woman, the figure in a myth or the dreamer of a dream, discovers and assimilates his opposite (his own unsuspected self) either by swallowing it or being swallowed. One by one the resistances are broken. He must put aside his pride, his virtue, beauty, and life, and bow or submit

to the absolutely intolerable. Then he finds that he and his opposite are not of differing species, but one flesh. (108)

Tompkins puts Campbell's notion of opposites becoming one in the context of Westerns: "In the end, the land is everything to the hero; it is both the destination and the way. He courts it, struggles with it, defies it, conquers it, and lies down with it at night" (81). On the grand stage of the deserts and plains of the West, the secular hero and the selected hero are molded by the dramas they enact and come to possess ". . . qualities required to complete an excruciatingly difficult task: self-discipline; unswerving purpose; the exercise of knowledge, skill, ingenuity, and excellent judgment; and a capacity to continue in the face of total exhaustion and overwhelming odds" (12). Besides being a proving ground, the landscape shapes the hero's sense of purpose and offers the solace of knowing that his struggles are not in vain. Through the landscape of the West, "the hero plays out his social relationships, answers his spiritual needs, and foreshadows his destiny" (82).

Such an encounter is an ancient theme. The land whispers to the seeker, offering portents and signs. In the *Old Testament*, Moses encounters a bush burning and yet not consumed; Ezekiel sees a wheel within a wheel; the wind blows, the horizon shimmers like sateen, and prescient dreams arrive. The *New Testament* offers a more recent example of the land in its depiction of Jesus' temptations, an interpretation of which is in Reynolds Price's lyrical *Three Gospels*.

For more than a month Jesus walked alone in the desert past Jericho, the crags and wastes by the hot Dead Sea, Earth's deepest pit. He thought [about] God's meaning for him and the time he'd have before the great coming. In the early days he thought he heard God's voice again "My son, I waited the ages for you through all the prophets, that you come at last and I might rest." For a while after that the time felt short.

Then vipers, jackals, a starved lion, and swarms of flies crossed Jesus' path in the sunstruck gullies . . . his own hunger sapped him and he was sleeping nights in gullies with no more cover than his seamless coat . . . [but] no creature more than sniffed his hand or licked the dry soles of his feet.

What came nearer to harming Jesus in those days was the tempting spirit that crossed his path in numerous forms. One form wore his mother's face and led a child by the hand toward him saying "This is my son"—the child was himself. Another form likewise wore Jesus' face but was old and smiling with sons and daughters that bore his traits and tended his age. A third was all the human beauty he'd known until now, all the hair he'd touched.

Eventually on the fortieth day Jesus fended the spirit off. By then he was high on a peak above Jericho. When the final tempter melted in air, Jesus howled to the rocks, gnawed thorny weeds and turned his lean face back to the north but not toward home. What he thought he'd understood in the desert burned to be told. . . . (247–248)

This translation bears out Campbell's description of the process wherein the hero assimilates his "opposite," which is essentially the subordination to the needs of the group the individual's desires for familial connection, long life, and the passionate embrace of another. The desert, the mountains, and the plains shape and teach. It is only speculation, but it is reasonable to believe that Jesus, by virtue of being part of a pastoral society and through the observation of the dynamics of nature, came to an understanding of one of the most ineffable principles of life: in order for something to live, something else must die. Perhaps it was in the desert that he fully saw the application of this reality to his own life. Would not the Western protagonist, having been raised on a ranch or farm and living intimately with the land, arrive at a similar epiphany?

At some point, the hero rejoins society. A loner and an outsider, the hero protects the community. He must be alone (or perhaps with a trusted partner); otherwise, the detachment critical to leadership during war is compromised. For example, the presence of a wife or children will cause a shifting of loyalty on the part of the hero, or at a minimum cause a hesitation that may be fatal. A case in point is Shane, from the novel of the same name, whose job is not to supplant Joe as the patriarch of the Starretts; it is to put away his love for Marian and confront Stark Wilson.

As Campbell writes, the hero's detachment comes because "destiny has summoned [him] and transferred his spiritual center of gravity from within the pale of his society to a zone unknown" (58). To create a hero who answers God's call makes sense as an inevitable result over evolutionary time of the transmutation of tribal ethical codes into religious ones designed to give a core belief system to nation-states. What better way to enforce a code than to attribute God's authorship to it as well as to warn of His severe retribution for its contravention? America is a land where Christianity has buttressed social ideals, enforced limitations on freedom of action, and provided points of reference. Manifest Destiny was a parallel in the minds of many to the Israelites' seizing of the Promised Land; the shedding of blood is common in its stories and foremost in its theology, required of adherents and especially of enemies, so violence was not necessarily an evil but rather a means to an end; the finality of Revelations also suggests the arrival of God's justice, so ineffably perfect, to supplant man's version, so imperfectly applied. However, because that which is inestimably holy cannot have an earthly presence except it inhabit a human carriage, God calls, even woos his ministers, teachers, and warriors.

The Mythology of the American Frontier gave this conceit a new spin by subordinating the Gospel of forgiveness and love to an *Old Testament* ethic of judgment. Frontier mythology is not universal but tribal, calling for righteous warfare against those who stand in opposition to a chosen people having come to claim a land of milk and honey.

Works Cited

Campbell, Joseph. *The Hero with a Thousand Faces.* Princeton: Princeton U.P., 1949.

Price, Reynolds. *Three Gospels.* New York: Scribner, 1996.

Tompkins, Jane. *West of Everything: The Inner Life of Westerns.* New York: Oxford, 1992.

Wilson, Edward O. "The Biological Basis of Morality." *The Atlantic Monthly.* April 1998: 53–70.

Individualism

Robert Bellah

The Ambiguities of Individualism

Individualism lies at the very core of American culture. Every one of the four traditions we have singled out is in a profound sense individualistic. There is a biblical individualism and a civic individualism as well as a utilitarian and an expressive individualism. Whatever the differences among the traditions and the consequent differences in their understandings of individualism, there are some things they all share, things that are basic to American identity. We believe in the dignity, indeed the sacredness, of the individual. Anything that would violate our right to think for ourselves, judge for ourselves, make our own decisions, live our lives as we see fit, is not only morally wrong, it is sacrilegious. Our highest and noblest aspirations, not only for ourselves, but for those we care about, for our society and for the world, are closely linked to our individualism. Yet, as we have been suggesting repeatedly in this book, some of our deepest problems both as individuals and as a society are also closely linked to our individualism. We do not argue that Americans should abandon individualism—that would mean for us to abandon our deepest identity. But individualism has come to mean so many things and to contain such contradictions and paradoxes that even to defend it requires that we analyze it critically, that we consider especially those tendencies that would destroy it from within.

Modern individualism emerged out of the struggle against monarchical and aristocratic authority that seemed arbitrary and oppressive to citizens prepared to assert the right to govern themselves. In that struggle, classical political philosophy and biblical religion were important cultural resources. Classical republicanism evoked an image of the active citizen contributing to the public good and Reformation Christianity, in both Puritan and sectarian forms, inspired a notion of government based on the voluntary participation of individuals. Yet both these traditions placed individual autonomy in a context of moral and religious obligation that in some context justified obedience as well as freedom.

In seventeenth-century England, a radical philosophical defense of individual rights emerged that owed little to either classical or biblical sources. Rather, it consciously started with the biological individual in a "state of nature" and derived a social order from the actions of such individuals, first in relation to nature and then in relation to one another. John Locke is the key figure and one enormously influential in America. The essence of the Lockean position is an almost ontological individualism. The individual is prior to society, which comes into existence only through the voluntary contract of individuals trying to maximize their own self-interest. It is from this position that we have derived the tradition of utilitarian individualism. But because one can only know what is useful to one by consulting one's desires and sentiments, this is also ultimately the source of the expressive individualist tradition as well.

Modern individualism has long coexisted with classical republicanism and biblical religion. The conflict in their basic assumptions was initially muted because they all, in the forms commonest in America, stressed the dignity and autonomy of the individual. But as modern individualism became more dominant in the United States and classical republicanism and biblical religion less effective, some of the difficulties in modern individualism began to become apparent. The therapeutic ethos to which we have devoted so much attention is suggestive of these because it is the way in which contemporary Americans live out the tenets of modern individualism. For psychology, as Robert Coles has written, the self is "the only or main form of reality."[1]

The question is whether an individualism in which the self has become the main form of reality can really be sustained. What is at issue is not simply whether self-contained individuals might withdraw from the public sphere to pursue purely private ends, but whether such individuals are capable of sustaining either a public *or* a private life. If this is the danger, perhaps only the civic and biblical forms of individualism—forms that see the individual in relation to a larger whole, a community and a tradition—are capable of sustaining genuine individuality and nurturing both public and private life.

There are both ideological and sociological reasons for the growing strength of modern individualism at the expense of the civic and biblical traditions. Modern individualism has pursued individual rights and individual autonomy in ever new realms. In so doing, it has come into confrontation with those aspects of biblical and republican thought that accepted, even enshrined, unequal rights and obligations—between husbands and wives, masters and servants, leaders and followers, rich and poor. As the absolute commitment to individual dignity has condemned those inequalities, it has also seemed to invalidate the biblical and republican traditions. And in undermining these traditions, as Toequeville warned, individualism also weakens the very meanings that give content and substance to the ideal of individual dignity.

We thus face a profound impasse. Modern individualism seems to be producing a way of life that is neither individually nor socially viable, yet a return to traditional forms would be to return to intolerable discrimination and oppression. The question, then, is whether the older civic and biblical traditions have the capacity to reformulate themselves while simultaneously remaining faithful to their own deepest insights.

Many Americans would prefer not to see the impasse as starkly as we have put it. Philosophical defenders of modern individualism have frequently presumed a social and cultural context for the individual that their theories cannot justify, or they have added ad hoc arguments that mitigate the harshness of their theoretical model. As we saw in chapter 5, therapists see a need for the social ties that they cannot really comprehend—they cry out for the very community that their moral logic undercuts. Parents advocate "values" for their children even when they do not know what those "values" are. What this suggests is that there is a profound ambivalence about individualism in America among its most articulate defenders. This ambivalence shows up particularly clearly at the level of myth in our literature and our popular culture. There we find the fear that society may overwhelm the individual and destroy any chance of autonomy unless he stands against it, but also recognition that it is only in relation to society that the individual can fulfill himself and that if the break with society is too radical, life has no meaning at all.

MYTHIC INDIVIDUALISM

A deep and continuing theme in American literature is the hero who must leave society, alone or with one or a few others, in order to realize the moral good in the wilderness, at sea, or on the margins of settled society. Sometimes the withdrawal involves a contribution to society, as in James Fenimore Cooper's *The Deerslayer*. Sometimes the new marginal community realizes ethical ends impossible in the larger society, as in the interracial harmony between Huckleberry Finn and Jim. Sometimes the flight from society is simply mad and ends in general disaster, as in *Moby Dick*. When it is not in and through society but in flight from it that the good is to be realized, as in the case of Melville's Ahab, the line between ethical heroism and madness vanishes, and the destructive potentiality of a completely asocial individualism is revealed.

America is also the inventor of that most mythic individual hero, the cowboy, who again and again saves a society he can never completely fit into. The cowboy has a special talent—he can shoot straighter and faster than other men—and a special sense of justice. But these characteristics make him so unique that he can never fully belong to society. His destiny is to defend society without ever really joining it. He rides off alone into the sunset like Shane, or like the Lone Ranger moves on accompanied only by his Indian companion. But the cowboy's importance is not that he is isolated or antisocial. Rather, his significance lies in his unique, individual virtue and special skill and it is because of those qualities that society needs and welcomes him. Shane, after all, starts as a real outsider, but ends up with the gratitude of the community and the love of a woman and a boy. And while the Lone Ranger never settles down and marries the local schoolteacher, he always leaves with the affection and gratitude of the people he has helped. It is as if the myth says you can be a truly good person, worthy of admiration and love, only if you resist fully joining the group. But sometimes the tension leads to an irreparable break, Will Kane, the hero of *High Noon*, abandoned by the cowardly townspeople, saves them from an unrestrained killer, but then throws his sheriff's badge in the dust and goes off into the desert with his bride. One is left wondering where they will go, for there is no longer any link with any town.

The connection of moral courage and lonely individualism is even tighter for that other, more modern American hero, the hard-boiled detective. From Sam Spade to Serpico, the detective is a loner. He is often unsuccessful in conventional terms, working out of a shabby office where the phone never rings. Wily, rough, smart, he is nonetheless unappreciated. But his marginality is also his strength. When a bit of business finally comes their way, Philip Marlowe, Lew Archer, and Travis McGee are tenacious. They pursue justice and help the unprotected even when it threatens to unravel the fabric of society itself. Indeed, what is remarkable about the American detective story is less its hero than its image of crime. When the detective begins his quest, it appears to be an isolated incident. But as it develops, the case turns out to be linked to the powerful and privileged of the community. Society, particularly "high society," is corrupt to the core. It is this boring into the center of society to find it rotten that constitutes the fundamental drama of the American detective story. It is not personal but a social mystery that the detective must unravel.[2]

To seek justice in a corrupt society, the American detective must be tough, and above all, he must be a loner. He lives outside the normal bourgeois pattern of career and family. As his investigations begin to lead him beyond the initial crime to the glamorous and powerful center of the society, its leaders make attempts to buy off the detective, to corrupt him with money, power, or sex. This counterpoint to the gradual unravelling of the crime is the battle the detective wages for his own integrity, in the end rejecting the money of the powerful and spurning (sometimes jailing or killing) the beautiful woman who has tried to seduce him. The hard-boiled detective, who may long for love and success, for a place in society, is finally driven to stand alone, resisting the blandishments of society, to pursue a lonely crusade for justice. Sometimes, as in the film *Chinatown,* corruption is so powerful and so total that the honest detective no longer has a place to stand and the message is one of unrelieved cynicism.

Both the cowboy and the hard-boiled detective tell us something important about American individualism. The cowboy, like the detective, can be valuable to society only because he is a completely autonomous individual who stands outside it. To serve society, one must be able to stand alone, not needing others, not depending on their judgment, and not submitting to their wishes. Yet this individualism is not selfishness. Indeed, it is a kind of heroic selflessness. One accepts the necessity of remaining alone in order to serve the values of the group. And this obligation to aloneness is an important key to the American moral imagination. Yet it is part of the profound ambiguity of the mythology of American individualism that its moral heroism is always just a step away from despair. For an Ahab, and occasionally for a cowboy or a detective, there is no return to society, no moral redemption. The hero's lonely quest for moral excellence ends in absolute nihilism.[3]

If we may turn from the mythical heroes of fiction to a mythic, but historically real, hero, Abraham Lincoln, we may begin to see what is necessary if the nihilistic alternative is to be avoided. In many respects, Lincoln conforms perfectly to the archetype of the lonely, individualistic hero. He was a self-made man, never comfortable with the eastern upper classes. His dual moral commitment to the preservation of the Union and the belief that "all men are created equal" roused the hostility of abolitionists and Southern sympathizers alike. In the war years, he was more and more isolated, misunderstood by Congress and cabinet, and unhappy at home. In the face of almost universal mistrust, he nonetheless completed his self-appointed task of bringing the nation through its most devastating war, preaching reconciliation as he did so, only to be brought down by an assassin's bullet. What saved Lincoln from nihilism was the larger whole for which he felt it was important to live and worthwhile to die. No one understood better the meaning of the Republic and of the freedom and equality that it only very imperfectly embodies. But it was not only civic republicanism that gave his life value. Reinhold Niebuhr has said that Lincoln's biblical understanding of the Civil War was deeper than that of any contemporary theologian. The great symbols of death and rebirth that Lincoln invoked to give understanding to the sacrifice of those who died at Gettysburg, in a war he knew to be senseless and evil, came to redeem his own senseless death at the hand of an assassin. It is through his identification with a community and a tradition that Lincoln became the deeply and typically American individual that he was.[4]

Notes

1. Robert Coles, "Civility and Psychology," *Dædalus* (Summer 1980), p. 137.

2. On individualism in nineteenth-century American literature see D. H. Lawrence, *Studies in Classic American Literature* (1923; Garden City, N.Y.: Doubleday, Anchor Books, 1951). On the image of the cowboy see Will Wright, *Sixguns and Society: A Structural Study of the Western* (Berkeley and Los Angeles: University of California Press, 1975). On cowboys and detectives see John G. Cawelti, *Adventure, Mystery, and Romance: Formula Stories as Art and Popular Culture* (Chicago: University of Chicago Press, 5976).

3. On the hero's avoidance of women and society see Leslie Fiedler, Love and Death in the American Novel (New York: Stein and Day, 1966), and Ann Swidler, "Love and Adulthood in American Culture," in Themes of Work and Love in Adulthood, ed. Neil J. Smelser and Erik H. Erikson (Cambridge, *Mass.: Harvard University Press,* 1980), pp. 120–47.

4. The best book on Lincoln's meaning for American public life is Harry V. *Jaffa, Crisis of the House Divided: An Interpretation of the Lincoln-Douglas Debates* (Garden City, N.Y.: Doubleday, 1959). Reinhold Niebuhr's remarks appear in his essay "The Religion of Abraham Lincoln," in *Lincoln and the* Gettysburg Address, ed. Allan Nevins (Urbana, Ill.: University of Illinois Press, 1964), p.72.

Savior in the Saddle: The Sagebrush Testament

Michael T. Marsden

As Frederick Jackson Turner pointed out, the birth of a new land demanded the simultaneous birth of a new culture, with its roots necessarily in the past, but its blossom in the timeless experience of the ever-extending and never-ending frontier.[1] This operative truth is acted out time and again as Western after Western unfolds on movie screens across this land. It is logical, therefore, to suggest that notions of a Savior, a Messiah, would have undergone a similar transformation from the Christian Savior of almost nineteen hundred years of European cultural refinement to a Christ equipped to serve the essentially different spiritual needs of a new and separate culture. Nowhere is this transformation more clearly seen than in the Western film.[2]

American heroes have a long tradition of serving as the Redeemer. For the Puritans, the wilderness of their Chosen Land was inhabited by devils, and these devils could be driven out only by the strongest and worthiest of men. If the land was to be settled, it had to be tamed and purified. It is of this challenge that the American hero, beginning with Daniel Boone, was born. And Boone's direct cultural descendant, the Western hero, became America's most permanent heroic creation, serving as Redeemer for generations of Americans.

However, it is interesting that, while criticism of the Western film has suggested the Savior-like nature of the Western hero, no extended treatment has been given to the divine, Savior-like qualities of this American creation. Harry Schein, for example, in an article entitled "The Olympian Cowboy,' suggests that in the western landscape one can discern "an Olympian landscape model, the Rocky Mountains—saturated with divine morality."[3] A little later in that article he suggests that Shane is "an American saint . . . and sits at God's right hand."[4] But these suggestions are never explored. Martin Nussbaum, in his article "The 'Adult Western' As An American Art Form," argues that the gun is a symbol of divine intervention into the American landscape, but he never entertains the implications of this regarding the nature of the Western hero.[5]

It is my purpose here to establish several of the religious parallels that abound in Western film, and then to crystallize them into a statement regarding the religious nature of the Western hero. The West of the American imagination is the landscape for this study, not the West as it was, but the West, as John Ford would say, as it should have been.

It is practically a commonplace for people to refer to the Western gunfighter-hero as an American parallel to the medieval knight.[6] While such mediations seem appropriate and stimulate interest, there is a very real danger that they will cloud the issue of the particular and unique nature of the American Western hero; he is an American god, who in the name of a divinely ordered civilization carries a Colt .45. As Gary Cooper succinctly put it, the five bullets in the cylinder were for law and order, and the one in the chamber was for justice. The Western formula clearly implies that the Messiah of the New Testament was unacceptable to a land of savagery, harsh landscape, and purple sunsets. The West needed a Christ who could survive the Great American Desert, and for much longer than forty days, and who could show himself equal to the American challenge, whether real or imagined. And this Savior would have to be equal to the wishes and dreams of a suffering people who wished to be delivered from the concretized evil that plagued their lives. The people longed for a Christ who would ride in, deal effectively with evil, and dispense justice with a finality that would make the angels envious and a skill that John Cawelti, in his book *The Six-Gun Mystique*, likens to that of a surgeon.[7] But this Western Savior must, of necessity, bring with him all the trappings of a just and at times wrathful God, as in the Old Testament. He could not be the loving and forgiving and merciful Christ of the New Testament but must be, rather, a Christ who has been modified, changed by contact with the western experience. The lawlessness of the frontier required a strong sense of divine justice untempered with mercy. The coming of the Western hero is a kind of Second Coming of Christ, but this time he wears the garb of the gunfighter, the only Savior the sagebrush, the wilderness, and the pure savagery of the West can accept.

A just God and a Savior, there is none besides me.   (*Isaiah* 45:21)

The West of the American imagination needed a clean, swift, sure, and final justice in a lawless land infested by outlaws, Indians, and a hostile and threatening environment. The Western film mythology, from the very beginnings of film history, combined the best myths available to forge a viable and lasting mythology which, until recently with the release of anti-Westerns such as *Bad Company* (1972), *Soldier Blue* (1970), and *Dirty Little Billy* (1972), has remained intact, and would appear to be able to weather even the tumultuous filmic assaults being waged against it during the last decade.

Finally, in dealing with the nature of the Western hero, it seems fruitful to view him as a coming together of certain elements from the Old and the New Testaments, and to see through him the creation of a Sagebrush Testament with its own ethos.

Behold the days come, saith the Lord, and I will raise up to David a just branch; and a King shall reign, and shall be wise; and shall execute a judgment and justice in the earth. (*Jeremiah* 23:5)

In 1916 William S. Hart starred in and directed an allegorical Western entitled *Hell's Hinges*. Hart plays the role of Blaze Tracy, who, as one title says, represents a two-gun "embodiment of the best and the worst in the early west." As the film opens he embodies primarily the worst. We find him in league with Silk Miller, owner of the local saloon, aptly named the Palace of Joy. The town is awaiting the arrival of a rather weak and selfish young parson who has been sent by his bishop to establish a church in the wilderness and prove himself as a clergyman. God does not, however, abide in Hells Hinges, a truth which the inexperienced parson and his lovely sister, Faith, must soon painfully face.

As Tracy first gazes at Faith, it is "one who is evil, looking for the first time on what is good." Later, Tracy, who was expected by the corrupt townspeople to take part in the elimination of the parson from Hell's Hinges, stands up for the clergyman and his congregation as they hold their first church service in a local barn. The dance-hall girls, rabble-rousers, and other nonbelievers decide to break up the ceremony by holding a dance on the same premises. But Blaze Tracy's two guns convince them to allow the Sunday service to continue.

When the parson's sister, Faith, attempts to "convert" Blaze, he utters: "I reckon God ain't wantin' me much ma'am, but when I look at you, I feel I've been ridin' the wrong trail." He seeks out religion because Faith holds stock in it, and there must therefore be some value in it. When the parson is lured into the lead dance-hall girl's boudoir, plied with drink, and seduced, it is Blaze who tells a parable to the bewildered good townspeople, who are now a leaderless flock. He tells them, in a Christlike and kindly New Testament manner, about Arizona, a renowned cowboy roper who set off to rope a calf, but the rope failed him. Thus, he says, it was the instrument they counted on that failed them, not their faith.

The evil townspeople are so depraved that they conspire to burn down the newly erected church. So effective have they been in destroying the parson that he is first in line with a willing hand and a lighted torch. But, before he can act, he is killed by the remaining good people who will shed blood to protect their church. After considerable bloodshed, and while Blaze is away on an errand of mercy, the church is burned down. The few remaining good people are literally sent into the desert, to await the return of the Savior who will seek revenge for the destruction of the church and the death of the parson. Blaze, living up to his first name, guns down Silk Miller and turns the whole town into a living inferno. He gives Hell's Hinges a "crown of fire," and forcefully damns it to eternity. In short, Faith is helpless in the West unless she has two blazing guns to defend her. The Western Savior needs the confrontation with civilization (formal religion) to tame him, but he can easily arrive at heroic stature because of his essential goodness.

In *Hell's Hinges* there is the obvious, but nonetheless effective illustration of the blending of certain divine qualities from the Old and New Testament to form a kind of Sagebrush Testament, which must of necessity result in the forging of a new Savior, who is of the sagebrush, but also superior to it.

The 1931 film *Cimarron*, the only Western ever to receive the Oscar for best picture, (Editor's note: The 1992 western *Unforgiven* also won an Oscar for Best Picture) contains another powerful illustration of the essential transformation of Christianity through the American imagination in the Western. Yancy Cravat (Richard Dix) is an incurable wanderer who finds himself in Oklahoma as a consequence of the land rush into the Indian territory, opened for settlement. In turn, he becomes a poet, gunfighter, lawyer, and editor and is successful at each. Being a leading citizen, he is bound to defend the forces of civilization over the forces of the lawless frontier. During one scene, in order to bring religion to the frontier, he himself preaches a sermon. He pulls out a Bible from his back pocket, and as he draws it forward it crosses the butt of his holstered gun as a warning to all who would attempt to usurp the forces of civilization. The saloon is his church, and instead of a crucifix in the background, there is the traditional saloon nude. Christ has come to the frontier, but he wears different garb and follows a new ethos, a modified ethos that was born of the confrontation with the land and savagery. In the middle of his sermon, Yancey Cravat uses his free hand to draw his sixgun and shoot down several unruly cowboys who are disrupting his preaching!

The Savior-like nature of the Western hero is nowhere more clearly manifested than in George Stevens's masterful *Shane* (1953). Alan Ladd at the beginning of the film moves slowly down the Grand Teton Mountains from the west. He is the new Christ, the frontier Christ, coming down from a western Olympus to help the cause of the farmers against the ranchers. We see Shane through the eyes of America's future, young Joey Starrett, through whom the tradition that Shane represents will be handed down. Shane is the pearl-handled-gun-toting Messiah who *can* save the endangered land from the forces of lawlessness. It is not by accident that Joey's parents are named Joe and Marion, standing in wait for the Messiah-son who will deliver them The suggestion by some critics that Joey may well be dreaming the entire story seems to work well here. For Shane is what Joey wants to become and what Joe and Marion want their son to become. Shane brings with him all the trappings of a wrathful God out of the Old Testament—omniscience, swift judgment or justice, and an anger born of injustice. But that "wrath" is only hinted at in the early parts of the film as some dangerous undercurrent in the man. As the film opens, he has attempted to hang up his guns, to live peacefully, kindly, and gently. But experience proves that evil must be dealt with directly, swiftly, and surely.

The Devil is personified in this film by the hired gunman, Jack Wilson (Jack Palance), who shoots down an innocent farmer to instill fear in the homesteaders.

When the farmers are burying their murdered compatriot and are considering giving up the land, it is Shane who, in the middle of a barren cemetery with the flimsy, false-fronted town to his back, reminds them about what is at stake in this epic struggle. He preaches his sermon on the mount effectively, and they depart reassured, determined, and unified. Shane, however, by unwillingly but obediently accepting the burden of the homesteaders, sacrifices his right to the good life. He was sent from the mountain to perform a task of salvation, and although he struggles mightily with his fate and wishes it were otherwise, he does not, in his moment of truth, hesitate to shoulder the burden of being a savior. He, finally, plays the hand he has been dealt.

But before he sacrifices himself he instructs Joey in the use of the gun. Martin Nussbaum has correctly observed that the gun is really a deus ex machina in the Western.[8] It is the "word" of the West, and must be understood and used correctly. The temptation is to limit one's interpretation of the gun to sexual suggestions, which are indeed clearly there in *Shane* as in other Westerns. Marion, for example, is both fascinated by the power Shane possesses through the gun and afraid of it. The Western hero must use the gun deliberately and sparingly so that, in the words of Judd in *Ride the High Country* (1962), he can "enter his house justified." Shane tells Marion and Joey that it is not the gun that is evil, but rather the way in which it is used. It is only a tool, he explains, neither good nor bad in itself. Shane leaves Joey instructed. And when Joey runs to town after Shane, watches over his hero, and finally warns him of the danger, he is found tested and true.

After the showdown, Shane, who incidentally has been wounded in the left side, and who is about to ride off into the mountains again, stops and lays his hand upon the head of young Joey, as if to consecrate him for the task ahead.[9] But this Messiah needs only one apostle, not twelve. For the Christianity of the American imagination, of the American Desert, is an individualistic one.

From *Shane* to the cynical "Dollars" films of the 1960s is a long leap, but the image of the Savior clings even to Eastwood's portrayal of the self-interested yet fated Messiah of a deserving few. In *Fistfull of Dollars* (1964—American release 1967), Eastwood rides into a Southwestern town on a mule. He is shot at, poked fun at, and swings from a cross-like beam. The whole scene suggests a Palm Sunday in reverse. As a consequence of doing battle with the evil forces in the town, he receives a terrible beating including, appropriately, a wound on the hand. He seeks sanctuary in a coffin, and is reborn again to fight evil, seeming to be invulnerable to shots in the heart by wearing an armor breastplate. In a touching sequence, suggestive of the Holy Family's flight from Bethlehem to the desert, Eastwood frees a captive mother, her helpless husband, and their young son and sends them off into the desert to seek refuge. Eastwood, "the man with no name," like the heroes of American-made Westerns, brings justice (and mercy) to this evil-ridden society through violence.

Eastwood returned in 1973 as the "no name" character in a Western of his own creation, *High Plains Drifter,* in which he eschews traditional religion because it did not intervene when the town had bullwhipped the Marshal to death in its streets. He comes to the town to execute an elaborate but just revenge upon its inhabitants. While pushing aside the parson who speaks empty Christian platitudes, "No Name" dispenses justice with an appropriateness that defies parallels. The cowardly townsfolk are, for example, led to believe they can be made courageous under his leadership. He, however, trains them and leaves them, taking with him their supposed courage. Called a Guardian Angel by some, the Devil by others, he turns out to be their judge and, like God, allows men to work out their own destinies, trapping and destroying themselves. As a final insult, he has them paint the whole town red, suggesting the crown of fire so memorable from *Hell's Hinges,* and he even paints "Hell" over the town's name on the sign at the edge of the town.

Alejandro Jodorowsky, a South American director, has successfully employed the convention of the Sagebrush Savior in his ultraviolent and enigmatic film *El Topo* (1971). El Topo rides into the desert with his son, abandons him to his own devices, and seeks adventure in the Great Desert. After numerous violent experiences, he is shot by a woman companion, left for dead, and rescued by a tribe of cave-dwelling mutants who are kept in underground confinement by the neighboring townspeople. While living among these strange people, he becomes a kind of pacifist Savior and eventually leads them to freedom from their confinement. But when they rush en masse into the Mexican village, they are promptly slaughtered by the forces of evil. El Topo, seeing the slaughter, grabs a rifle and, declaring in turn that he is justice and then God, consecrates the bullets with his words. He becomes the personification of violence, seemingly invulnerable to bullets himself. The film ends in a holocaust as El Topo destroys the villains with his rifle and then immolates himself, Buddhist monk fashion, in the middle of the main street, etching forever in the minds of the viewers the inevitability of justice through violence.

Films such as *El Topo* serve as illustrations of the viability of the Savior convention, as the Western is adapted to the cultural needs of other nations which seek to develop it as a unique folk-pop art within their own cultural contexts and thus reexamine it in that milieu.

Criticism of the Western film must take into account the transformation of a Christian mythology as much as the transformation of other cultural traditions. The Western hero cannot simply be a Christ transported out of the New Testament any more than he can be a slightly altered medieval knight. For in the American imagination, the New Testament message of love and mercy does not provide solutions any more than the American judicial system does. The answer lies in divine intervention, through a hero who combines the most useful qualities of the Old Testament God and the New Testament Christ, to create a Sagebrush Savior who is kind, yet strong; who is just, yet firm. This hero is the only hero the Western can abide by in a wilderness which is ever ready to snuff out civilization as it weakly struggles to exist in flimsy wooden churches, schools, and town halls, strung out like cross-bearing telephone poles against the ever-widening horizon. The hero must be superhuman, and he must, above all, be invulnerable to the human weaknesses shared by those whom he must defend and protect. If he is to be the answer to the dreams and prayers of the troubled, he must ride tall, shoot straight, and remain eternally vigilant for the causes of right.

But in order to create the needed hero the Western had to borrow from numerous sources to form the truly viable and invulnerable Savior who rides in, provides a definite and final solution to the problem, and rides out as inevitably and often as our psyches dictate. He, like the Christian Messiah, must always be with us, ever ready to sweep down on the evil towns and destroy them so they can be rebuilt to house families and civilization and the dreams of men. He may exist only in the American imagination, but he has the will of a people to give him strength and their hearts to give him immortality.

NOTES

1. *The Turner Thesis Concerning the Role of the Frontier in American History,* ed. George Rogers Taylor (Boston: D. C. Heath,1956).

2. I should like to express my appreciation to Jack Nachbar for many hours of stimulating conversation on the topic of Western films, and for providing the catalystic conception that the Western hero was more of the Old Testament than the New Testament.

3. Harry Shein, "The Olympian Cowboy." *American Scholar,* 24 (Summer 1955): 317.

4. Ibid., p. 319.

5. Martin Nussbaum, The 'Adult Western' As an American Art Form," *Folklore,* 70 (September 1959): 464.

6. See, for example, Joseph J. Waldmeir, "The Cowboy, The Knight, and Popular Taste," *Southern Folklore Quarterly,* 22, no. 3 (September 1958): 113–120.

7. John G. Cawelti, *The Six-Gun Mystique* (Bowling Green, Ohio: Bowling Green State University Popular Press, 1970), p. 59.

8. Nussbaum, p. 464.

9. Joey was, of course, played by Brandon de Wilde, who later starred in *Hud* as the teenage nephew of Hud who turned away in disgust from all that he represented. Brandon de Wilde died at the age of thirty-three, as did, in 1973, Carl B. Bradley, who played the Marlboro cowboy in a national advertising campaign. The author does not wish to suggest anything more than that such curiosities in light of the Christ parallels prove to be interesting musings for the imaginative.

Wade in the Water: Wyatt Earp's Transformation in *Tombstone*

Stephen Cook

"And I will execute great vengeance upon them with furious rebukes; and they shall know that I am the Lord, when I shall lay my vengeance upon them."

Ezekiel 25:17

In the 1993 western *Tombstone*, the second half of the movie has as a foundation the major premise established through prophecy in the beginning scene: someone will come to quell the anarchy of the Cowboys, a ruthless gang of killers, each of whom will answer personally for his sins, which are grievous, to be sure. A dying Morgan Earp, shot in the back and lying on a pool table sodden with his blood, is face to face with his brother Wyatt and delivers the pronouncement: "You're the one." Moments later, Morgan dies, and in Wyatt's grief and with his brother's blood on his hands, he steps out into the street, there to be drenched by a torrential storm in a scene reminiscent of birth—blood and water signify this—and baptism as well, a cleansing and an anointing emblematic of Wyatt Earp's calling as God's Bringer of Justice. It is also in these moments that he is made separate for his holy task, for when his wife and mistress approach him from opposite directions, he rejects them both, pleading to be left alone.

Ensuing scenes reinforce that separation as his family and Wyatt leave Tombstone for Tucson, where all but Wyatt board a train. There in the depot, Wyatt Earp and his Immortals—Doc Holliday, Turkey Creek Johnson, Texas Jack Vermillion, and a former Cowboy known simply as McMasters—confront two of the gang sent to finish off the Earps, Frank Stilwell and Ike Clanton. Clanton survives, spared, but Wyatt slashes Clanton's face with a spur to emphasize the message Clanton is to bring to the Cowboys: "You called down the thunder, well now you got it. . . . The Cowboys are finished, you understand me. I see a red sash, and I kill the man wearing it. . . . The law is coming. You tell 'em I'm coming and Hell's coming with me. . . . Hell's coming with me."

With these scenes and others, screenwriter Kevin Jarre creates an American jihad, a narrative set in fact yet drawn from the Old and New Testaments, starring a hero who embodies human as well as superhuman qualities. Still, in the script Wyatt Earp is more mythological than real, for Jarre roots *Tombstone* deeply in the central premise of American heroic mythology: in order for community to survive and to flourish, the sacrifice of altruistic individuals is absolutely necessary. To amplify on this idea, I must reiterate that this "altruistic hero" takes two forms. The first is a secular hero while the second is "the chosen one," selected by God or ordained by Fate to fulfill the role of savior.

Jarre makes Wyatt Earp the latter kind of hero; indeed, three times Morgan Earp says to Wyatt, "You're the one," and as I state earlier, the last time most poignantly seconds before Morgan dies. The redundancy is not because of bad writing; rather Jarre understands the need to transport his main protagonist from the secular (a character who bravely steps forward) to the selected (a character that is initially reluctant but is ultimately compelled, thrust forward by events). To accomplish this task, Jarre fills *Tombstone* with images of and allusions to Christianity, rightly assuming that many if not all references will be familiar to a large number of viewers who are capable of understanding these landmarks. Other viewers will see primarily the movie's action, witty dialogue, and charismatic characters. They will also understand that on a basic level, the movie is about a conflict between good and evil, a battle that seemingly causes Wyatt Earp to devolve to the level of the Cowboys. Jarre anticipates that many viewers may arrive at this conclusion, so he uses Doc Holliday to explain to the other members of the Immortals that Wyatt's motives are not ones of revenge for one brother slain and another wounded. Instead, Holliday assures his fellow riders (and us) after joking that Wyatt is "down by the creek walking on water" that Wyatt is consumed by the holy mandate for a "reckoning."

More submerged in the screenplay and less accessible to the casual viewer is the prophecy made by a Mexican priest in the opening scene. The incensed padre begins to quote Revelations 6:8: "And I looked, and behold a pale horse: and his name that sat on him was Death, and Hell followed with him. And power was given unto them over the fourth part of the earth, to kill with the sword, and with hunger, and with death, and with the beasts of the earth." However, the gunfighter Johnny Ringo guns down the priest before he can recite the second sentence, for the well-educated Ringo knows what is to come, and he understands the death sentence inherent in the words. The observant viewer will also note the way in which Jarre and director George Cosmatos tie the Cowboys to the "fourth part of the earth": the camera quite clearly shows us that Curly Bill Brosius, the leader of this gang, wears knee-high boots with four aces engraved on each.

Jarre and Cosmatos make it plain that God has *called* Wyatt Earp to be His warrior, like Gideon or David or an avenging angel in The Book of Revelations. *Tombstone* is thus part of a lineage of American films for which the challenges to "the chosen one" are the kelsom of their plots. It is on behalf of "the causes of right" that Wyatt Earp and his Immortals wreak havoc on the Cowboys, ignoring the stylized rituals of gunfighting, for these outlaws are little more than "bugs" as Morgan labels them.

Therefore, one of the principal arguments of the script is that even the most sentient of viewers should conclude early on that the Cowboys have flat got it coming.

The opening scene leaves no doubt about the wickedness of these men whose red sashes show solidarity with each other as well as a deeper allegiance to evil. Old Testament writers traditionally used red hues as symbols of transgression as in Isaiah 1:18: "Though your sins be as scarlet, they shall be white as snow; though they be red like crimson, they shall be as wool." The leader of the Cowboys, Curly Bill Brocius, is especially demonic-appearing, regularly wearing a red shirt to complement the sash and sporting a devilish mustache and goatee. Still, it is not in caricature but in their actions that the Cowboys' natures are revealed. In revenge for the deaths of two of them at the hands of some Federales, the rest of the gang rides into a Mexican town to confront these officers, one of which is getting married. In a gun battle, the police are killed, except for the groom who is initially unwounded, but then shot in the knee to make him prostrate. Still, defiant, the groom yells, "You go to Hell," which is both an expression of that defiance and a prophecy. Curly Bill kills the groom at that point, and the bride is dragged into the church to be raped. Curly Bill declares himself the "Founder of the Feast," then sits with other Cowboys at the banquet table prepared for the wedding party. For Curly Bill to make such a pronouncement is sacrilegious because Christian theology ties the concept of feasts to the sacraments, one of which is marriage: "[Religious feasts] manifested the beneficence of God towards his creatures. By these feasts man not only acknowledged God as his provider but recorded the Lord's unbounded and free favour to [his] chosen people whom he [has] delivered, by personal intervention, in the world" (*New Bible Dictionary* 365).

However, God is watching—the opening shot of the movie reveals a Mexican church with a cross at its summit, presiding over all—and He uses the priest as a messenger until the doomed Ringo, who has made his own Faustian deal with the Devil, drops the priest with a single shot. Ringo translates and interprets the priest's words for the other Cowboys, and Cosmatos immediately cuts to Earp descending from a train: the director cinches the connection between the prophecy and the lawman at that point. The threat to community is also established by a camera shot of the terrorized face of a Mexican child in that little village, and Jarre and Cosmatos repeat this theme as a means of winning the viewers' assent to the carnage directed against the Cowboys in the second half of the movie. The movie continues to emphasize the threat of the Cowboys. Curly Bill, stoned on opium, howls at the moon, shoots at the stars, and kills Marshal White as part of a pretense of surrendering his guns. Virgil Earp steps into the street to rescue a child chasing a ball from being run over by the Cowboys riding at breakneck speed. This last incident finally causes Virgil Earp's wall of indifference to crumble. He can take no more: "I walk around this town and look these people in the eye, and it's just like someone slappin' me in the face. These people are afraid to walk down the street, and I'm tryin' to make money off that like some goddam vulture. If we're gonna have a future in this town, it's got to have some law and order." Virgil takes over Fred White's job and swears in Morgan Earp as his deputy. In Virgil, we see a classic secular hero, whose call to action comes not from God or Fate but from the community itself, in particular, those who cannot defend themselves.

In Tombstone, conflict increases, and it is in those contested streets close by the O.K. Corral that the Earps and Doc Holliday meet four members of the Cowboys: Tom and Frank McLaury and Ike and Billy Clanton. Only Ike survives, his personal enmity multiplied many times over by the members of the gang, now implacable foes of the Earps, who are clearly protectors of the community, roles the movie emphasizes: on a Sunday morning patrol of Tombstone, the Earps appear while a church with a crucifix at its peak is at the top of the screen, the chime of its bells calling good citizens to worship. The Earps are not free to attend, however, for even though they wear split-tailed preacher coats, their mission is in the streets of that beleaguered town. The juxtaposition of the church with the Earp brothers is obvious as is the repetition of the theme of evil when a drunken Johnny Ringo confronts them, saying, "I want your blood. I want your souls."

Indeed, it is next for the lawmen to suffer as foretold by the tarot cards held by Allie, Virgil's wife: the Tower of Babel, Death, and the Devil. Morgan is killed by a shot in the back, and Virgil is so badly wounded in another ambush as to lose the use of his left arm. Confusion reigns as the Cowboys and their ally County Marshal Behan make a grab for power. It is these terrible moments that lead Wyatt into the street, to accept his separation and anointing as well as his exile into the wilderness.

It is there that Doc Holliday's presence is most important. Dying from tuberculosis, his pallor is reminiscent of the pale horse alluded to by the Mexican priest. Wyatt and Doc are thus spiritually linked, and one can make an argument that Doc is a selected hero. What is certain is that Doc's physical gift of reflexes complements his friend's sense of mission. The battle is thoroughly joined, and no quarter is given or asked, especially during a ferocious firefight at a creek in the desert, where the Immortals are pinned down and at risk of being wiped out. However, Wyatt Earp rises and, seemingly impervious to bullets, wades into the water, killing Curly Bill and other members of the gang. Earp's actions are evidence of his "selected" status, for they transcend the reality of physics. In essence, Wyatt is bulletproof. It is after the battle that Doc makes the joking reference to Wyatt walking on water and also explains the distinction between "revenge" and a "reckoning." In acting as interpreter of Wyatt's actions, Doc reveals the intense symbiosis between the two men. Both are solitary figures finding companionship in few others. Texas Jack inquires after the firefight at the creek as to why Doc rides with them when he is so ill as to be spitting up blood. Doc's reply is bedrock simple: "Wyatt Earp is a friend of mine." "Hell, I got lots of friends," Jack retorts, but again Doc's words are abbreviated yet profound: "I don't."

Doc most clearly shows his friendship at the end in two significant moments. The first is when he rises from a sickbed to confront Johnny Ringo in Wyatt's stead. Earp is not fast enough, and he knows it. Still, Wyatt goes to confront Ringo, but arrives only after the duel is completed, won by Doc, badge on his chest, moments after the camera offers the viewer an upward look at him, bathed in effusive light. Ringo has fallen, tottering at first as Doc urges Ringo to fire back, to put Doc out of his physical pain. However, there are remnants of the Cowboys to be killed or to be dispersed, and it is for Doc to give up the ghost in Glenwood Sanitarium, oddly enough without his boots on and having received the last rites from a priest, who instead of pronouncing a sentence dispenses grace and redemption. The priest's visitation is wryly observed by Doc as further evidence of his hypocrisy, but Wyatt offers his own keen insight: "You're not a hypocrite, Doc; you just like to sound like one." There is no question that Doc Holliday has earned his redemption.

Before death, Doc renders his final service to Wyatt Earp, who has been coming daily to visit. The former lawman is lost: once wealthy, he has nothing; his wife Maddie is dead from an opium overdose; his family is away from him in California; his best friend is soon to be a corpse; last, he has no sense of direction. When Doc requests that Wyatt no longer come to visit, Wyatt tells him that he does not know what to do with himself or how to claim the "normal life" he so desires. Doc gently reminds Wyatt, "There is no normal life, only life" itself, then urges his friend to find Josephine Marcus, to "grab that spirited actress and make her your own." These words are Doc's last act of friendship and are a benediction for the remainder of Wyatt's days. In turn, Wyatt's last words to his friend are, "Thanks for always being there."

Wyatt Earp's transformation is nearly complete. Initially self-centered, he has come to understand the preeminent need for community to flourish in the face of rogue individualism; early on a spiritual skeptic who mocks his brother Morgan's interest in some kind of transcendence, he has accepted and fulfilled God's calling; rigorously amoral, saying "what do I care" when Curly Bill gets off after murdering Marshal White, he is now a vessel emptied and ready to be filled, for part of the mythology of the altruistic hero is the recompense he receives, bestowed by God and a grateful community. In Wyatt's case, he claims certain immediate rewards: Josephine accepts his marriage proposal, and they remain together for nearly fifty years, ultimately moving to golden California, where in a wonderful notation by Jarre that shows the melding of history and myth, we learn that early-day movie stars, among them William S. Hart, bear Wyatt Earp's casket to his grave.

What then do we make of *Tombstone?* Not intended to be a historical document, the movie therefore does not report but rather interprets. Thus, for example, it is irrelevant that Doc Holliday at one point fires eighteen shots from two six-shooters. A more serious question concerns the extremely violent nature of the film, which leads some viewers to conclude that Wyatt Earp becomes an assassin, and while that outlook has *some* truth, it simply does not go far enough, for it ignores the careful building of meaning throughout the movie, allusions and symbols that take the viewer into the realm of American heroic mythology where Wyatt Earp becomes *God's* trigger man.

WORKS CITED

"Feasts." *New Bible Dictionary.* 3rd edition. Ed. D. R. W. Wood. Downers Grove: Intervarsity Press, 1996.

The Holy Bible. King James Version.

Tombstone. Directed by George Cosmatos. With K. Russell and V. Kilmer. 1993.

THE MATRIX

Stephen Cook

Eighty-three years after *Hell's Hinges*, the Wachowski Brothers' thriller/urban western *The Matrix* echoed many of the same themes offered by *Hell's Hinges* and *Tombstone*. In a desolate future controlled by soulless machines, humans are raised in a factory setting to be nothing more than batteries for those machines. A group of human guerrilla fighters led by Morpheus operates from his hovercraft called the Nebuchadnezzar, the name an allusion to the Babylonian king in the Old Testament Book of Daniel. Nebuchadnezzar goes mad at one point in the text but is restored to soundness of mind after receiving a revelation. Morpheus also "sees," looking past the Matrix, a rosy façade of "normalcy" projected by the machine hierarchy, knowing instead that behind the illusion is the "desert of the real." Morpheus and his crew have been looking for "the one" whose coming "the oracle" has prophesied. Neo is the fulfillment of the prophecy, ordained by fate to liberate humans from the metal pharaohs who rule them. Early on, *The Matrix* alludes to Neo's uniqueness: when Neo the computer hacker sells bootleg programs to a fellow hacker, the buyer says as part of his thanks, "You're my savior, my own personal Jesus Christ."

Even so, Morpeus and his gang of rebels must work to convince Neo of his destiny as the leader who will ultimately lead his people to "Zion" and to prepare him to meet the bionic Agent Smith and others like him constructed to eliminate any disturbances or rebellions by humans. In the characters surrounding Neo the "selected hero," we see prototypical "secular heroes," with the exception of Cipher, who is the Judas of the crew and pays for his treachery with his life.

After enduring a series of rigorous physical and mental tests, Neo has an O.K. Corral–style showdown with Agent Smith, but because of the betrayal of Cipher, Neo's chances of success are tenuous. It is only when Neo fully repudiates his slave name of Thomas A. Anderson that he has the power to "enter" Agent Smith's chest, causing Smith to explode. The other agents are so intimidated that they flee. The surviving members of the crew are saved, among them Trinity, Neo's love interest, who at one point resuscitates Neo with a kiss. This turnaround on the traditional theme of the life-restoring kiss is but one way in which Trinity is a heroine for the Twenty-First Century. She's tough, unflappable, and deadly in combat against the Matrix and its henchmen. Neo's commentary upon meeting her is significant, as is her reply:

> "I thought you were a guy."
> "Most guys think I'm a guy."

Also worth noting is the diverse ethnicity of the crew. Both factors indicate profound changes in American mythology, which has traditionally placed the White Male at its center.

The Matrix clearly defends the traditional American secular values of freedom, self-governance, and the non-negotiable possession of one's own being, yet—as does director Thomas Ince in *Hell's Hinges* and as do screenwriter Kevin Jarre and director George Cosmatos in *Tombstone*—the Wachowski Brothers take the essence of the narrative and its important symbols from within a Christian framework.

WORKS CITED

The Matrix. Dir. by the Wachowski Brothers. With Keanu Reeves and Laurence Fishburne. 1999.

American Heroic Mythology

Study Questions

1. How does the author of "The Altruistic Hero" define the terms "selected hero" and "secular hero"?
2. Why do successful societies encourage altruism, and what methods do cultures use to promote sacrifice?
3. "The Altruistic Hero" argues that individuals who become either selected or secular heroes must be people of "goodness." How is "goodness" defined? Why must a hero be "good" at his or her core?
4. In the world of nature, how does death sustain life? What are the ways in which the deaths of heroic individuals sustain the group or the community? What other forms of altruism are necessary for a community to survive?
5. In the essay "Individualism," how does Robert Bellah describe "that most mythic individual hero, the cowboy"?
6. Bellah and his colleagues tell us that sometimes a hero loses his way and becomes a rogue individual. According to the author of "Individualism," what keeps the heroic individual from going astray and being a force for evil?
7. According to Michael Marsden, how has the myth of the cowboy become intertwined with Christian theology?
8. After reading Marsden's description of the silent movie *Hell's Hinges* in "Savior in the Saddle: The Sagebrush Testament," describe the ways in which *Hell's Hinges* is an allegory.

Study Questions—Tombstone (1993)

1. How does the opening scene introduce the central premise of *Tombstone* as a battle between good and evil, according to the author of "Wade in the Water: Wyatt Earp's Transformation in *Tombstone*"?
2. Apply Bellah's analysis of individualism to the movie. Which individuals are in service to the community? Which individuals have crossed the line into what Bellah calls "nihilism"? (For another dramatic study in the implications of this question, watch the Antoine Fuqua film *Training Day*.)
3. What images in *Tombstone* represent community most vividly (and poignantly)?

4. How does the movie use repetition, for example, the way in which the number four keeps coming up, or the reiteration of the phrase, "You're the one," or the way in which the crucifix appears again and again?

5. How is the theme of transformation by moving west revealed in *Tombstone*? By the way, at the end of the movie, what state do Wyatt and Josephine move to?

6. Look at the hats the characters wear. How do the hats reveal the personalities of those who wear them?

7. Compare the characters of Hawkeye (From *Last of the Mohicans*) and Wyatt Earp. How are they similar, and how are they different? How has the frontiersman become the cowboy—what is the nature of that transition?

8. Look at the character of Josephine Marcus. Does she play a significant role or is she merely "eye candy"?

9. How does the traditional Western theme of men showing mastery over other men reveal itself in *Tombstone*? Where do images of guns as phallic symbols show up?

10. According to Doc Holliday, there is a difference between "revenge" and a "reckoning"? What do you think he means?

11. Some observers have said the real love affair in *Tombstone* is between Doc and Wyatt, not between Wyatt and Josephine. What do you think?

12. *Tombstone* is, at its core, a drama about white males battling it out for supremacy (although it is certainly true that the community will be affected by whether or not the rule of law wins out). However, the viewer will see in the background many women and people of color. Does this bit of inclusiveness make the movie more democratic and realistic, or is this aspect simply a matter of tokenism?

13. *Tombstone* implies that two characters—Billy Breckenridge (Sister Boy) and Mr. Fabian (The actor)—are gay. What do you think? How do the other characters in the movie treat these characters? How do the screenwriter (Kevin Jarre) and the director (George Cosmatos) intend for us to see Billy and Mr. Fabian?

Suggested Essay Topics

1. Read "Wade in the Water: Wyatt Earp's Transformation in *Tombstone*," and apply its ideas to the Western. What are the ways *Tombstone* shows Wyatt Earp as a "selected hero"? More specifically, how does screenwriter Kevin Jarre use Christian theology to present Wyatt Earp as "the one," a man who must serve as a redeemer to the citizens of the beleaguered town?

2. Analyze *Tombstone* in light of ideas presented in "The Altruistic Hero" and "Individualism." How is the movie a vehicle for teaching altruism and heroism? How does the film reinforce the American fascination with individualism, both virtuous and nihilistic? How are images of Christianity used to portray a battle between good and evil?

3. Watch *The Matrix*. How does the movie posit Neo as a "selected hero"? Is *The Matrix* a Western? Why or why not?

4. Watch *Spiderman*, and evaluate it in light of what you have learned about heroic mythology.

5. Watch *The Departed* (winner of the best picture Oscar for 2006). Is the movie a battle between good and evil, or does it posit a world devoid of morality, a place where all that truly matters is the use of force? Analyze the characters in light of what you've learned about American Heroic Mythology. What characters are outlaws? Which ones are "secular heroes" if any? In the final scene, does Detective Dignam become a "rogue individual" or is he a "secular hero" operating under the aegis of what Bellah calls the hero's "special sense of justice"?

6. Watch *Malcolm X*. Evaluate the movie in light of what you have learned about American Heroic Mythology. Is Malcolm X a redeemer figure? Does the mythology that has sprung up around him posit Malcolm X as a "selected hero"?

7. What conclusions can we draw about American culture that one of the principal figures in our heroic mythology is a Messiah/Redeemer/Jesus figure concerned not with mercy but with justice attained through violence? To paraphrase Marsden, Is faith helpless without the application of force?

8. William Donald Hamilton was an evolutionary biologist for whom "Hamilton's Rule" (rB>C) is named. The formula represents the biological basis for altruism: relationship X Benefit > Cost. Write a paper in which you analyze Hamilton's Rule and speculate on the existence of an "altruistic gene." For help on this question, read "The Selfless Gene," by Olivia Judson in *The Atlantic*, October 2007. You may also wish to read "The Hidden Cost of Heroism," by Christopher McDougall in *Men's Health*, November 2007.

THE REEL WEST

The Western is one of a handful of organic art forms in America. Jazz and Gospel also qualify, and if sports are art, then lacrosse and basketball are native activities. However, beginning with Buffalo Bill's Wild West Show and dime novels, the Western came to dominate our imaginations like nothing else. The Western defined for us ideas of right and wrong, civilized and uncivilized, masculinity and femininity, and in particular, the characteristics, look, and behavior of the hero-figure. Ideas and pictures from the Western permeated our culture like rain percolating into soil and becoming groundwater. Perceptive image-builders and advertisers appeal to this national sub-conscious, selling everything from cigarettes to action-figures to presidents. For example, in the November 2005 issue of *Vanity Fair*, Evgenia Peretz writes in "High Noon in Crawford" of the way in which political consultant Karl Rove set about to transform George W. Bush into "that American archetype of honesty, courage, and unshakeable conviction: the cowboy" (222).

Peretz explains the overall strategy:

The plan . . . was hatched in the late 90s, when the Connecticut-born Texas governor, who attended Andover and Yale, [decided] to run for the presidency. The first thing Bush needed was a ranch. In 1999, he picked one, a 1,600-acre spread in Crawford . . . He'd spend roughly 20 percent of his presidency there—more than any modern president has been on vacation—so the press would get a steady diet of him in his cowboy hat, walking tall down dusty roads. (222, 224)

Clearly, Bush is not a *real* cowboy; he would be hard-pressed to rope a steer and take his dally around a saddle horn. What he did was to take on the appearance of a cowboy, thereby surrounding himself with myth and mystique greatly appealing to people in the heartland of this country. Bush's message was and continues to be that the Sheriff is in town and that the community is under his skilled and capable protection. He is a man with a steady hand. If you doubt that Rove was successful, do a google search on the number of times Bush has been compared to a cowboy in the last five years, especially by the European press.

In this section, the commentary of three critics with the sharp eyes of raptors will flesh out the ideas presented in this introduction. Thomas Schatz gives an overview of the Western, focusing on some of the classics in the genre. Jane Tompkins' Introduction to her book *West of Everything: The Inner Life of Westerns* provides a feminist interpretation of the Western by someone who loves westerns and yet is troubled by many of its themes. Richard Slotkin, author of *Gunfighter Nation*, shows in "Gunsmoke and Mirrors," how Westerns, as they grew in sophistication, offered political and social commentary on the events of the day. A fourth essay, "Material and Metaphorical—Horse and Rider in *Lonely Are the Brave*," analyzes the contributions of horses to Westerns, in particular the role of a palomino named Whiskey in a Kirk Douglas classic. Finally, study questions for *Red River* will provide an entryway into what many critics consider the Golden Age of Hollywood Westerns produced between the late 1940s and mid-1960s.

Remember, when you watch a Western, do not look for strictly literal truth. A revolver built to carry six bullets may fire eight or twelve. Rather, look at the mythology presented and understand that something does not necessarily have to be literally true to be true nonetheless in the vision it provides.

THE WESTERN

Thomas Schatz

"This is the West, sir.
When the legend becomes fact, print the legend."
—Newspaper editor in *The Man Who Shot Liberty Valance*

WESTERN AS GENRE

The Western is without question the richest and most enduring genre of Hollywood's repertoire. Its concise heroic story and elemental visual appeal render it the most flexible of narrative formulas, and its life span has been as long and varied as Hollywood's own. In fact, the Western genre and the American cinema evolved concurrently, generating the basic framework for Hollywood's studio production system. We might look to Edwin S. Porter's *The Great Train Robbery*, in 1903 as the birth not only of the movie Western, but of the commercial narrative film in America; and to Thomas Ince's mass production of William S. Hart horse operas during the teens as the prototype for the studio system.

The origins of the Western formula predated the cinema, of course. Its genealogy encompassed colonial folk music, Indian captivity tales, James Fenimore Cooper's *Leather-Stocking Tales*, nineteenth-century pulp romances, and a variety of other cultural forms. These earlier forms began to develop the story of the American West as popular mythology, sacrificing historical accuracy for the opportunity to examine the values, attitudes, and ideals associated with westward expansion and the taming and civilizing of the West. Not until its immortalization on film, however, did the Western genre certify its mythic credentials. The significance and impact of the Western as America's foundation ritual have been articulated most clearly and effectively in the cinema—the medium of twentieth-century technology and urbanization. And it was also in the cinema that the Western could reach a mass audience which actively participated in the gradual refinement and evolution of its narrative formula.

THE EARLY FILMS

As America's first popular and industrial mass art form, the commercial cinema assumed a privileged but paradoxical function in its development of the Western myth.

As a narrative mass medium, the cinema provided an ideal vehicle for disseminating the Western formula to the culture at large; as a commercial industry, it embodied those very socioeconomic and technological values which the Western anticipated in tracing the steady progression of American civilization. The height of the Western's popularity—from the late 1930s, through the '50s—spanned an era when the American West and its traditional values were being threatened and displaced by the Modern Age Twentieth-century technology and industry, the Depression with its Dust Bowl and flight to the cities, the ensuing World War and the birth of atomic power, the Cold War and the Korean conflict—these and other historical factors overwhelmed America's "Old West" and at the same time enhanced its mythic status. In constructing and gradually formalizing the actions and attitudes from the past on a wide screen, the Western genre created a mythical reality more significant and pervasive—and perhaps in some ways more "real"—than the historical West itself.

As cultural and historical documents, the earlier silent Westerns differ from the later Westerns. In fact, these earlier films have a unique and somewhat paradoxical position: Although they were made on the virtual threshold of the Modern Age, they also came at a time when westward expansion was winding down. Certain early cowboy heroes like "Bronco Billy" Anderson and William S. Hart did lay the groundwork for the heroic and stylized mythology of movie Westerns. But many other films, like *The Covered Wagon* (1923) and *The Iron Horse* (1924), were really historical dramas, depicting as accurately as possible the actuality of westward expansion. (In fact, *The Great Train Robbery* related events that had occurred only a few years previously and as such was something of a turn-of-the-century gangster film.) But eventually, the cumulative effects of Western storytelling in the face of contemporary civilization's steady encroachment served to subordinate the genre's historical function to its mythical one. In other words, efforts to document the historical West on film steadily gave way to the impulse to exploit the past as a means of examining the values and attitudes of contemporary America.

It's important to note in this context that during the Depression, as Hollywood moved into the sound era, the historical epics, which had dominated mainstream Western film production in the teens and '20s, faded from the screen, and the genre survived primarily in the form of low-budget "B" productions. These films rounded out the newly introduced double features and also served to provide John Wayne, who made dozens of these "B" Westerns, with considerable acting experience. Occasional Westerns like *The Virginian* (1929), *Cimarron* (1930), and *The Plainsman* (1936) attracted the attention of mass audiences, but both the technical restrictions of early "talkies" and Hollywood's preoccupation during the '30s with contemporary urban themes effectively pushed the Western out of mainstream production.

The Western returned to widespread popularity in the late 1930s. The growing historical distance from the actual West along with developments in film technology—especially a quieter, more mobile camera and more sophisticated sound recording techniques—gave the genre new life. The tendency today is to laud John Ford's *Stagecoach* in 1939 for regenerating the Western movie formula, although Ford's film was only one of several popular mainstream Westerns produced in 1939 and 1940, among them *Jesse James, Dodge City, Destry Rides Again, Union Pacific, Frontier Marshal* (all 1939), *Sante Fe Trail, Virginia City, The Westerner, The Return of Frank James, Arizona,* and *When the Daltons Rode* (1940). The following war years proved to be a watershed period for the genre and for Hollywood filmmaking in general-but by then the Western's basic structural design was well established and its gradual refinement already begun.

THE LANDSCAPE OF THE WEST

When we step back to get a broader picture, we notice that the Western depicts a world of precarious balance in which the forces of civilization and savagery are locked in a struggle for supremacy. As America's foundation ritual, the Western projects a formalized vision of the nation's infinite possibilities and limitless vistas, thus serving to "naturalize" the policies of westward expansion and Manifest Destiny. It is interesting in this regard that we as a culture have found the story of the settlement of the "New World" beyond the Alleghenies and the Mississippi even more compelling than the development of the colonies or the Revolutionary War itself. Ironically, the single most evocative location for Western filmmaking and perhaps the genre's most familiar icon (after the image of John Wayne) is Arizona's Monument Valley, where awesome stone formations reach up to the gods but the desolate soil around them is scarcely suitable for the rural-agricultural bounty which provided America's socioeconomic foundation. The fact is, of course, that Hollywood's version of the Old West has as little to do with agriculture-although it has much to do with rural values—as it does with history. The landscape with its broad expanses and isolated communities was transformed on celluloid into a familiar iconographic arena where civilized met savage in an interminable mythic contest.

The Western's essential conflict between civilization and savagery is expressed in a variety of oppositions: East versus West, garden versus desert, America versus Europe, social order versus anarchy, individual versus community, town versus wilderness, cowboy versus Indian, schoolmarm versus dancehall girl, and so on. Its historical period of reference is the years following the Civil War and reaching into the early twentieth century, when the western United States, that precivilized locale, was establishing codes of law and order as a basis for contemporary social conditions. The opening of virtually any Western "cues" us in to these oppositions: cowboys pausing on a hillside during a cattle drive to gaze at the isolated community in the distance (*My Darling Clementine*, 1946); a lone cowboy, who after riding into a pastoral valley, is accused by an anxious homesteader of gunslinging for land-hungry local ranchers (*Shane,* 1953); a rider on a mountainside watching railroad workers blast a tunnel above him and outlaws rob a stagecoach below (*Johnny Guitar,* 1954); the distant cry of a locomotive whistle and a shot of a black, serpentine machine winding toward us through the open plains as the steam from its engine fills the screen (*The Man Who Shot Liberty Valance,* 1962).

JOHN FORD'S *STAGECOACH*

Even as early as Ford's 1939 film, *Stagecoach,* these oppositions are presented concisely and effectively. Ford's film marks the debut of Monument Valley in the Western genre, a fitting arena for the most engaging and thematically complex of all prewar Westerns.

The film opens with a shot of Monument Valley, framed typically beneath a sky which takes up most of the screen. Eventually we hear two riders approaching from across the desert and then see them coming toward us. As the riders near the camera, Ford cuts from this vast, panoramic scene to the exterior of a cavalry camp, and the horizon is suddenly cluttered with tents, flagstaffs, and soldiers. The riders gallop into the camp, dismount, and rush into the post. In the next shot, a group of uniformed men huddle around a telegraph machine. Just before the lines go dead, the telegraph emits a single coded word: "Geronimo."

This sequence not only sets the thematic and visual tone for Ford's film with economy of action and in striking visual terms, but also reflects the basic cultural and physical conflicts which traditionally have characterized the Western form. In Hollywood's version the West is a vast wilderness dotted with occasional oases—frontier towns, cavalry posts, isolated campsites, and so forth-which are linked with one another and with the civilized East by the railroad, the stagecoach, the telegraph: society's tentacles of progress. Each oasis is a virtual society in microcosm, plagued by conflicts both with the external, threatening wilderness and also with the anarchic or socially corrupt members of its own community. Ford's stagecoach, for example, is journeying to Lordsburg (what better name for an oasis of order in a vast wasteland?) through hostile Indian country. Its passengers must contend not only with Indian attacks but also with the conflicts which divide the group itself. The stagecoach carries a righteous sheriff, a cowardly driver, an alcoholic doctor, an embezzling bank executive, a whiskey drummer, a gold-hearted prostitute, a genteel gambler, an Eastern-bred lady, and the hero, an escaped convict bent upon avenging his brother's murder and, simultaneously, his own wrongful imprisonment.

In this film, as in the Western generally, the conflicts within the community reflect and intensify those between the community and its savage surroundings. The dramatic intensity in *Stagecoach* only marginally relates to the disposition of the hero, whose antisocial status (as a convict) is not basic to his character but results from society's lack of effective order and justice. Wayne portrays the Ringo Kid as a naïve, moral man of the earth who takes upon himself the task of righting that social and moral imbalance. He is also a living manifestation of the Western's basic conflicts. Like the sheriff who bends the law to suit the situation, the banker who steals from his own bank, the kindly whore, or the timid moralizer who sells whiskey, Ringo must find his own way through an environment of contrary and ambiguous demands.

Ford's orchestration of the community's complex, contradictory values renders *Stagecoach* a truly distinctive film, setting it apart both dramatically and thematically from earlier Westerns. Within a simplistic cavalry-to-the-rescue and shoot-out-on-Main-Street formula, Ford's constellation of social outcasts represents a range of social issues from alcoholism to white-collar crime to individual self-reliance. Through these characters Ford fleshes out values and contradictions basic to contemporary human existence.

The appeal of the stagecoach's passengers derives from their ambiguous social status. Often they are on the periphery of the community and somehow at odds with its value system. Perhaps the most significant conflict in the Western is the community's demand for order through cooperation and compromise versus the physical environment's demand for rugged individualism coupled with a survival-of-the-fittest mentality. In *Stagecoach*, each of the three central figures—Ringo, Doc Boone (Thomas Mitchell), and Dallas (Claire Trevor)—is an outcast who has violated society's precepts in order to survive: Ringo is an accused murderer and escaped convict sworn to take the law into his own hands, while Doc Boone has turned to alcohol and Dallas to prostitution to survive on the frontier.

We are introduced to Dallas and Doc Boone as they are being driven out of town by the Ladies' Law and Order League, a group of puritanical, civic-minded women dedicated to upholding community standards. This scene is played for both comic and dramatic effect, but it does establish conformity and Victorian moralizing as elements of a well-ordered society. This initial view of the community's repressive and depersonalizing demands eventually is qualified by the film's resolution, however. Ringo and Dallas finally are allowed by the sheriff to flee to Ringo's ranch across the border. As the two ride away to begin a new life together, the camera lingers on Doe Boone, ever the philosopher, who muses, "Well, they're saved from the blessings of civilization." Beneath his veneer of cynicism, however, is an optimistic vision: the uncivilized outlaw-hero and a woman practicing society's oldest profession have been united and go off to seek the promise of the American West's new world.

THE CHANGING VISION

The gradual fading of this optimistic vision, more than anything else, characterizes the evolution of the Western genre. As the formula was refined through repetition, both the frontier community and its moralistic standard-bearers are depicted in increasingly complex, ambiguous, and unflattering terms. The Western hero, in his physical allegiance to the environment and his moral commitment to civilization, embodies this ambiguity. As such he tends to generate conflict through his very existence. He is a man of action and of few words, with an unspoken code of honor that commits him to the vulnerable Western community and at the same time motivates him to remain distinctly apart from it. As the genre develops, the Westerner's role as promoter of civilization seems to become almost coincidental. Eventually, his moral code emerges as an end in itself.

The stability of the Westerner's character—his "style," as it were—doesn't really evolve with the genre. Instead, it is gradually redefined by the community he protects. Both the hero and the community establish their values and world view through their relationship with the savage milieu, but as the community becomes more civilized and thus more institutionalized, capitalistic, and corrupt, it gradually loses touch with the natural world from which it sprang. Because the Westerner exists on the periphery of both the community and the wilderness, he never loses touch with either world. His mediating function between them becomes increasingly complex and demanding as the society becomes more insulated and self-serving.

Actually, the image of the classic Westerner who mediates the natural and cultural environments while remaining distinct from each does not emerge as a mainstream convention until the mid-'40s. In earlier films, the narrative conflicts were usually resolved with the suggestion that the Westerner might settle down within the community which his inclination toward violence and gunplay has enabled him to protect. The promise of marriage between Ringo and Dallas is indicative of this tendency, although their shared outlaw status and their eventual flight to Mexico undercut any simplistic reading of the film's prosocial resolution. A typical example of this tendency is William Wyler's 1940 film, *The Westerner*. In this film, the hero, Cole Hardin (Gary Cooper), mediates a violent confrontation between anarchic cattlemen and defenseless, idealistic homesteaders. These distinct communities are depicted in two narrative movements. The first shows Hardin's arrival and near lynching in a lawless cattle town run by the outrageous Judge Roy Bean (Walter Brennan), the self-appointed "law west of the Pecos." The second follows the hero's gradual assimilation into the community of homesteaders and his courtship of the farmer's daughter, Jane Ellen (Doris Davenport).

Bean's and Jane Ellen's worlds are locked in the familiar cattleman-homesteader struggle for control of the land, and Hardin is the only character who can function effectively in both worlds. Thus Wyler's film (from Jo Swerling's script) develops the classic configuration of the anarchic world of Male Savagery pitted against the civilized world of Woman and Home. The heroic Westerner, again, is poised between the two. Throughout the first half of the film, in which the competing ideologies are established, this configuration remains in perfect balance. Eventually, however, Hardin is won over by the woman-domesticator and turns against Bean, throwing off the film's narrative equilibrium. After Hardin prevails against Bean in a climactic gunfight, the Westerner is able to settle down with Jane Ellen in "the promised land."

Nothing could he more damaging to the hero's image, of course. He has compromised his self-styled, renegade world view by acquiescing to civilization's emasculating and depersonalizing demands. The earlier silent Westerns and their later low-budget counterparts had understood the logic of sending the Westerner "into the sunset" after the requisite showdown, thereby sustaining the genre's prosocial function while reaffirming the hero's essential individuality. Perhaps it was John Ford's experience with silent Westerns that motivated him to temper the marital and communal values of *Stagecoach's* resolution, or perhaps it was his intuitive understanding of what made the Western genre work. But certainly the ambiguous ending of Ford's film renders it decidedly more effective than most of the Westerns of its day. It was not actually until World War II and the ensuing post-war productions, though, that the Western hero and his particular role within the Western milieu would be radically reconsidered along the lines previously established in *Stagecoach*.

SHANE: THE INITIATE-HERO AND THE INTEGRATION OF OPPOSITES

This motif is used most effectively, perhaps, in *Shane*. The story is filtered through the consciousness of a young boy (Brandon De Wilde as Joey Starrett), and much of the film's clarity of vision and idealized simplicity derives from his naïve perspective. The actions of the principal characters, the setting of a lush green valley, even the distant Rocky Mountains, attain a dreamlike quality under George Stevens' direction and Loyal Grigg's cinematography.

The film opens with Shane (Alan Ladd) riding into the pastoral valley where ranchers and homesteaders are feuding. (As in *The Westerner*, "open range" and fenced-in farmland manifest the genre's nature/culture opposition.) Shane is a man with a mysterious past who hangs up his guns to become a farm laborer for Joe Starrett (Van Heflin), the spokesman for the homesteaders in their conflict with the villainous Ryker brothers.

The film is a virtual ballet of oppositions, all perceived from Joey's viewpoint. These oppositions become a series of options for him—and us—that he must negotiate in order to attain social maturity. The following diagram summarizes these oppositions.

SHANE

Joe Starrett	Wilson
Family	Ryker brothers
Homesteaders	Ranchers
Domestication	Male isolation

Woman's world ....Man's world
Fence ....Open range
Crops, sheep ....Cattle
Farm tools............................Guns
Social law.............................Primitive law
Equality ....Survival of the fittest
Future ....Past

Not only does this diagram indicate the elaborate *doubling* of the narrative, but it also points up the hero's mediation of both the rancher-homesteader conflict and the boy's confused notions of his ideal father figure. Although Starrett is the bravest and most capable of the homesteaders—and the only one respected and feared by the ranchers—he is basically a farmer of rural sensibilities and simple values. Starrett is clearly no match for Shane in either Joey's or his wife's (Jean Arthur) eyes, although the family proves strong enough to withstand the interloper's influence. By the end of the film, Marion's attraction to Shane complements her son's, although her family and her role as mother-domesticator remain her first concerns. In accord with her son's (and the genre's) sexual naiveté, the thought of Shane's and Marion's romantic entanglement is only a frustrating impossibility. Among Joey's parting cries to Shane as he rides away at the film's end is, "Mother wants you."

This sexual-familial conflict is, however, tangential to the film's central opposition between fenced land and open range. Nevertheless, it does reaffirm Shane's commitment to the values of home and family rather than those of power and capital. During the course of the film, Shane offers his services to the other farmers, but he is never really accepted because of his past and his stoic, detached manner. The cattlemen, who are generally seen drinking in the local saloon or else out harassing "sodbusters," show more respect for Shane than do the farmers, and attempt to recruit him at higher pay. Shane refuses, so the Rykers bring in Wilson (Jack Palance), a *doppelganger* from Shane's gunfighting past. Here, as in many genre films involving a violent, nomadic hero, the only real difference between the protagonist (Shane) and his antagonistic double (Wilson) has to do with their respective attitudes about social order and the value of human life.

The film ends with Shane knocking Starrett out with his pistol after a fierce fist-fight. He knows he must face Wilson and the Rykers alone. Joey follows Shane to town to watch the confrontation in the deserted saloon. Shane prevails against the men but is wounded, and he rides off into the mountains as Joey's calls echo after him. Those mountains, which like Shane's mysterious, violent past had remained in the background throughout the film, emerge now as his Olympus, as the Westerner's mythic realm beyond the reality of dirt farms and ramshackle towns.

But while Shane's heroic stature is affirmed, there is still a shade of ambiguity which tempers that stature. Just before the gunfight in the darkened saloon, Shane suggests to Ryker that "his days are numbered." "What about you, gunfighter?" asks Ryker. "The difference is, I know it" replies Shane, who then turns to the black-clad Wilson. The two simply stare at one another before the exchange of ritual dialogue that will initiate the gunfight. As in an earlier scene when the two had met and silently circled each other, a mutual understanding and respect is implicit in the look they exchange in addition to the promise of a violent, uncompromising confrontation. After the gunfight Shane tells Joey that "There's no living with the killing," but it's clear enough from the relationship established between Shane and Wilson that there's no living without it either. . . . These men know their fate all too well. They purposefully end their days in a fashion that they could control and that we in the audience come to expect.

As these various examples indicate, the Westerner is motivated to further the cause of civilization by his own personal code of honor, which seems to be existentially derived. Often this code leads him to an act of vengeance. The vengeful hero is different from the classic Westerner in that his past-either his entire past or an isolated incident-is of immediate concern and provides him with a clear sense of mission. But he does share with the classic hero his characteristic function: he is an isolated, psychologically static man of personal integrity who acts because society is too weak to do so. And it is these actions that finally enforce social order but necessitate his departure from the community he has saved. In *Stagecoach, Winchester 73* (1950), *The Searchers* (1956), *One-Eyed Jacks* (1961), *Nevada Smith* (1966), and countless other revenge Westerns, the hero rids society of a menace, but in so doing, he reaffirms his own basic incompatibility with the community's values.

Occasionally the hero will accept a job as lawman to carry out his vengeance, as in *Dodge City* and *My Darling Clementine*, but once he has satisfied his personal drives, he leaves the community to fend for itself. In those films, it is assumed that the hero's elimination of the power-hungry town boss and his henchmen has purified the community and given it lasting social order. The destruction of the Clantons at the O.K. Corral by the Earp brothers and Doc Holliday in *My Darling Clementine* serves both to avenge the murder of James Earp and also to project an image of an orderly Tombstone into the indefinite future. As Wyatt Earp and his brother (Henry Fonda and Ward Bond) ride off across Monument Valley after their gunfight, the new schoolmarm from the East waves to them, framed in long-shot against the infinite expanse of desert and sky. With this image Ford captures and freezes forever—like the English poet John Keats' ageless figures on a Grecian urn—the Western's principal characters and their contradictory yet complementary ideals.

THE CHANGING HERO: THE "PSYCHOLOGICAL" AND "PROFESSIONAL" WESTERNS

As an element of our national mythology, the Western represents American culture, explaining its present in terms of its past and virtually redefining the past to accommodate the present. The image of the Western community in Hollywood movies tends to reflect our own beliefs and preoccupations, and the Western's evolution as a genre results both from the continual reworking of its own rules of construction and expression and also from the changing beliefs and attitudes of contemporary American society.

As American audiences after World War II became saturated with the classic Western formula and also more hardbitten about sociopolitical realities, the image of the Western community changed accordingly, redefining the hero's motivation and his sense of mission. Hence the "psychological" Westerns of the late 1940s and the 1950s that traced the Westerner's neuroses (and eventual psychoses) stemming from his growing incompatibility with civilization as well as the cumulative weight of society's unreasonable expectations.

One of the more notable examples of this development is Fred Zinneman's *High Noon*, in which a local lawman (Gary Cooper) awaits the arrival of outlaws bent on avenging his having sent their leader to prison. The wait for the arrival of the outlaws provides the dramatic tension in the film, which is heightened by the fact that the townspeople ignore or evade Cooper's appeals for assistance. After he and his Quaker wife (Grace Kelly), a woman committed to nonviolence for religious reasons, finally confront and dispose of the outlaws, Cooper throws his badge into the dirt and leaves the community to fend for itself.

Howard Hawks' *Rio Bravo* (1958), supposedly a belated answer to Zinneman's "knee-jerk liberalism," describes a similar situation in an even more claustrophobic and helpless community. From Hawks' typically machismo perspective, however, the local lawman (John Wayne, with deputies Dean Martin, Walter Brennan, and Ricky Nelson) continually rejects offers of aid from the frightened citizenry, insisting, "This is no job for amateurs." Wayne and his cohorts prevail, and thus both the heroes and the community emerge with integrity intact. While *High Noon* and *Rio Bravo* each project substantially different views of the community and its redeemer-hero, both underscore the hero's incompatibility with that community. Ultimately, it is the hero's professional integrity and sense of responsibility to his job as lawman which induce him to act as an agent of social order.

The "professional" Western was, in fact, Hollywood's own answer to the psychological Western, much as Hawks' film had answered Zinneman's. In general, the psychological Western poses the question: how can the morally upright, socially autonomous Westerner continue to defend a repressive, institutionalized, cowardly, and thankless community without going crazy? The professional Western answers this question in one of two ways. The Westerner either works for pay and sells his special talents to the community that must evaluate his work on its own terms or else he becomes an outlaw.

The prospect of the classic, morally upright Westerner turning from his self-styled code of honor is closely related to the changing view of society in the Western.

As the community's notion of law and order progressively squeezes out those rugged individualists who made such order possible, the Westerners turn to each other and to the outlaws they had previously opposed. At this point, the "honor among thieves" that the Westerner can find with other lawless types is preferable to buckling under to the community's emasculating demands.

Consequently, many recent Westerns incorporate a group that is led by an aging but still charismatic hero figure and whose demand of payment, either as professional killers or as outlaws, undercuts the classic Westerner's moral code. Thus the professional Westerns of the past two decades, most notably *Rio Bravo, The Magnificent Seven, The Professionals, El Dorado, The Wild Bunch, True Grit, Butch Cassidy and the Sundance Kid, The Cowboys, The Great Northfield Minnesota Raid, The Culpepper Cattle Company*, and *The Missouri Breaks*.

Gone in these films is the isolated, heroic cowboy with no visible means of support whose moral vision and spiritual values set him apart from—and essentially above—the community he defends. Now he is cynical, self-conscious, and even "incorporated"; these traits render him increasingly unheroic. more like one of us. Still, despite his gradual descent from heroic demigod (superior in many ways to nature as well as to other men) in early Westerns to a psychologically more complex and generally more sympathetic character, the Westerner does maintain distinct traces of his isolated sense of honor. He strikes a romantic pose even in the face of extinction.

Sam Peckinpah's *The Wild Bunch* (1969), for example, describes the exploits of an outlaw collective (William Holden, Ernest Borgnine, Warren Oates, Edmund O'Brien, Ben Johnson, et al.) in their sustained rampage through the American Southwest and in Mexico just before the outbreak of World War I. Whereas the outlaw collective violates with equal disregard the laws of God, man, and nature, the real villain of the piece is progress. Big business, typified by the banks and the railroad, forces the Bunch out of the United States and into a confrontation with a corrupt Mexican bandit army. When one of their own group is captured and tortured by the Mexican bandits (whose leader has given up his horse for an automobile and is doing business with German warmongers), the Bunch undertakes a final, suicidal act of heroism—something that is very much in America's "national interest." In one of the most spectacular showdowns ever filmed, the Wild Bunch and the bandit army destroy each other in a quick-cut, slow-motion dream of blood and death.

This paradoxical resolution is in much the same vein as those in *The Magnificent Seven* and *Butch Cassidy*. In both of these films, although outlaw collectives are forced by time and civilization to practice their trade outside the United States, they retain a certain allegiance to their heroic code with its basis in American ideology. And in all three films, the outlaw collective regenerates the sense of group mission—one similar to that which had been subdued by advancing civilization on the American frontier. This sense of mission still determines the behavior and attitude of the collective, and as such it almost becomes an end in itself: the heroic mediator's social function emerges as a self-indulgent, formalized ritual.

Sam Peckinpah has understood and articulated, perhaps better than any Western filmmaker since John Ford, the concept of the Westerner who has outlived his role and his milieu. Particularly in *Ride the High Country* (1962), *Major Dundee* (1964), *The Wild Bunch* (1969), and *The Ballad of Cable Hogue* (1970), Peckinpah evokes a strong sense of irony and nostalgia in his presentation of a cast of aging heroic misfits. His men are hopelessly—and even tragically-at odds with the inexorable flow of history. The most evocative of these films is *Ride the High Country*, made in the same year as Ford's *The Man Who Shot Liberty Valance*. (Both films express regret over the passing of the Old West and its values.) The film stars Randolph Scott and Joel McCrae, two familiar cowboys from countless '40s and '50s Westerns, who are now reduced to tending bar and sharpshooting in a Wild West show. The opening sequence in *Ride the High Country* immediately establishes the hero's displacement in the new West and shows what he must do to contend with it. McCrae (as Steven Judd) arrives in town having given up his bartending job to guard a mine shipment, happy to return to the type of work which had sustained him through his more productive years. The town itself is modern, with automobiles, policemen, and even a Wild West show, where Judd finds his former deputy, Gil Westrum (Randolph Scott), reduced to a sideshow attraction. This opening sequence not only pits the old West against the new, but it also sets up an opposition between McCrea/Judd and Scott/Westrum. The former has retained his idealistic desire to continue as an agent of social order; the latter manifests a pragmatic willingness to make a profit off his former lawman status. Judd recruits Westrum to help him with the mine shipment, although Westrum agrees only because he assumes he'll eventually grab it for himself. Judd's reactionary idealism and Westrum's self-serving adaptability provide the central conflict throughout the film. This split is intensified by the presence of an initiate-hero (Ron Starr as Heck Longtree) who must decide between the two opposing world views. The initiate ultimately rejects Westrum's scheme to rob the shipment, and Westrum himself finally elects to join Judd and Longtree in a climactic showdown with another band of outlaws. The flexible, practical Westrum and the initiate Longtree survive the gunfight, but Judd falls, mortally wounded.

The film's closing shot is an over-the-shoulder, point-of-view shot from ground level, where we gaze with the dying Judd at the "high country" in the distance. As in the closing sequence in *Shane* (although this film is much bleaker in its outlook), the Westerner's status is reaffirmed in mythic proportions. However, instead of riding into the mountains as Shane had done, into that timeless terrain beyond the reach of civilization, Judd must be satisfied with only a dying glimpse of them.

But not even Peckinpah's jaded vision can match that of Robert Altman's remarkable 1972 Western, *McCabe and Mrs. Miller*. In Altman's film, the reluctant hero miraculously prevails against three killers only to freeze to death as he lies wounded and drifting snow covers him. Actually, the plot in Altman's film is somewhat similar to that in *Shane*. A charismatic figure with a violent but shadowy past makes his presence felt in a community and finally confronts single-handedly those power-hungry forces seeking control of the town.

The two films have little in common otherwise. Whereas Shane rode into a lush, pastoral valley wearing fringed buckskins and a six-gun, McCabe (Warren Beatty) rides into the dismal, rain-drenched town of Presbyterian Church in a suit and a derby and carrying a concealed derringer. Rather than working the land, McCabe provides the mining community with its first whorehouse. In McCabe, it is not the land which must be protected, but rather the business which has become the lifeblood of that particular community: McCabe's brothel. Marion Starrett's pure woman-domesticator is countered here by Constance Miller (Julie Christie), an experienced madam and prostitute (sex is simply a commodity of exchange), who expands McCabe's meager enterprise into the realm of big business.

The final showdown is precipitated when McCabe refuses to sell out his share of the "house' to an unseen corporation. As McCabe conducts an elaborate, cat-and-mouse gun battle through the streets with three hired killers sent by the corporation, the other townspeople are busy fighting a fire in the community's half-built church. In an ironic counterpoint to the sunlit communal celebration on the church foundation in Ford's *My Darling Clementine* (1946), here the townsfolk work together to save a church which few of them would ever consider attending. In reality, the church in *McCabe* is just an empty shell, a façade as hollow as the values and the future of the community itself. McCabe's genuine act of heroism goes unnoticed as the townspeople work futilely to rescue a formal edifice without spiritual substance. Against his own better judgment, and against his beloved Mrs. Miller's protestations, McCabe finally joins those countless other Western heroes, reaffirming his own individual identity, protecting his own homestead and reinforcing the Western's essential theme that "a man's gotta do what he's gotta do."

———

JOHN FORD AND THE EVOLUTION OF THE WESTERN

. . . With each successive Western after *Stagecoach*, Ford's attitude toward the classic Western formula became increasingly self-conscious, both stylistically and thematically. Gradually, he shifted his cinematic and narrative emphasis from the "subject matter" of the genre to its narrative form and cultural function. The question of influence is always difficult, even when considering so inventive a filmmaker working within so conventional a form. When we examine Ford's contributions to the genre, however, it seems fairly simple to determine that he was among the most (if not the most) influential of Western film directors. Further, the evolution of Ford's treatment of the genre is indicative of its overall historical development. In order to examine this development in some detail, we will compare and contrast four Ford Westerns produced in consecutive decades) all of which were widely popular when they were released and are now considered among Hollywood's greatest Westerns: *Stagecoach* (1939), *My Darling Clementine* (1946), *The Searchers* (1956), and *The Man Who Shot Liberty Valance* (1962).

STAGECOACH AS AN ADVANCE IN THE GENRE

As I have already discussed, *Stagecoach* involves a straightforward narrative of classic Western concerns: the legendary, psychologically uncomplicated and stable hero (John Wayne as the Ringo Kid) helps protect the occupants of a stage from an Indian attack so that he can reach Lordsburg and avenge his brother's murder. After single-handedly ridding the town of the menacing Plummer brothers, Ringo leaves with Dallas to ride into the sunset and the promise of a new life beyond the limitless horizon.

Stagecoach, often criticized as being cliched or conventional, actually represented a considerable advance in imagery and thematic complexity over previous and then-current Westerns—despite its essentially one-dimensional characters, its cavalry-to-the-rescue climax, and its "escape hatch" solution to Ringo's outlaw status. The film is visually unprecedented, both in its depiction of Monument Valley as the archetypal Western milieu and also in Ford's sensitive, controlled camerawork. Ford neatly balances the vast expanse of the valley against the enclosed, socially defined space of the stagecoach, the way stations, and other interior locations. He establishes a visual opposition that intensifies the hero's divided self (uncivilized renegade versus agent of social order) and the genre's essential nature/culture opposition.

Stagecoach also anticipates Ford's narrative and visual concern for community ritual, which became more pronounced in his later Westerns. As Ford well understood, these rituals—dances, weddings, funerals, and in this case, a childbirth—are virtually punctuation marks of the genre itself. They formally articulate and define the community and its collective values.

Ford establishes both his characters and his dominant themes by tracing the travelers' reactions to a variety of familiar events that emphasize many of society's values: the "democratic" balloting to decide whether to press on in the face of Indian attacks; a group meal in which seating arrangements and body language indicate the social status and attitudes of the participants; the unexpected birth of a baby to one of the travelers. The childbirth sequence is especially significant, complicating the journey's progress but also positing the savage wilderness as a potential utopia for future generations. It is during this crisis that Ringo's fellow renegades, Doc Boone and Dallas, verify their heroic credentials. They add a moral and humanistic dimension to the stagecoach's world in microcosm. The other passengers may represent more traditional roles of a civilized society, but these two transcend such a civilization characterized by its concern for social status and material wealth.

After Boone sobers up and successfully delivers the baby, Dallas cares for the mother and child through the night. As she shows the newborn child to the group, she and Ringo form a silent union (in a telling exchange of closeups) that is realized in their later embrace. With this silent exchange, Ford isolates Ringo, Dallas, and the child as a veritable Holy Family of the frontier, and the motif is strengthened by the couple's final flight into the desert at film's end. It is thus the family, the nuclear social unit, that brings together Westerner and Woman and offers the promise of an ideal frontier community.

CLEMENTINE: A UTOPIAN WESTERN

My Darling Clementine (1946), like Stagecoach, closes with a figurative embrace between Westerner and Woman, but in that later film, the redeemer-hero rides off alone. There is only a vague suggestion that he will return to Clementine (Cathy Downs) and the community. In fact, *Clementine* is much less naïve than *Stagecoach* in its recognition of the hero's basic inability to reconcile his individual and social roles. Still, it might well be considered more naive in its idealized portrayal of Wyatt Earp (Henry Fonda) as the stoic, self-reliant redeemer.

Ringo's character was essentially one-dimensional and static, but Ringo's outlaw status (although unjustified) gave an ambiguous edge to his prosocial, redemptive actions. *Clementine's* hero and community, on the other hand, are depicted in the most positive light the Arizona sun could produce, and in that sense it is the more overtly mythic, classical Western of the two. The elements Ford had introduced in *Stagecoach*—sound, iconography (Monument Valley and John Wayne), and the orchestration of themes, values, and characters—solidify in *Clementine* into an unyielding and unqualified ritual form, celebrating the promise of the epic-heroic figure and the utopian community.

Like Ringo (and later Ethan Edwards in *The Searchers*), Earp is motivated by vengeance: after the Clantons kill his younger brother and steal his cattle, Earp accepts the job as Tombstone's marshal (which he had rejected earlier) and vows over his brother's grave to avenge his death. As Earp says over his brother's grave early in the film, "Maybe when we leave this country, kids like you will be able to grow up and live safe." Although his primary motives involve blood lust, Earp's legal status renders him beyond reproach. Only one aspect of *Clementine* offsets Earp's spit-and-polish demeanor and provides an ambiguous edge to the narrative—the presence of Doc Holliday (Victor Mature) as Tombstone's resident saloon keeper and charismatic authority figure.

The device of using another central character who shares the hero's prosocial allegiance but not his motivation or world view appears frequently in Westerns. This "double" generally points up both the primitive and the cultivated characteristics of the hero and his milieu. Earp and Holliday emerge as oppositional figures on various levels: Earp is the archetypal Westerner, Holliday is a well-educated, Eastern-bred doctor; Earp is a stoic, laconic militarist who uses force only when necessary, Holliday is cultured and articulate but also prone to violent outbursts; both run the town with self-assured authority, but Earp disdains Holliday's penchant for gunplay; Earp is a natural man who operates on instinct and savvy, Holliday is a cultivated man seeking refuge in the West from a failed romance and a demanding career.

Holliday is an interesting and somewhat unusual character within the Ford constellation. Like Doc Boone and later Dutton Peabody in *Liberty Valance,* he is cultured enough to quote Shakespeare but cannot live with himself or the savage environment without alcohol. Unlike the drunken philosophers in these films, however, his age and physical abilities are roughly on a par with the hero's, so he counters Earp on considerably more than just an attitudinal level.

The sharpest distinction between Earp and Holliday, of course, involves the film's namesake, Clementine Carter. Clementine has followed Holliday from Boston, virtually stepping over the dead gunfighters the temperamental doctor has left in his wake. Once she catches up with Holliday in Tombstone, Clementine must confront her own "primitive" double—the character of Chihuahua (Linda Darnell), a saloon girl of questionable breeding. Complementing the film's dominant law-and-order opposition, then, which pits the Earps and Holliday against the Clantons, are the foursome of Wyatt, Doc, Clementine, and Chihuahua, who form a fascinating network of inter-relationships.

It is finally (and predictably) Clementine who tempers Earp's character. She gives a touch of humanity to his rigid attitude and takes the edge off his mythic stature. Apparently, as long as the Eastern figure is either a woman or an aging, philosophical alcoholic (this is invariably the case in Ford's Westerns), then he or she conceivably has something to contribute to the settling of the wilderness. Holliday's character is doomed from the start, however, and only time will tell whether a faster gunman or his diseased lungs will finish him. Through Earp and his mission, Holliday is able to die heroically in the climactic gunfight. Thus he joins Chihuahua, his female counterpart, who had died earlier under his own apparently misguided scalpel.

Like *Stagecoach, Clementine* was filmed on location in Monument Valley and on black-and-white film stock. The visual style in *Clementine* is considerably more lyrical and expressive than in the earlier film, however, especially in those daylight sequences where Ford frames the desert and monuments beyond the town in elaborate compositions. There is little sense of the horizon beyond the community in this film. This is partially because of the preponderance of night sequences, most of which focus either upon Doc's alcoholic rages or the Clantons' maniacal carrying-on. In the daylight sequences, we generally are only able to glimpse the horizon through man-made structures like fenceposts, boardwalks, and so on.

In the oft-cited church sequence, one of those rare moments when it seems as if the entire narrative is concentrated into a single image, Ford orchestrates an array of visual opposition. We see the contrast of earth and sky, of rugged terrain against horizon, of Monument Valley's vast panorama framed by the rafters and flagstaffs of the half-built church, of man and nature. In an eloquent ritual sequence, the townspeople hold a Sunday square dance, an interesting juxtaposition to the anarchic behavior of Tombstone's nighttime revelers. Earp approaches with Clementine, and the preacher orders the townspeople to stand aside "for the new marshal and his lady fair." As the two dance, framed against the sky, the genre's array of prosocial values and ideals coalesces into an extremely simple yet eternally evocative image.

Those ideals are affirmed as the Earps clean up Tombstone—just as Ringo had cleaned up Lordsburg—in a violent, climactic gun battle, But whereas the gunfight in *Stagecoach* occurs offscreen (Ford shows us Ringo from low-angle falling and firing his rifle, then the camera pulls in on the anxious Dallas), in *Clementine* it is an elaborate, murderous ballet. Ford contends that he choreographed the O.K. Corral sequence after the "real" Wyatt Earp's own description of the legendary battle; the conflict does seem like a military operation. Despite its ties with history, though—and there are few in this mythic tale—the gunfight is not staged in a naturalistic manner. Rather, it seems to be a dream of voices, gunshots, and dust.

The gunfight is initiated when a stagecoach passes the corral, raising clouds of dust. The six participants move in and out of the frame and the dust, firing at one another until only Wyatt and his brother Morgan (Ward Bond) remain standing. This ritualistic dance of death serves both to contrast and complement the earlier dance in the half-built church: social integration is viable only if community order is maintained. With that order ensured, Wyatt promises Clementine, who is now the new schoolmarm, that one day he will return. He and his brother then leave the community and ride westward across Monument Valley.

Ford's Masterpiece: *The Searchers*

The Searchers is the story of an obsessive, nomadic hero (Wayne as Ethan Edwards) who arrives home after a three-year disappearance. Edwards had fought in the Civil War and then had vanished, apparently somewhere in Mexico. The day after he turns up, a band of renegade Indians massacre his family. We learn that Ethan's former sweetheart, Martha (Dorothy Jordan), now his brother's wife, had been sexually violated before she was killed, and that her two daughters were kidnapped by the Indians. The massacre sets Ethan and a young initiate-hero, Martin Pawley (Jeffrey Hunter), off on an epic, decade-long journey throughout the West (Monument Valley).

The object of their pursuit is the leader of the renegade Indian band, Scar (Henry Brandon), who has taken the sole living captive from the massacre as his squaw. Pawley, himself a one-eighth Cherokee who had been found in his infancy by Ethan and had been raised by the Edwards family during Ethan's prolonged absence, is intent upon returning his foster sister to civilization. Ethan's intentions are a good deal less altruistic.

He is bent upon killing Scar to avenge his brother's wife's death, and he also plans to kill the captive squaw whom he considers unfit to return to the world of the White Man.

Throughout Ethan and Martin's search, the linear, chronological aspects of the complex narrative are subordinate to its oppositional structure, which centers on Ethan's character. The search itself does provide a temporal framework for the story, but the events depicted do not really fit into a cause-and-effect pattern. Instead, they progressively reveal and qualify the Westerner's contradictory, multi-faceted personality. The entire film, in fact, might be read as a procession of characters with whom Ethan is doubled.

Upon his initial return, Ethan is set in opposition with his brother Aaron, a simple man of the earth who had remained in Texas and had wed Ethan's sweetheart, raised a family, and cultivated the wilderness in the name of civilization. This nomad-homesteader opposition is accentuated on the morning after Ethan's return when the Reverend-Captain Samuel Johnson Clayton (Ward Bond) thunders into the Edwards' household to enlist Aaron and Martin's aid in his pursuit of Scar's renegade band. Clayton is also a composite of contradictions, although he seems sufficiently comfortable with his dual institutional role of lawman and clergyman. His prosocial beliefs and functions offset Ethan's nomadic, antisocial nature both spiritually and socially. Even though they once were officers for the Confederacy, the men now sit on opposite sides of an ideological fence. Unlike Clayton, Ethan did not attend the Confederate surrender, and he still relishes his status as rebel. "I figure a man's only good for one oath at a time," he tells Clayton. "I still got my saber . . . Didn't turn it into no plowshare, neither." This attitude sets Ethan against both Aaron, the man who allowed himself to be domesticated by a woman and the land, and also Clayton, the warrior who now fights for both the laws of man and God.

Ethan's only law is his own, fashioned from his long-standing rapport with the wilderness. His character is shown throughout as being ignorant and unsympathetic to civilization and its ways, but his understanding of the desert expanse and his natural environment far surpasses that of any other white man in the film. He is in touch with his surroundings but out of touch with his people, and he clearly likes it that way.

Ethan's only connection with civilization is his feeling for Martha. For him, she transcends the distinction between the civilized and the savage. From the opening shot of the film when Martha glimpses Ethan approaching across the desert and welcomes him back into the familial fold, Ford subtly indicates that she is his reason for returning. After the massacre when Ethan comes back to the burnt-out homestead, she is the only family member to whom he calls out. Once he finds her body, Ethan's deepest fears and anxieties are animated, and his obsessive search is set in motion.

The thematic core of *The Searchers* revolves around a series of male/female relationships involving sexual union, sexual taboo, and sexual violation: Ethan and Martha,

Aaron and Martha, Scar and Martha, and by extension Scar and Martha's daughter Lucy (whom he rapes and kills after the massacre) and also daughter Debbie (whom he eventually takes for his squaw). Scar's sexual violation of Martha and her daughters, and Ethan's maniacal desire to avenge the deed by killing the Indian as well as his own niece, draw the two men into an intense and perverse rapport.

The relationship between Westerner and Woman had been a significant but generally subordinate motif in earlier films, but here it emerges as a dominant, motivating factor in the narrative. In a classical Western like *My Darling Clementine,* the hero's repression of his sexual and domestic inclinations was a positive character trait: as high priest of order in the West, he was committed to an unspoken code of chastity and self-enforced solitude. In *The Searchers,* the hero's sexual repression—based in his guilt-ridden feelings about Martha and her daughters' violation—assumes psychotic proportions and finds release only when Ethan finally scalps Scar. That task completed, and his obsessions restored to their proper subliminal realm, Ethan turns his back on both the white and Indian cultures and wanders across the desert into oblivion.

While Scar and his renegade band appear to be a rather traditional threat to the civilized homesteaders, Ford's depiction of Indian culture and of the Scar-Ethan relationship appears to radically transform the Western's traditional portrayal of inhuman "Redskins." Unlike *Stagecoach,* where the Indians were simply natural hazards and had no individual or cultural identity, here they are the creators of an autonomous civilization which virtually mirrors the whites (In discussing *The Searchers,* Ford once stated: "The audience likes to see Indians get killed. They don't consider them as human beings—with a great culture of their own—quite different from our own. If you analyzed the thing carefully, however, you'd find that their religion is very similar to ours.")

Because of this sympathetic portrayal of Indian culture, Scar and Ethan are cast in a curiously similar social status. Both are renegades from their own civilizations who violently avenge their respective families. Scar's two sons had been killed by whites years earlier, and his slaughter of Ethan's family is simply one in a series of retributions. Like Ethan, Scar knows the language and the cultural codes of his enemy, and like Ethan he has cultivated a hatred for that enemy so intense that it ultimately seems to transcend the original motivating desire for vengeance.

Scar and Ethan's relationship as brothers under the skin is enhanced by Ford's casting a blue-eyed (but well-tanned) Anglo, Henry Brandon, as Scar. Ford prided himself on casting of real Native Americans in his Westerns, but authenticity in this case was less vital than rhetorical and symbolic expression. Scar's physical characteristics distinguish him from his own people and accentuate his rapport with the Westerner. Their physical and motivational similarities are intensified when Ethan and Scar finally meet late in the film. In a bristling confrontation in Scar's camp, Ford mirrors not only their dialogue ("You speak good English"/"You speak good Comanche"), but he also mirrors our own perceptions of the two men. By filming the confrontation in a rare exchange of over-the-shoulder shots, he encourages the audience to assume Scar's as well as Ethan's viewpoint.

Ultimately, the similarities between Ethan and Scar, between protagonist and antagonist, underscore Ford's evolving conception of the conflicts and threats within the Western milieu. No longer does the Westerner have to deal with faceless "Injuns" who throw the defenseless community into chaos; now the threat involves that very same nomadic, self-reliant individuality which society cannot tolerate and which is shared by both the hero and the Indian. Ironically, this incompatibility between Ford's hero and society grows to a point where the hero's very presence generates disorder. The coincidence of Ethan's and later, Scar's unannounced arrivals into the precariously balanced community, coupled with their similar moral codes and renegade reputations, finally make it rather difficult to distinguish between Demon Indian and Redeemer Westerner.

Ethan's absolute, uncompromising, and obsessive character is continually juxtaposed with the initiate-hero, Martin Pawley. Martin embodies the opposites which Ethan cannot tolerate—he, like the captive Debbie, is both Family and Indian, both civilized and savage, both loved and hated. Martin accepts his dualities, however, and his capacity for reason and compromise repeatedly undercuts Ethan's manic quest for revenge. When Ethan tries to stir up Martin's blood lust by telling him that one of the scalps on Scar's lodgepole belongs to Martin's mother, Martin replies, "It don't make no difference." Martin learns the ways of the desert and the land from Ethan, but his ultimate goal is to return Debbie to her people and to settle a homestead with his childhood sweetheart, Laurie (Vera Miles). Martin is the one who finally kills Scar, not aggressively but in an act of self-defense, and this enables him to return to Laurie in Texas and to commit himself to rural and domestic values which Ethan had been unable (or unwilling) to do years earlier with Martha.

Significantly, though, once Martin honors that commitment, his role as initiate-hero evaporates, and he all but disappears from the narrative. The film's final moments focus not upon Martin's integration into the community but upon Ethan's inability to do so. Although finally able to embrace Debbie and return her to civilization, reaffirming his fundamental belief in Woman and Family, Ethan cannot commit his own life to those values. In the film's closing shot. Ethan stares through the doorway at the family's reunion celebration (and beyond it to the audience), then turns and slowly walks off across Monument Valley as the door closes and leaves the screen in darkness. This image reprises the film's opening shot, wherein Martha had opened a door to reveal Ethan approaching from the distance. This visual motif reaffirms our own perspective from inside the secure, if somewhat repressive, confines of society. It also demonstrates the hero's basic inability to pass through that doorway and enjoy civilized existence. Like the dead Indian whose eyes Ethan had shot out early in the search,

Ethan is doomed to wander forever between the winds, endlessly traversing the mythic expanse of Monument Valley.

FORD'S FAREWELL TO THE WESTERNER

If we were to look to a small ranch outside the community of Shinbone some six years later, we might be able to hazard a guess about Ethan's fate after the close of *The Searchers*. Made between *Two Rode Together* (1961) and *How the West Was Won* (1963, in which Ford directed the Civil War episode), *The Man Who Shot Liberty Valance* is Ford's nostalgic and bittersweet farewell to the Westerner and his vanishing ideals.

The story is deceptively simple: Ransom Stoddard (Jimmy Stewart), an aging United States senator, has returned to the prosperous and progressive town of Shinbone where he had begun his career as a lawyer. Accompanied by his wife, Hallie (Vera Miles), Stoddard comes to town to attend the funeral of Tom Doniphon, a forgotten cowboy. The funeral must be financed by the county because Doniphon died without money, home, or even a handgun. At the inducement of an aggressive newspaper editor, Stoddard explains his presence and the significance of Doniphon through an extended flashback that takes up most of the film.

The flashback traces Stoddard's journey West fresh out of law school, his confrontation during the trip with a brutal, psychopathic outlaw (Lee Marvin as Liberty Valance), and his befriending of a charismatic but essentially aloof local rancher, Doniphon, played, of course, by John Wayne—here regenerating the epic Westerner. Stoddard promotes statehood for the community, while Valance is hired by ranchers "north of the Picket Wire" to prevent it, and the conflict between Stoddard and Valance intensifies until they meet in a traditional gunfight. Valance is killed, and Stoddard goes on to build a career as "the man who shot Liberty Valance."

We later learn (in a flashback within a flashback, a narrative device we hardly expect within the Western's usually straightforward story construction) that Doniphon, not Stoddard, was responsible for killing Valance. In this act of heroic self-destruction, Doniphon bequeaths to Stoddard the leadership of the community and, even more significantly, the hand of his "gal" Hallie.

After Stoddard completes the flashback story, the newspaper editor tears up his notes and throws them into the fire, delivering the film's—and Ford's—definitive self-critical statement: "This is the West, sir. When the legend becomes fact, print the legend." *Liberty Valance* is, in effect, Ford's effort to print both the fact and the legend, both history and myth, and to suggest how the two interpenetrate one another. Ford is no longer primarily concerned with the vision of contemporary America drawn from stories about its past; instead, he concentrates on the very process whereby our present demands for a favorable vision distort and manipulate the past. Whereas *Stagecoach* and *My Darling Clementine* overtly celebrated the culture's idealized self-image, *Liberty Valance* deconstructs and critiques that image, finally acknowledging the necessary role of myth and legend in the development of history and civilization.

To examine the Western's amalgam of fact and fiction, Ford creates a world of formal artifice, a timeless theatrical realm in which the allegory is enacted. Abandoning the wide expanse of Monument Valley and the filmic "realism" of wide-screen color and location shooting, Ford shot *Liberty Valance* in black and white, and almost all of the flashback episode was performed on a sound stage. The opening and closing sequences of the film establish Shinbone roughly at the turn of the century, and are shot in exteriors under natural light. When Stoddard begins his flashback, however, Ford depicts the stagecoach amid the artificial trappings of a Western studio set under artificial studio lighting. In case we missed the point, a masked figure (who turns out to be Valance) comes from behind a *papier-mâché* boulder, dressed in a white, floor-length overcoat, and shouts, "Stand and deliver." He proceeds to rob the stage and terrorize its occupants, tearing apart Stoddard's law books after giving him a brutal lesson in "Western law."

With this initial flashback, Ford establishes conflict dramatically (Stoddard versus Valance) and thematically (Eastern versus Western law), as well as chronologically ("new" versus "old" Shinbone) and filmically (the actual Shinbone versus the stylized realm of the flashback).

Thus, Ford's distinction between fact and legend involves not only character, story, and thematics, but also the structuring of space (exterior versus studio, nature versus artifice) and time (present versus past). Whereas all Westerns address two time frames—the old West and the immediate present—*Liberty Valance* addresses three. Placing the *act of telling* (i.e., Stoddard's flashback "confession" to the reporter in turn-of-the-century Shinbone) between past and present reinforces Ford's concern with the *process* of mythmaking. The film's narrative framework, the stark stylization of the flashback story, and Ford's treatment of the principal figures all give the flashback a remarkable dreamlike quality. It is shown as the aging Stoddard might have imagined it. Stoddard himself looks much the same in the flashback as in the opening despite the quarter-century lapse—only his whitened hair indicates the advancing years. We never actually see Doniphon in the new Shinbone sequences, although his presence is felt even before the flashback when Stoddard opens the casket and orders the mortician to put Doniphon's boots and spurs on him. Doniphon, like Valance, has no business in the new Shinbone, with its telephones, paved sidewalks, and irrigation projects. Stoddard's "social man" has outlived the legendary Shinbone of his own imagination to survive in the modern world, but Doniphon and Valance, two self-consciously mythic figures, are consigned to the realm of memory and legend.

There are three mediating characters in *Liberty Valance*. First, the newspaper editor in the new Shinbone—vastly different from Dutton Peabody (Edmund O'Brien), the *Shinbone Star's* founding editor (as witnessed in the flashback) and another of Ford's philosophical drunks—who functions much like Ford the filmmaker, mediating legend and fact, myth and history, past and present. Then there is Tom Doniphon, who mediates Valance's primitive savagery and Stoddard's naive idealism. Finally, we have Hallie, who like the editor—and the audience—must decide between Stoddard and Doniphon, between the promise of "a garden of real roses" and the cactus rose. Before Stoddard begins his flashback, Hallie rides off to Doniphon's deserted, burnt-out home to pick a cactus rose, and she eventually leaves it on his casket. The rose represents the torn allegiance felt by Hallie, Ford, and the audience between garden and desert, between nature and civilization.

Although Stoddard is the narrative focus and the guiding sensibility of the film—it is, after all, his story—the cactus rose is the film's emotional and thematic core, its symbol of a lost age when civilization and wilderness coexisted in a precarious but less compromising balance. (Tom often brought Hallie cactus roses when he came courting.) Ford does not mean, however, to condemn Hallie's choice of Stoddard any more than he means to indict the Western genre itself. Hallie's choice ultimately is as inevitable as ours: We were destined to follow a certain historical path in order to reach our present cultural condition, and we keep rewriting history to convince ourselves that we have taken the "right" path, that our destiny represents the fulfillment of promises made and kept.

As Stoddard's train winds back East to Washington in the film's closing sequence, he and Hallie agree to return eventually to Shinbone to live out their lives. What draws them back West, it seems, is a sense of loss and the ghost of Tom Doniphon—who was, as Ford said, "the central character, the motivation for the whole thing." Ringo, Wyatt Earp, and Ethan Edwards never lost sight of the horizon, and each was able to escape an enclosing, repressive society, avoiding what Doc Boone had termed "the blessings of civilization." No such option was available to Tom Doniphon, however. His killing of Valance, which he himself describes as "cold-blooded murder," is finally an act of self-destruction. As surely as he eliminates Valance and saves Stoddard, he is committing himself to a life of isolated uselessness.

The ideal union of Westerner and Woman in the family, the one social institution revered by all of Ford's essentially antisocial heroes, has regressed from a reality (Ringo and Dallas) to a promise (Wyatt and Clementine) to an untenable situation (Ethan and Martha) to an outright impossibility (Tom and Hallie). With the steady enclosure of the genre's visual and thematic horizons, the hero's options are reduced to one single, inexorable reality: Doniphon does not ride off into the sunset or across Monument Valley, but into the Valley of Death.

With Tom Doniphon's death, Ford bids farewell to the Westerner and his heroic code. *The Man Who Shot Liberty Valance* is a fitting epitaph. It traces the death of that code and the basis for its mythic legacy. Some critics have noted the similarities in story and character between this film and *My Darling Clementine*, but the evolution of Ford's perspective and the genre's changing thematic emphases render the differences of those films more significant than their similarities. Time has turned Ford's—and the genre's—initial optimism into a mixture of cynicism and regret. Stoddard's glad-handing politician and Hallie's overwhelming nostalgia are the only elements remaining of the genre's faded utopian vision.

No filmmaker understood or articulated that vision with the style, sensitivity, and consistent quality of John Ford, and although the Western genre survives him, it will be forever in his debt. Not only was Ford the best of Hollywood's Western storytellers, but he brought to that story a depth and complexity that place his Westerns among the most significant films of the American cinema.

West of Everything:
The Inner Life of Westerns

Jane Tompkins

I make no secret of the fact: I love Westerns. I love to hear violins with the clip-clop of hooves behind them and see the cactus-punctuated sky spread out behind the credits. When the horses pound toward the camera and pull up in a cloud of dust, my breath gets short.

Physical sensations are the bedrock of the experience Westerns afford. Louis L'Amour says in the first sentence of *Hondo* (1953) that the hero "rolled the cigarette in his lips, liking the taste of the tobacco," that he "squint[ed] his eyes against the sun's glare." "His buckskin shirt," L'Amour says, "seasoned by sun, rain, and sweat, smelled stale and old."

L'Amour puts you inside the hero's shirt, makes you taste what he tastes, feel what he feels. Most of the sensations the hero has are not pleasurable: he is hot, tired, dirty, and thirsty much of the time: his muscles ache. His pain is part of our pleasure. It guarantees that the sensations are real. So does the fact that they come from nature: the sun's glare, not the glare of a light bulb; a buckskin shirt, not a synthetic wash-and-wear. For Westerns satisfy a hunger to be in touch with something absolutely real. It is good that the eye has to squint at the sun, since what the eye craves is the sun's reality.

I often imagine the site of the Western—the place it comes from and goes to, humanly speaking—to be like the apartment in a certain *New Yorker* cartoon. A woman is ironing a big pile of laundry—naked light bulb overhead, cats sitting around on the floor, crack in the wall—while through the door of an adjoining room you see her husband, sitting in the bathtub and calling to her, "Hon, I think it's time we took a big ride into the big sky country." The Western answers a need to get out of the apartment and into fresh air, sunlight, blue sky, and open space.

Don't fence me in.

Not just any space will do. Big sky country is a psychological and spiritual place known by definite physical markers. It is the American West, and not just any part of that but the west of the desert, of mountains and prairies, the West of Arizona, Utah, Nevada, New Mexico, Texas, Colorado, Montana, Wyoming, the Dakotas, and some parts of California.

This West functions as a symbol of freedom, and the opportunity for conquest. It seems to offer escape from a mechanized existence, economic dead ends, social entanglements, unhappy personal relations, political injustice. The desire to change places also signals a powerful need for self-transformation. The desert light and the desert space, the creak of saddle leather and the sun beating down, the horses' energy and force—these things promise a translation of the self into something purer and more authentic, more intense, more real.

The hero of Owen Wister's *The Virginian* (1902), says in a moment of rare self-revelation: "Often when I have camped here, it has made me want to become the ground, become the water, become the trees, mix with the whole thing. Not know myself from it. Never unmix again" (280). In Westerns the obsession with landscape is finally metaphysical. The craving for material reality, keen and insistent as it is, turns into a huger even more insatiable. "My pa used to say," says a character from Louis L'Amour's *Galloway* (1970), "that when corruption is visited upon the cities of men, the mountains and the deserts await him. The cities are for money but the high-up hills are purely for the soul." The same is true of the Western. Thriving on physical sensation, wedded to violence, dominated by the need for domination, and imprisoned by its own heroic code, the Western appeals finally beyond all these to whatever it is the high-up hills betoken.

———

From roughly 1900 to 1975 a significant portion of the adolescent male population spent every Saturday afternoon at the movies. What they saw there were Westerns. Roy Rogers, Tom Mix, Lash LaRue, Gene Autry, Hopalong Cassidy. From the twenties through the early seventies there here hundreds of nationally distributed feature films which gave the general population the same kind of experience on a more sophisticated level. Some of these films—*High Noon* (1952) ("Do not forsake me, oh my darling"), *Shane* (1953) ("Come back, Shane")—have become part of the permanent repertoire of American culture. Western radio shows in the thirties and forties were followed by TV shows in the fifties and sixties. In 1959 there were no fewer than thirty-five Westerns running concurrently on television, and out of the top ten programs eight were Westerns (Nachbar, x). John Wayne, the actor whose name is synonymous with Western films, became the symbol of American masculinity from World War II to Vietnam. Throughout the twentieth century, popular Western novels by Zane Grey, Ernest Haycox, Max Brand, Luke Short, and Louis L'Amour have sold hundreds of millions of copies. In 1984 L'Amour alone had 145 million books in print.

People from all levels of society read Westerns: presidents, truck drivers, librarians, soldiers, college students, businessmen, homeless people. They are read by women as well as men, rich and poor, young and old. In one way or another Westerns—novels and films—have touched the lives of virtually everyone who lived during the first three-quarters of this century. The arch-images of the genre—the gunfight, the fistfight, the chase on horseback, the figure of the mounted horseman outlined against the sky, the saloon girl, the lonely landscape itself—are culturally pervasive and over-powering. They carry within them compacted worlds of meaning and value, codes of conduct, standards of judgment, and habits of perception that shape our sense of the world and govern our behavior without our having the slightest awareness of it.

This book asks what the Western hero has meant for the way Americans living in the twentieth century have thought about themselves, how the hero's aspirations have blended with theirs, and how his story has influenced people's beliefs about the way things are. For what the hero experiences is what the audience experiences: what he does, they do too. The feeling of being "in a Western"—the kind of experience that is and the effects it has—are what I am attempting to record. Westerns play, first and last, to a Wild West of the psyche. The images, ideas, and values that become part of an audience's way of interpreting life come in through the senses and are experienced first as drama. To comprehend how they've shaped people's attitudes and behavior, to understand them in an intellectual or conceptual way, one must begin with their impact on the body and the emotions.

The first half of this book highlights some of the genre's main features—death, women, language, landscape, horses, cattle—pays attention to the look and feel of their presence, and asks some questions. Why is the Western haunted by death? Why does it hate women and language so much? What messages does the landscape send? Why are there horses everywhere, and why don't people pay them more attention? What is implied by the fact that the raising of cattle for human consumption forms the economic basis of the life that Westerns represent?

Some of the answers are problematic and raise questions about the values to which Westerns have educated us. For Westerns believe that reality is material, not spiritual; they are obsessed with pain and celebrate the suppression of feeling; their taciturn heroes want to dominate the land, sometimes to merge with it completely—they are trying to get away from other people and themselves.

The second half of the book looks at these issues by studying outstanding examples of the genre that generate the image of the West people carry in their minds: *The Virginian, Riders of the Purple Sage* (1912), the Buffalo Bill Historical Center, and a best-selling novel by Louis L'Amour. Though it's the West not of actuality but of representation I'm dealing with here—words and pictures, not flesh and blood—fiction and fact interpenetrate continually when one considers the life of Western writers in relation to their work. Owen Wister, Zane Grey, and Louis L'Amour in different ways all lived what they wrote. And Buffalo Bill spent the last half of his life playing out the first half theatrically.

Unlike most books on the Western, this one treats novels and films together. For when you read a Western novel or watch a Western movie on television, you are in the same world no matter what the medium: the hero is the same, the story line is the same, the setting, the values, the actions are the same. The media draw on each other: movies and television programs are usually based on novels and short stories; conversely, when you read *Hondo*, you're likely to think of John Wayne. So when I say "Western" I mean everything from a comic book or a fifteen-minute radio show to a feature film or a full-length novel. What matters is not the medium but the identity of the imaginative world. Just as you know, when you turn the television on, whether you're watching a science fiction serial or a sitcom, you know you're in a Western.

———

One of the things that lets you know when you're in a Western is the presence of Indians. Yet, to the surprise of some, including myself, Indians will not figure significantly in this book.

When I sat down to watch Western movies in 1986 (the novels are a somewhat different story), I expected to see a great many Indians. I'd written a piece on Indian museums and a long article on how historians of colonial New England had represent native peoples in their work. I was primed. As I watched, an Indian would appear, like the Indian woman in *The Searchers* (1956) who attaches herself to the young male lead. Her name was "Look." This woman is treated so abominable by the characters— ridiculed, humiliated, and then killed off casually by the plot—that I couldn't believe my eyes. The movie treated her as a joke, not as person. I couldn't bear to take her seriously; it would have been too painful. I kept on looking.

But the Indians I expected did not appear. The ones I saw functioned as props, bits of local color, textural effects. As people they had no existence. Quite often they filled the role of villains, predictably driving the engine of the plot, threatening the wagon train, the stagecoach, the cavalry detachment—a particularly dangerous form of wildlife. But there were no Indian characters, no individuals with a personal history and a point of view. There was the buffoonish old man in *Red River* (1948) who wins a set of false teeth from Walter Brennan, and then they trade the teeth back and forth for the rest of the film, comic relief to take the edge off the relentlessness of the drive. Surely that Indian didn't count. Still I waited, but after a while, I forgot.

Confronted, finally, with the fact that I'd left out what everyone assumed was a major element of Western narratives, I began to think back over the movies I'd seen, trying to remember what I might have missed. *Shane, High Noon, Gunfight at the OK Corral* (1969). No Indians. *My Darling Clementine* (1946), *The Wild Bunch* (1969), *The Big Country* (1958). None that I could remember. *Duel in the Sun* (1946), *Wagonmaster* (1950), *Rio Bravo* (1959), *Warlock* (1959), *Man Without a Star* (1955), *Will Penny* (1968), *Destry Rides Again* (1939), *Jesse James* (1939). Again I couldn't remember any Indians, though they might have been there. They must have been in *She Wore a Yellow Ribbon* (1949), but not that I could recall. I tried a different tack.

Images of Indians sprang to mind, detached from any one picture. That yipping sound on the sound tracks that accompanies Indian attacks, the beat of tom-toms growing louder as you near the Indian encampment. The encampment itself—tepees, campfires, dogs and children running around, squaws in blankets. Most vividly, a line of warriors—war paint, feathers, spotted horses—appearing suddenly on a ridge.

But no people. Now and then a weak imitation, like Henry Brandon playing "Scar" in *The Searchers*. It was bizarre. Either I had managed to see seventy-five to eighty Western films that by chance had no serious representations of native people in them, or there was something wrong with the popular image of Westerns. I remembered the Indians in Cooper's novels—Uncas, Chingachgook, Hardheart—ethnographically incorrect, maybe, but still magnetic, compelling. There were no such characters in the movies I had watched. Logic would suggest that in his flight from women and children, family life, triviality, and tameness, the Western hero would run straight into the arms of the Indian, wild blood brother of his soul, but it doesn't happen. Indians are repressed in Westerns—there but not there—the same way women are.

And when they do appear they are even more unreal. At least women in Westerns are not played by men. At least horses are not played by dogs, or cattle by goats. Faked scenery is more convincing than fake Indians are. In movies about the Roman Empire, real Romans don't play the roles. There aren't any Romans anymore, so Charlton Heston is OK. But when there are thousands and thousands of Native Americans alive, why should Jeff Chandler play Cochise? Why should Henry Brandon play "Scar"? How do you take Charles Bronson and Anthony Quinn seriously, when they're surrounded by nameless figures who are natives? An Indian in a Western who is supposed to be a real person has to be played by a white man. The Indians played by actual natives are extras, generic brand; those with bit parts are doodles in the margin of the film. Of course there are exceptions—everyone will think of some. *Cheyenne Autumn* (1964), for example, though it has no memorable Indian characters, really does attempt to represent the native point of view. But what I have been describing is the norm.

Since this book was written, one movie has appeared that represents Native Americans in a serious, sympathetic way: Kevin Costner's *Dances with Wolves* (1990). Here the Lakota Sioux (played by themselves) are attractive and believable, individually and as a group. They draw you to them, their closeness is palpable—the family you never had, the community you never belonged to—and you know why the protagonist deserts the army to become one of them. Their lives make sense. But Costner's triumph in this respect emphasizes the sad history that makes his film so distinctive.

The absence of Indians in Western movies, by which I mean the lack of their serious presence as individuals, is so shocking once you realize it that, even for someone acquainted with outrage, it's hard to admit. My unbelief at the travesty of native peoples that Western films afford kept me from scrutinizing what was there. I didn't want to see. I stubbornly expected the genre to be better than it was, and when it wasn't, I dropped the subject. Forgetting perpetuates itself. I never cried at anything I saw in a Western, but I cried when I realized this: that after the Indians had been decimated by disease, removal, and conquest, and after they had been caricatured and degraded in Western movies, I had ignored them too. The human beings who populated this continent before the Europeans came and who still live here, whose image the Western traded on—where are they? Not in Western films. And not in this book either.

———

While the Western may have been wrongly credited for giving us Indians, its general reputation as a serious representation of life has been vastly lower than what it deserves. People think of Westerns as light entertainment, adolescent and escapist, but there is nothing trivial about the needs they answer, the desires they arouse, or the vision of life they portray. One of the hallmarks of the genre is an almost desperate earnestness. This passage from the opening of *Heller with a Gun* (1955), an early L'Amour novel, exemplifies in miniature the kind of experience the Western likes to put its readers through, and it shows that whatever else they may be doing, Westerns are not getting away from seriousness, or from the demands of hard work, or from living a significant life:

> It was bitter cold. . . .
>   He came down off the ridge into the shelter of the draw with the wind kicking up snow behind him. The sky was a flat slate gray, unbroken and low. The air grew colder by the minute and there was a savage bite to the wind. . . .
>   He was two days out of Deadwood and riding for Cheyenne, and the nearest shelter was at Hat Creek station, probably fifty miles along.
>   Wind knifed at his cheek. He drew deeply on his cigarette. Whoever followed him had the same problem. Find shelter or die. The wind was a moving wall of snow and the evening was filled with vast sound. (5)

This is a typical opening for a L'Amour novel. A man is alone in a blizzard with a murderer on his trail. Thirty-six hours later, this particular hero rides into Hat Creek Station out of the forty-below weather, having overpowered the man who was trying to kill him. The chapter ends as follows:

> His mind was empty. He did not think. Only the occasional tug on the lead rope reminded him of the man who rode behind him.
>   It was a hard land, and it bred hard men to hard ways. (15)

The final sentence, in itself a kind of mini-Western, epitomizes familiar clichés. It represents physical strength as an ideal. It says that the hero is tough and strong, that the West made him that way; and it says this in simple language that anyone could understand. But it does not represent an escape from work. The protagonist is caught in a snowstorm, in below-zero weather, fifty miles from the nearest shelter; he is in pain and trapped in a situation he cannot escape except by monumental effort. He is able to reach it only through dogged persistence and the exercise of an unrelenting purpose. It is the ability to endure pain for a long time that saves him.

In fact all the qualities required of the protagonist are qualities required to complete an excruciatingly difficult task: self-discipline; unswerving purpose; and a capacity to continue in the face of total exhaustion and overwhelming odds. At the most literal level, then, the experience the scene reproduces for its readers is that of work rather than leisure, of effort rather than rest or relaxation. Whatever it may be an escape from for its audience, this scene is not an escape from the psychological demands of work.

It is, however, an escape from something else. Though it reproduces with amazing thoroughness and intensity the emotional experience of performing intolerable labor, it removes the feelings associated with doing work from their usual surroundings and places them in a locale and a set of circumstances that expand their meaning, endow them with an overriding purpose, and fill them with excitement. In short, hard work is transformed here from the necessity one wants to escape into the most desirable of human endeavors: action that totally saturates the present moment, totally absorbs the body and mind, and directs one's life to the service of an unquestioned goal. What the reader and the hero feel at the end of the episode is a sense of hard-won achievement. The laboriousness of the experience, its mind-numbing and back-breaking demands, are essential to the form of satisfaction the narrative affords.

Rather than offering an alternative to work, the novels of Louis L'Amour make work their subject. They transfer the feelings of effort and struggle that belong to daily life into a situation that gives them a point, usually the preservation of life itself. In story after story the hero undergoes an ordeal that exacts superhuman exertions. Protagonists crawl across deserts on their hands and knees, climb rock faces in the blinding sun, starve in snowbound cabins in the mountains, walk or ride for miles on end with all but mortal wounds, survive for long periods of time without water, without shelter, without sleep. Although the settings are exotic and the circumstances extreme, these situations call on the same qualities that get people out of bed to go to work, morning after morning. They require endurance more than anything else; not so much the ability to make an effort as the ability to sustain it. It isn't pain that these novels turn away from. It isn't self-discipline or a sense of responsibility. Least of all is it the will to persevere in the face of difficulty. What these novels offer that life does not offer is the opposite of a recreational spirit. It is seriousness. They posit effort and perseverance not only as necessary to salvation but as salvation itself. It is when your own life doesn't require of you the effort, concentration, and intensity of aim that L'Amour heroes need to stay alive that you want to be out with them in a Wyoming blizzard with a murderer on your trail fifty miles from Hat Creek Station.

The desire to test one's nerve, physically, as a means of self-fulfillment is illustrated in a somewhat prosaic but nevertheless telling way in a joke someone sent to *Reader's Digest*. The anecdote helps to explain why L'Amour's audience might be looking not for an escape from work but for quite the reverse:

> Last summer my wife and I met a couple at a restaurant. After an enjoyable lunch, the women decided to go shopping, and I invited the man to go sailing. Later, while we were out on the water, a storm blew up. The tide had gone out, and we were downwind trying to work our way back through a narrow channel. At one point the boat grounded and we had to climb overboard and shove with all our might to get it back in deeper water. As my new friend stood there, ankle deep in muck, the wind blowing his hair wildly, rain streaming down his face, he grinned at me, and with unmistakable sincerity said, "Sure beats shopping!"

The men in this joke, like the heroes in L'Amour's novels, are braving the elements. Drenched to the skin, pushing a boat off a sandbar, they are having the time of their lives. They enjoy themselves so much not because they are out on a pleasure trip but because they are meeting a challenge, a challenge whose value is defined by contrast with the activity the women are engaged in—shopping. Shopping, in this context, not only implies nonmale activity, it embodies everything that readers of Westerns are trying to get away from: triviality, secondariness, meaningless activity. That the qualities devalued here are associated with women is essential to the way Westerns operate as far as gender is concerned. Requiring no effort of the will, no test of strength or nerve, shopping is seen here as petty and inconsequential; whatever paltry resources it calls on, however it is performed, shopping makes no difference. It isn't serious.

Ordinary work—in fact, ordinary life—is too much like shopping. It never embodies what the hero's struggle to get out of the blizzard embodies: the fully saturated moment. But this is not because life in the twentieth century involves people in all those transactions the Western hero traditionally rejects—the acquisition of material goods, the desire for social status, the search for luxuries. What Westerns criticize in daily life is not the presence of things, technology, laws, or institutions per se, but the sense that life under these conditions isn't going anywhere. If Westerns seem to long for the out-of-doors, for a simplified social existence, for blizzards and shoot-outs, and fabulous exploits, it isn't because their readers want to give up TV and computers and fast foods and go back to life on the frontier. It's that life on the frontier is a way of imagining the self in a boundary situation—a place that will put you to some kind of ultimate test. What distinguishes the life of the L'Amour hero from that of his readers isn't that he can build a fire in the snow, kill ten bandits with six bullets, or get on his horse and ride out of town whenever he wants to; it is that he never fritters away his time. Whatever he does, he gives it everything he's got because he's always in a situation where everything he's got is the necessary minimum.

In the foreword to the thirtieth-anniversary edition of *Hondo*, his most famous novel, L'Amour declares that working people are not only his intended audience but the subjects of his stories as well:

> I sing of arms and men, not of presidents, kings, generals, and passing explorers, but of those who survived their personal, lonely Alamos, men who drove the cattle, plowed the furrows, built their shelters against the wind, the men who built a nation. (vi)

L'Amour's epic description of life in the Old West suggests that the hunger Westerns satisfy is a hunger not for adventure but for meaning. What these books offer their readers is not free time but its very antithesis: pressure so acute that time disappears. The trouble with ordinary work isn't, as people generally assume, that it demands too much of you but that it doesn't demand enough. F.O. Mathiessen once wrote of Herman Melville that his novels called the whole soul of man into being; that is what, in their way, the novels of Louis L'Amour aim to do.

———

The whole soul of man. "Man?" What about woman?

When they speak of their youthful afternoons at the movies, the men I talk to invariably have a certain ruminative tone in their voices, smiling inwardly at something I can't see. "Every Saturday," they say, "for years, I used to go . . ." and then they mention some (to me) extraneous circumstance, like how much they paid, or the name of the movie theater, or what they used to eat. Then, invariably, they list the names of the heroes—Roy Rogers, Gene Autry, Tom Mix, Lash LaRue; they try to remember them all, as if they were baseball statistics—and sometimes they say which one they liked best. They pronounce these names like the words to a prayer whose meaning they have forgotten, and trail off into a silence I used to think was significant but which may just be a nostalgic blur. Or it may be full of things they can't articulate. These conversations, at any rate, are maddening. Here am I trying *manfully* to write about Westerns, starting from zero and getting bleary-eyed in the process, and there they are with this huge backlog of knowledge and experience to draw on—I'll never catch up—from which they draw nothing but a list of names.

With women it's different. Either you draw a blank when you ask them about Westerns or you get something less formulaic and more personal. When they do have a history with the genre, women are split into two camps: those who identified with the hero and those who didn't or couldn't. Annie Oakley and Dale Evans were for this second group. One friend said she loved "Bonanza" so much that she had to invent a female character so that she could participate as a woman, and spent a long time deciding whether to be the fourth wife or one of the Cartwright children. Another friend told me she could identify with the male heroes but only the nonwhite, non-WASP ones, Tonto and Zorro. Another was so crazy about Gene Autry as a child that she wore guns around all the time and for two years refused to answer to anything but "Gene." I identified with everybody—the Lone Ranger, Tonto, Silver, and if there was a woman in the story, with her, too, though sometimes she was just too different from the men to be anybody I'd want to be.

I used to listen to "The Lone Ranger" on the radio on Monday, Wednesday, and Friday evenings at seven-fifteen. I loved the sound of hoofbeats, the *William Tell Overture*, the nasal intonation of the Lone Ranger's voice when he spoke to Tonto, the cry "Hi-ho, Silver, away!" But I wasn't really a fan. It wasn't the Lone Ranger or Gene Autry who laid the groundwork for my later love of Westerns, it was horses. From the age of eight to about thirteen, I was horse-crazy. I lived for summers when I took riding lessons, wanted my parents to buy me a horse, fantasized about horses, drew pictures of them, read books about them, collected statues of them, pretended to *be* a horse.

Up comes the inevitable Freudian query: horse as penis? I don't know. To me, at age eight, a penis was an embarrassing-looking thing that hung down between a boy's legs. I certainly didn't want one. But horses and riding were my experience of happiness and freedom. Horses smelled good and made me feel physically alive. Riding showed me that right effort could be followed by accomplishment, made me feel competent, and gave me an experience of risk and daring that I craved. It was the best thing life had to offer.

With late adolescence this enthusiasm wore off, and it wasn't until I was almost forty that I read my first L'Amour novel. But as soon as I did I was back in the saddle again. This time I fell in with the heroes. They worked hard, and so did I. They kept going under adverse circumstances, and so did I. Often, after finishing a L'Amour book, I would feel inspired to go back to some difficult task, strengthened in the belief that I could complete it if only I didn't give up. Westerns made me want to work, they made me feel good about working, they gave me what I needed in order to work hard.

So although Westerns have traditionally been fare for men and not for women, women can feel engaged by them. In fact, since stories about men (at least in our culture) function as stories about all people, women learn at an early age to identify with male heroes. Socialized to please others, women also acquire early on the ability to sympathize with people whose circumstances are different from their own. Hence they regularly identify across gender lines in reading and in watching movies and television.

Feminist theorists have shown how movies force women to look at women from the point of view of men, seeing women as sex objects, forcing women to identify against themselves in order to participate in the story. Westerns do this more than most narratives, and the attitudes toward oneself that form over a lifetime of seeing oneself trivialized and degraded are extremely difficult to undo. But in the very act of harming women in this way Westerns also force men into parts that are excruciating to perform, parts that, given the choice, they probably would not have wanted to play.

In fact, what is most interesting about Westerns at this moment in history is their relation to gender, and especially the way they created a model for men who came of age in the twentieth century. The model was not for women but for men: Westerns insist on this point by emphasizing the importance of manhood as an ideal. It is not one ideal among many, it is *the* ideal, certainly the only one worth dying for. It doesn't matter whether a man is a sheriff or an outlaw, a rustler or a rancher, a cattleman or a sheepherder, a miner or a gambler. What matters is that he be a *man*. That is the only side to be on. The most poignant expression of this sentiment, so characteristic of the genre, comes in the late, and in many ways uncharacteristic, film *The Wild Bunch*. Robert Ryan, leader of a gang of louts hired by the railroad to catch a gang of thieves to which he used to belong, has just heard one of his crew say something derogatory about the gang they're chasing. And he replies, "We're after *men*, and I wish to God I was with them."

That, I think, is the way the audience of a Western feels when things are going right. "I wish to God I was with them." I feel that way a lot when I watch Westerns, and sometimes I feel exactly the reverse.

———

I am simultaneously attracted and repelled by the power of Western heroes, the power that men in our society wield. I've been jealous of power, and longed for it, wanted the experiences that accompany it, and seen the figures who embody it as admirable, worthy to emulate, and sexually attractive. I have also been horrified by the male exercise of power and, like most women, have felt victimized by it in my own life. In a sense my engagement with the Western has been an attempt to understand why men act the way they do and to come to terms with it emotionally.

So I came to this project with a mixture of motives, not unlike the motives with which men originally came to the West: curiosity, awe, and a desire to subdue and possess. There was the feeling that if I could understand what made these Western heroes so attractive, I could gain some advantage over men, turn the knowledge against them when I needed to. In a sense, I suppose, I wanted to do to Western heroes what my own culture, in the form of Western novels and movies, had done to women, had done to me. I wanted to hold men up to scorn.

But though I have felt contempt and hatred for the Western hero, for his self-righteousness, for his silence, for his pathetic determination to be tough, the desire to *be* the Western hero, with his squint and his silence and his swagger, always returns. I want to be up there in the saddle, looking down at the woman in homespun; I want to walk into the cool darkness of the saloon, order a whiskey at the bar, feel its warmth in my throat, and hear the conversation come to a sudden halt. I want these things and I don't want them, because I have found in my own life, and through reading and watching Westerns, that the price for these experiences, or rather, for the power they represent is too high. The price the Western exacts from its heroes is written in the expression on Gary Cooper's face throughout *High Noon* as he tries to get help in confronting Frank Miller's gang. The expression is one of fear, distaste, determination, and inward pain. It is impossible not to share that pain with Western heroes if one is trying to understand them. Consequently, my attitude toward the hero is always shifting. Outrage, disdain, admiration, emulation, compassion.

A word about pain. Westerns invite their audiences to undergo a considerable amount of it. And for a long time I imagined it was only *other* readers and viewers who responded to this invitation, albeit subliminally. The attraction to suffering, I thought, was a pathology found especially in men who, as a class, were always trying to prove that they could take it. Never did it occur to me that I loved the pain I was describing, and that in fact *everything* I said about the Western hero—and, by implication, his audience—was in varying degrees true of me as well.

Gunsmoke and Mirrors

Richard Slotkin

You get the picture: John Wayne is leading a cavalry charge to rescue helpless victims from the Apaches. The strong, silent marshal—Gary Cooper, Henry Fonda, James Stewart—steps into the empty street to face the menace at the far end and makes Dodge City, or Tombstone, or "this whole valley" safe for women and children.

The western is an essential part of American mythology—the body of traditional tales, historical fables and heroic fantasies through which we remember our past. Movie images taught generations of children how to play cowboys and Indians. And those children, grown up, have used western movie symbols [. . .] as a way of simplifying the problems we confront and making terribly clear just what it is that "a man's gotta do" about them[. . . .]

The myth is rooted in history: two centuries of westward expansion, during which white settlers cleared the wilderness and fought Indians and Mexicans for possession of the continent. Because the nation grew prosperous through the continual conquest of new lands, richly endowed with exploitable natural resources, we came to equate democracy with freewheeling individualism, mobility, perpetual growth, ever rising expectations. Because the winning of the West required the subjugation of nonwhites, Americans learned to divide humankind into "savage" and "civilized" races. We are a violent society, in part because the frontier experience linked the idea of human dignity with gunplay. "God may have made men," the saying goes. "Samuel Colt made them equal." But only a handful of Americans actually experienced the reality of the West. Most Americans, past and present, have known the frontier only through its myths.

Motion pictures were invented just as the real frontier was passing away, and they became our most important medium for translating fact into myth and extracting lessons from our past. The history of modern movies begins with the first western, Edwin S. Porter's *The Great Train Robbery* (1903), which pioneered cinematic storytelling.

The westerns had special advantages. Story composition was easy: Filmmakers could draw on a vast literature of novels, dime novels, stage melodramas and Wild West shows, full of ready-made plots and characters. They could also draw on surviving remnants of "the real thing." In the first decades of the new century most of the western landscape was unaffected by modernization, and many frontier heroes and villains—Buffalo

Bill, Wyatt Earp, the outlaws Henry Starr and Emmett Dalton—were still available to appear on camera. When Thomas Ince filmed *Custer's Last Fight* in 1912, many of the participants served as actors and technical advisers.

Most silent westerns were formula films, featuring well-established stars like Bronco Billy Anderson, W. S. Hart and Tom Mix in predictable, melodramatic plots. The "realism" of these films was mostly illusion. The constant repetition of movie images taught audiences what the West was supposed to look like, who westerners were, how they were likely to act. The setting was almost always the typical board-front desert town inhabited by the usual suspects: an outlaw with noble moral instincts, a school-marm who loves and redeems him, a villainous gambler or Mexican bandit, ably assisted by a dance-hall slut. The viewer could rely on the haberdashery—white hats, black hats—to distinguish good guys from bad guys. Whatever the story, the audience could count on at least one thrilling horseback chase and a climactic shoot-out to settle the black hats once and for all. But as the industry prospered and horse operas gained in popularity, a larger, more ambitious sort of western was developed: the historical epic, which celebrated the winning of the West as the triumph of civilization over savagery, of whites over Indians, of the locomotive over the buffalo. A wave of epics followed the successes of James Cruze's *The Covered Wagon* in 1923 and John Ford and Thomas Ince's *The Iron Horse* in 1924, and westerns reached a new height of popularity in 1926–27, just as the economic boom of the Roaring Twenties was approaching its zenith.

The Great Depression that followed the stock market crash of 1929 nearly wiped out the western. The epic western celebrated the progress and prosperity of the American past: Perhaps there was too painful a contrast between such images on screen and the breadlines in the street. The grim ironies of the gangster film seemed more appropriate, and the musical comedy or the swashbuckling romance offered an escape from both the pain and the irony.

Then in 1939 all the studios decided simultaneously that the time had come to bring back the western. They were responding to the mood of the moment: The New Deal had restored confidence in our power to cope with the Depression. Now, with war looming in Asia and Europe, the time seemed right for films that offered a more hopeful and patriotic reading of the American past—a task for which the western had been the traditional vehicle.

This "renaissance of the western" began a 30-year period in which westerns were the most popular form of action picture in theaters and later on television. The renaissance westerns made several permanent contributions. They were modeled on the historical epics of the silent era, and they firmly established the principle that westerns are movies about American history. Studio research departments went to great lengths to develop stories with some genuine historical basis and to provide authentic costumes and hardware, from six-guns to stagecoaches and period locomotives. Most of these films begin with rolling titles, as solemn as high school textbooks, which carefully set the historical scene: "Nebraska, 1869. The Civil War was over and now the transcontinental railroad. . . ." Virtually all these films drew on a mere 40 years of western history—from the gold-rush wagon trains of 1849, through the Civil War, to the Plains Indian wars, the transcontinental railroads and the heyday of the range cattle business (1870–90). Yet their power was such that this narrow slice of time has come to symbolize the whole history of expansion that preceded it.

In the movie version of western history, 40 years of cowboys and Indians, six-guns and Stetsons outweigh two centuries of long rifles, buckskins and colonial rangers battling the French and Indians.

Since this wave of productions also sent writers rummaging through history, the kinds of stories a western could tell became more various. And since the history in these films was being looked at for patriotic purposes, the renaissance westerns also established the practice of looking to the frontier past for imaginative solutions to current problems—industrial conflict, social justice, war and peace. Films like *Dodge City* and *Union Pacific* (1939) and *Western Union* (1941) associated the western with the heroic phase of America's industrial growth. *Dodge City* set the pattern. The film opens on a race between a stagecoach and a locomotive of the new railroad: That's the symbol of America's future. Progress!

Iron men and iron horses, you can't beat 'em." Warner Bros. emphasized the patriotic purpose of the film by premiering it in *Dodge City* itself, amid a historical pageant described by studio flacks as "one of the biggest things that has ever been put on in the history of show business."

But westerns also took up the thornier issues of war and social justice. *Santa Fe Trail* (1940) starred Errol Flynn as J.E.B. Stuart and a young Ronald Reagan as George Custer, leading the cavalry in an effort to keep political fanatics (John Brown's abolitionists) from organizing an army to take over the state of Kansas.

One of the most popular of the new westerns was *Jesse James* (1939), directed by Henry King: a sympathetic portrait of the outlaw as a folk hero, a Robin Hood who battles greedy railroad men. King's folk epic took the gangster film's dark and critical view of American capitalism, gave it populist appeal by shifting the action from the modern city to the agrarian past and managed to blend a critique of economic exploitation into a story that still ends by celebrating American progress. The cult of the outlaw (as one film historian has called it) has proved one of the most durable subjects on the western, from *The Return of Frank James* and *When the Daltons Rode* (1940) to *Butch Cassidy and the Sundance Kid* (1969) and *The Outlaw Josey Wales* (1976).

The outbreak of World War II briefly arrested the further development of the western. From 1942 to 1945 the war film became the dominant form of action movie. But after victory and demobilization, as soldiers came home to Brooklyn and Texas,

Hollywood came home to the western, picking up pretty much where the renaissance left off.

From an artistic as well as a commercial point of view, the years 1946 to 1960 may have been the western's gold age. By the time of the Korean war the western had developed a symbolic language both rich in meaning and widely understood.

The town-tamer western—films ranging from John Ford's classic interpretation of Wyatt Earp in *My Darling Clementine* (1946) to Fred Zinneman's bleak and dis-illusioned *High Noon* (1952)—dealt with crime as an obstacle to progress and starkly posed questions about law and justice, individual responsibility and social solidarity. Increasingly, the heroes of these films appeared as loners who have to uphold the code of heroic values—you can't run away from a fight—in the face of public misunder-standing and social cowardice. The cult of the outlaw metamorphosed into the gun-fighter movie—*The Gunfighter* (1950), *Shane* (1953), *No Name on the Bullet* (1959), *Last of the Fast Guns* (1960)—a highly stylized action film that transformed the west-ern shoot-out into a ritual. Here was a new kind of hero, neither a populist outlaw nor an elected sheriff, but a professional killer.

Gunfighter heroes were telling symbols for cold war America: alienated men, watch-ful as any paranoid, faster on the draw but menaced by every kid with a gun—at once the most powerful and the most vulnerable of men.

The formalization of the western allowed filmmakers to explore all sorts of for-bidden or difficult subjects. In the era of McCarthyism and the black-list, when polit-ical expression of any kind was dangerous for a filmmaker, westerns provided safe vehicles for disguised commentary on the toughest issues of the day, including civil rights and the cold war. In 1950, *Broken Arrow* and *Devil's Doorway* showed Indians as sympathetic figures, victims of mistreatment and prejudice who were willing to make peace with whites.

But westerns also mirrored the harder face of cold war politics. Beginning with Ford's famous "cavalry trilogy" of 1948–50 *(Fort Apache, She Wore a Yellow Ribbon, Rio Grande)*, the western provided a way to treat the concerns of the war film—choice of enemy, preparedness, whether to attack first or defend—in the language of the western. Ford's *Rio Grande* was released on November 15, 1950, at a critical point of the Korean war, when the issue was whether or not General Douglas Mac Arthur should cross the Yalu River and risk World War III by attacking Red China. On the same screen that showed John Wayne as Colonel Kirby Yorke, glaring across the Rio Grande at Apache sanctu-aries that fussy diplomats forbade him to attack, newsreels were showing McArthur star-ing through his binoculars across the Yalu into China. In *Rio Grande* the myth of the western hero tells Yorke (and the audience) what is the right and necessary thing to do: He must disobey his government, cross the river and "get it done." The idea occurs that perhaps a similar imperative guides—or ought to guide—the newsreel general as well.

Westerns continued to serve as vehicles for political mythmaking, particularly after 1960 when John F. Kennedy identified his forward-looking, activist administration as the New Frontier. The slogan characterized the young President's personal and political style: a mixture of idealism and militaristic tough-mindedness that made Kennedy (in the words of political columnist Joe Klein) "the ultimate existential gunslinger." Filmmakers played out two of the most important initiatives of the New Frontier: support for the civil rights movement at home and counterinsurgency in the third world—especially Vietnam. The late '50s and early '60s saw a spate of civil rights westerns dealing with themes of integration and racial tolerance. *Trooper Hook and The Tin Star* (1957) dealt with interracial (white-Indian) relationships. In *Walk Like a Dragon* (1960) a Chinese immigrant Americanizes himself by learning the arts of the gunfighter.

The counterinsurgency theme became dominant in western movies during the New Frontier. In *Vera Cruz* (1954) and most notably in *The Magnificent Seven* (1960), Hollywood anticipated the direction of American policy by sending a group of American gunfighters south of the border to aid democratic Mexican peasants fighting oppressive foreign dictators and native warlords. These films set the pattern for what might be called the Green Beret western, in which American gunfighters in Mexico symbolically act out the program of counterinsurgency that Kennedy and his advisers had designed for the third world.

The development of these westerns paralleled the course of our engagement in the Vietnam war. As the public began to question the way the war was being fought, westerns also began to raise questions about the logic of our policy. In Sam Peckinpah's masterpiece, *The Wild Bunch* (1969), several American outlaws confront a Mexican military dictator who has imprisoned and tortured their comrade, a Mexican campesino with revolutionary sympathies. But the classic rescue scene, and the traditional final shoot-out between democratic good and evil tyranny, soon degenerates into a general massacre of rescuers and rescued, dictators and civilians—the perfect visualization of the phrase, spoken by an American captain in 1968, that came to embody the ultimate absurdity of the war: "We had to destroy the city in order to save it."

When the Vietnam war ended, so did the western's 30-year boom. Other genres have taken over some of the western's themes. The town-tamer and gunfighter westerns gave way to fables of gunslinger cops and urban vigilantes in the *Death Wish* and *Dirty Harry* series. *Star Wars* and *Star Trek* replaced the cavalry and counterinsurgency westerns, substituting the "final frontier" of outer space for the wild frontier of the Old West.

The westerns that have appeared since 1980—films like *Heaven's Gate*, *Silverado*, the two *Young Guns* movies and *Dances with Wolves*—reflect the disruption of a Hollywood tradition that began with *The Great Train Robbery*. Directors like John Ford learned their craft by working on westerns within the studio system. The new directors have studied westerns, which is not the same thing. Their westerns seem self-conscious and more than a little nostalgic, as if they are aware that they are dealing with a classic form that really belongs to an older Hollywood.

But in the right hands, this approach can still produce interesting and powerful films. *The Outlaw Josey Wales* shows Clint Eastwood's understanding of the cult of the outlaw. The film combines historical reconstruction with a response to a contemporary issue, the bitter aftermath of Vietnam. There is no mistaking the meaning of the film's final line, in which Josey forgives his last enemy: "We all died a little in that damned war."

Eastwood's most recent western, *Unforgiven* (1992), has the spareness, intensity and depth of a genuine classic. It starts out as a straightforward variation of the *Shane* formula—the great gunfighter, who has been morally redeemed by the love of a good woman, arrives to help the helpless.

But the movie develops into a subtle study in human character and the character of myth: The unfolding action and the well-designed interactions between Eastwood and his supporting players gradually reveal that something essential in the soul of gunfighter Bill Munny has remained unredeemed by the life and sainted memory of his dead wife. His power comes from neither the justice of his cause (which is dubious) nor the purity of his soul but from the fact that he still has a killer's heart and mind and is able to take a life without hesitation or afterthought.

Dances with Wolves and *Unforgiven* call our attention to the dark side of the western, the dark side of American cultural myth—the side that sees violence as essential to progress and to the vindication of one's moral character, that sees a massive (but miraculously precise and selective) shoot-out as a viable solution to almost any given problem; the side that divides the world along lines of race and culture and dehumanizes those on the other side of the border by identifying them as savages and outlaws. But as these films suggest, the western can be more than a device for reinforcing a mythology of violence and division. Because it is so closely identified with American history, the western provides superb opportunities for artists to reexamine our past and reimagine our myths.

As we contemplate our common history from the perspective of 1993, even the Indian wars can be seen as civil wars. If that is so, perhaps the best westerns of all are waiting to be made.

Material and Metaphorical— Horse and Rider in *Lonely Are the Brave*

Stephen Cook

In American Culture, the horse is both physical and metaphorical. It is also simultaneously indigenous and imported, having disappeared in North America about ten thousand years ago and then reintroduced by explorers and colonists. The Pueblo Uprising of 1680 allowed hundreds of head of Spanish stock to escape, and Southwestern Amerindians like the Comanche, Kiowa, and Apache seized many of these free-range horses. Through this new-found dialectic between horse and rider, these tribes were reborn and others after them, creating the Plains Horse Culture, a period of roughly 150 years during which formerly earthbound peoples discovered the freedom of raptors and created societies so efficient as to allow for leisure, the acquisition of wealth, and the creation of art. This historical development was nothing new; for well into antiquity, whatever the culture, the horse gave worker, warrior, or traveler the decided advantages of strength, speed, and maneuverability. Societies came to embody mobility and mastery, but these qualities were the gifts of horses.

In America, by 1915, the lives of the Plains Tribes were in a shambles, but in the larger society, the horse was a mainstay and equal in numbers to the human population. However, the advent of the automobile and the assembly line making cars affordable for the masses started a transition wherein the horse became less utilitarian and more symbolic, but even as metaphor, the horse continues to carry the load. As it did yeoman service in reality, what the horse is and represents are made subservient to qualities embodied and represented by humans. A horse may demonstrate enormous courage and steadiness, but it is the resolve of the hero on its back that we largely see and make note of. Therefore, in Westerns the horse is a silent partner, one taken for granted in the same way as landscape. Yet like the natural world that provides the setting, horses make Westerns possible. If anyone doubts that the horse is, as Jane Tompkins writes, where "everything in the genre is hidden" (90), he or she only need engage in an exercise that Tompkins suggests:

> "A fiery horse with the speed of light, a cloud of dust, and a hearty hi-ho Silver! The Lone Ranger! These words, declaimed to the sound of the *William Tell Overture*

accompany the opening shot of "The Lone Ranger"—a close up of a big white horse, ridden at a gallop by a masked rider. As the words "THE LONE RANGER"cover the image, we hear *bang, bang*. The camera pulls back. The Lone Ranger and Silver gallop down into a sage-dotted valley, draw up momentarily in front of a butte, wheel, then take off again, Silver's white mane and tail waving in the wind. Now try to imagine the same sequence without the horse. . . . (89)

This task may seem obvious and even simplistic, yet two examples will fully illustrate Tompkins' meaning. Look at a scene from Walter Hill's *The Long Riders*. The James-Younger Gang has come to Northfield, Minnesota. The gang robs the First National Bank, but the town rises up against the Gang, blocking both ends of the street on which the bank is located and raining gunfire from the tops of buildings. The bank robbers mount their horses and race back and forth through the street, being shot to pieces, one killed and most of the others severely wounded. The Gang escapes Northfield by riding into the windows of a storefront and exiting through a similar bank of windows at the rear.

The scene is hard to watch because of the carnage, and yet it also moves at breakneck speed, inducing in this viewer a greatly elevated pulse. What is instructive is an exercise I suggest, one like the suggestion Tompkins proffers: As you watch The *Long Riders*, keep your eyes on the horses rather than the men riding them. It's not easy to do—our inclination is to follow the human forms rather than the horses propelling them.

As a contrast and as a way to reveal just how spavined we human beings appear dismounted, those readers who have seen *Monty Python and the Holy Grail* need only remember the percussive sounds of two halves of a coconut being knocked together and the ludicrous motions of actors pretending to be horseback. To this observer, it is clear that horses bring to the Western genre many of its most adrenalized moments, obviously transporting a rider on screen yet also a viewer, for while the images of horses are electronically projected onto a screen, they still represent something non-technological. In this primal scenery, we see ". . . something people [can] have close contact with, something they [can] press against with their bodies. Something that is alive, first of all, something big, powerful, and fast-moving" (Tompkins 93).

Thus, horses bring physicality to the Western, even a "perilous, sexually-charged, rapturous potentiality . . ." (95). In *The Missouri Breaks*, rustler Tom Logan courts Jane Braxton, the daughter of a prominent rancher, the man who has brought the psychotic "regulator" Lee Clayton to clean out thieves such as Tom and his gang. On an idyllic horseback ride, Tom and Jane ride a single horse face to face, Jane's legs wrapped around Tom's waist. The walk of the horse becomes a gentle foreplay. In *The Right Stuff*, we see a much more aggressive preliminary, replete with heavy breathing. The test pilot Chuck Yeager is horseback in the Mojave Desert of California, riding close by Edwards Air Force Base. He pauses to watch the fueling of the X-15, and it is a moment of wonderful juxtaposition between the quivering horse and the aircraft from which rolls wave after wave of heat, making it appear equally alive. Yeager rides to Pancho's, a watering hole for pilots, bureaucrats, and officers, where he makes an agreement to pilot the X-15 the following day and then engages in a kind of charade with his wife Glynnis at the bar, making it appear that he is trying to pick her up. She leaves first and rides into the desert, followed shortly by Yeager. He pursues her at breakneck speed past Joshua trees until a branch from one catches him across the chest and sweeps him from the saddle. He breaks a rib but punches through the sound barrier the next day.

The sensuality inherent in riding brings us to a consideration of why people still ride. Of course, in many parts of the world horses continue to have a connection to work. However, a tractor has it all over a horse except in very steep terrain. Vehicles, by and large, are superior in terms of providing movement from place to place. Because of these realities, in this country, the vast majority of riding is for pleasure and profit derived from catering to the excitement horses bring to the senses. It seems to me that people ride or watch horses being ridden in order to locate some hidden connection to pre-modern life. For one directly involved, riding is like sailing, exploring, surfing, or swimming in an ocean or river—one confronts the elements; one submits to the various degrees of challenge offered by the experiences; one accepts the possibility of becoming lost, of injury, even of death, and one thereby gains a realistic sense of one's true importance, coming to see that we humans are not much: chemicals and perhaps a little more. The price of this kind of sharpening of one's life is the possibility that forces beyond our control may compel us to mingle with the stars. Thus, the connection between sensuality and being horseback is no surprise, for while there is the obvious movement of the hips and the traditional romance associated with a mounted figure, the reality is that riding horses, or catching a wave, or risking a current, or taking an unknown path are about the risks inherent in really, truly loving. Is it not so that danger gives love an excitement? We know that love can lay us open, exposing us to injury or intimacy, sometimes both. The serious endurance riders I know are folks who regularly invest time and money and who endure aches, pains, and injuries in order to ride. Why? For love. For passion. It's not complicated.

And one reason the Western will always be with us in spite of observers who annually write its obituary is because of the presence of horses who ". . . fulfill a longing for a different kind of existence . . . [one that is] [a]nti-modern, anti-urban, and anti-technological . . ." (Tompkins 93). However, the paradox is that this desire for a simpler, less-complex time also presents "an emotional double-bind, filling us with longing for a mode of life that [the western] declares extinct before our very eyes" (103). Few if any movies represent this dichotomy more than *Lonely Are the Brave*, based on the novel The *Brave Cowboy* by Edward Abbey. In *Lonely Are the Brave*, a sleek palomino named Whiskey and its rider, the protagonist, a man named Jack Burns, embody Abbey's jaundiced view of technology and his concomitant mourning for lost connections with the natural world. In the opening scene of the movie, the viewer initially supposes that Burns and Whiskey are living in the Nineteenth Century, but that illusion is shattered by Air Force jets flying overhead, breaking the sound barrier. As the roar subsides, screenwriter Dalton Trumbo returns the viewer to the essentials: desert, horse, and cowboy. Burns and Whiskey engage in an exchange that is playful, yet serious, for this process establishes a compact of trust, one Thomas McGuane details, especially in regard to a saddle horse named Cayenne:

> He really taught me the coming and going aspects of a using horse; how their feet move in the rocks, when they're winded; how much water they need when they're hot, how you shouldn't let them eat when you're gathering cattle or they learn to dive at a gallop because idle hunger has struck; why you should get down when your lariat is caught under your horse's tail, why nose flies make them throw their heads in your face, why geldings make that noise at a trot, why Old Paint will always walk off and leave you; how a horse will, finally, sell out for grain, how a horse can get you home from the mountains in the dark when a mule can't; and above all, how when you do such things long enough with one horse, you begin to see things in him, to look deep in his eyes and to make your deal, which is a kind of interchange of respect. ("Roping, from A to B" 208–209)

Burns saddles Whiskey and points her in the direction of Duke City, New Mexico. His plan is to get put in jail so that he may break out, taking with him a friend jailed for civil disobedience. However, Burns and Whiskey must first cross the main highway into town. They barely escape being hit. The scene foreshadows the end of the film, emphasizing how the iron of horseshoes against slick asphalt creates an inability of horse and rider to find purchase in a hostile world of machinery. Even when Burns and Whiskey make their way safely across the highway, they catch their breath in the shadow of an auto wrecking yard. Above them soar stacks of old cars, piled on top of each other, and the visual effect is of the enormous weight of steel bearing down on flesh and blood.

Burns does get tossed in jail, but he does not convince his friend Paul Bondi to escape. Paul stays to do his time so that he may resume a life with his wife Jerry, a woman who has some sort of history with Burns. However, it's clear that Burns long ago chose a solitary life. The men share more than a connection to Jerry; they also share a Jeffersonian approach to the world. Still, the two men stand in sharp contrast, for Paul is rational and is willing to compromise. He longs for a return to his domestic life. Burns is stubborn and pig-headed, having chosen a beautiful yet anachronistic existence, one clearly doomed. That Burns is a goner is abundantly clear early on in the book and the film—what other reason could there be for the narrative thread comprised of the inexorable movement of a truck hauling toilet seats cross country and into Scissors Canyon, New Mexico?

The cargo of the truck shows Abbey's dark humor and cynicism and is a counterpoint to the romance of Burns's life. Art Hinton, the truck driver, also offers the reader a contrast. Minutes away from the inevitable collision with Burns and Whiskey, Hinton, as described by Abbey, is "numb, foggy, sick in the stomach and tired, all broken up inside: like a sack of old junk" (291). On the other hand, Burns, though wounded by a bullet in the movie version, is very much alive and nearly home free— all he needs to do is cross the ribbon of asphalt on the floor of the canyon, and nobody will find him, especially since the pursuing sheriff, out of a grudging admiration, is disinclined to continue the search. However, Burns cannot escape his fate as we see in the last scene from *Lonely Are the Brave*. He and Whiskey attempt to cross over the highway that confronts them, and at a critical moment, Whiskey balks, and they are hit by the truck Art Hinton is driving. Motorists rush to Burns' aid, and as he "looks pathetically up into the camera, his rain-wet face like a baby's in its innocence, he resembles nothing so much as Whiskey . . . beautiful, innocent, uncomprehending flesh struck down by a machine" (Tompkins 102). Police officers arrive, and the last paragraph of *The Brave Cowboy* reads: "From the black arroyo came the scream of the horse, then the sound of the first shot and another scream;—while over the great four-lane highway beside them the traffic roared and whistled, and thundered by, steel, rubber and flesh, dim faces behind glass, beating hearts, cold hands—the fury of men and women immured in engines" (Abbey 297). In the novel, Burns screams in grief and frustration and pain; however, in the movie, he dies quietly, but only after reassuring himself that Whiskey is gone. In either version, the bond between man and animal is clear.

"Immured" is an excellent word choice by Abbey, for it means "entombed." Perhaps he means it literally, but for all his polemics in opposition to the American culture of consumption, Abbey seems to have been in favor of inflatable rafts, beer in aluminum cans, and pick-up trucks. I believe that rather than argue categorically against technology, he opposed the ways in which we submerge ourselves in it, rarely if ever surfacing for a taste of the natural world.

It also seems true to me that many Americans like their padded existences. Still, there are others who have a longing for the pre-technological world, and some of these folks have ties to horses. Of them, a few grizzled hold-outs and antiquarians continue to employ horses for work, but the true use of horses is to awaken ancient rhythms in riders, to re-acquaint them with the wheel of the seasons, and to bridge the great divide between animal and human by reinvigorating instinct (McGuane "Horses" 4).

WORKS CITED

Abbey, Edward. *The Brave Cowboy.* New York: Avon, 1956.

Lonely Are the Brave. Dir. by David Miller. With Kirk Douglas, Gena Rowlands, and Walter Matthau. 1962.

McGuane, Thomas. "Roping, from A to B." *An Outside Chance.* New York: Farrar, 1969 207–225.

———. "Horses." *Some Horses.* New York: Lyons, 1999. 1–20.

Monty Python's Search for the Holy Grail. Dir. by Terry Gilliam and Terry Jones. With Graham Chapman, John Cleese, Terry Gilliam, Eric Idle, Terry Jones, and Michael Palin. 1974.

Tompkins, Jane. *West of Everything: The Inner Life of Westerns.* New York: U of Oxford P, 1992.

The Long Riders. Dir. by Walter Hill. With David Carradine, Stacy Keach, Dennis Quaid, and Christopher Guest. 1980.

The Missouri Breaks. Dir. by Arthur Penn. With Marlon Brando and Jack Nicholson. 1976.

The Right Stuff. Dir. by Philip Kaufman. With Scott Glenn, Ed Harris, and Sam Shepard. 1983.

THE REEL WEST

STUDY QUESTIONS

1. In "The Western," Thomas Schatz writes, " . . . the Western genre created a mythical reality more significant and pervasive—and perhaps in some ways more 'real'—than the historical West itself." How is it possible for myth to be real?
2. Schatz also calls the Western " . . . America's foundation ritual . . . ." What is he talking about?
3. What principal themes do John Ford's Westerns explore?
4. What role does landscape play in Ford's Westerns?
5. In what ways do Ford's Westerns reflect America during the historical periods in which they were made?
6. Jane Tompkins repeats an old cliché: "Don't fence me in." How does this old saying reflect an American attitude?
7. Describe the hero's relationship with nature, according to Tompkins. What qualities are called out in the hero by a life lived on the land?
8. What is Tompkins' attitude toward Westerns?
9. How do Westerns treat women and Native Americans, according to Tompkins?
10. How does Richard Slotkin define the Western in "Gunsmoke and Mirrors"?
11. How does Slotkin define "the dark side" of the Western?
12. Find two or three examples of how Westerns reflect or comment on a particular period in American history, according to Slotkin.
13. In what ways do Westerns depend on horses, according to the author of "Material and Metaphorical: Horse and Rider in *Lonely are the Brave*"?
14. What qualities do horses bring to Westerns? How do they represent ancient connections to the natural world?
15. Can you think of a time when a wild or domestic animal taught you an important lesson about life?

STUDY QUESTIONS—*RED RIVER* (1948)

1. The world of the cowboys in *Red River* is a masculine one. What rules govern the behavior of men in this world? To what extent do these rules still apply to American men in the 21st Century?

2. Tess Millay and Tom Dunson's fiancé are women with speaking roles in *Red River*, but do their parts really matter? After all, they are the *only* women with speaking roles. Analyze the importance of their characters.

3. What sort of man is Tom Dunson? Does he change or remain static? Does Dunson cross the line into what Robert Bellah calls "nihilism"? Is Dunson a Captain Ahab of the plains? (Did you notice that the last name of the cattle buyer in Abilene is Melville?)

4. Describe Matt Garth. Is he truly weak and soft-hearted? Why does he give Dunson such free-rein over himself?

5. How is Dunson's attitude about land acquisition a parallel to American history, in particular the 19th Century idea of Manifest Destiny?

6. Consider the character of Quo. Is his portrayal racist, or does *Red River* take him seriously and treat him well?

7. The cattle drive can be seen as a metaphor for capitalism in America. How? Why? Is Dunson a model for men and women who want to build empires in America, or does Garth represent a different and ultimately more successful management style?

8. Offer an educated guess: When Dunson reads the Bible over the graves of men he has killed and buried, does he read from the *Old Testament* or the *New Testament?* For help on this question, consult Michael Marsden's essay, "Savior in the Saddle: The Sagebrush Testament."

Suggested Essay Questions

1. Compare *Red River* with *The Searchers*. Both are Westerns starring John Wayne, but Howard Hawks directed *Red River*, and John Ford directed *The Searchers*. What similarities and differences do you see? In particular, pay attention to the endings of both movies. Which ending is more emotionally satisfying? Which ending is more realistic? What message does each picture offer about the hero's place in the community?

2. Watch *The Searchers*, *The Cowboys*, *True Grit*, and *The Shootist*. What similar values do these four movies articulate, and what messages about masculinity do they offer the viewer? Use Jane Tompkins' essay as a starting point for this analysis.

3. Do research to prove or disprove this assertion: *High Noon* was (and continues to be) Fred Zinneman's critique of McCarthyism.

4. Write a research paper on the Negro Cinema, which between 1916 and 1950 produced many Westerns with all-Black casts. Some of the titles of these movies are *The Crimson Skull*, *Trooper of Company K*, *The Homesteader*, *The Bull-Dogger*, *Black Gold*, *Rhythm Rodeo*, *Look-Out Sister*, *The Flaming Crisis*, *Harlem Rides the Range*, and *A Chocolate Cowboy*. Focus your paper on whatever is most interesting or surprising to you in the course of your research.

5. Write a research paper on the ways horses transformed the lives of Native Americans.

6. Watch *Lonely are the Brave* and *Hidalgo.* Describe the relationships between horse and rider in each movie. How do they complement one another, and how do the horses reveal their personalities? Is it too much to say that the horses featured in each movie reveal character? In other words, can Whiskey and Hidalgo be said to possess courage and a sense of self?

7. William Kittredge writes in "Taking Care of Our Horses," "After horses were domesticated on the high steppes of Central Asia, a couple of different kinds of cultures evolved. One was made up of farming people who stayed home to tend crops—their villages evolved into cities and kingdoms. . . . The others were horse people who followed herds through the seasons, and never had a true home—they became warriors, employed by the kingdoms, inhabiting a horseback, traveling version of the right life."

Think back to our discussion of the farmer and cowboy figures. Clearly, the origins of these archetypes are very old. What qualities cause people to choose one kind of life over the other? What does Kittredge mean by "the right life"?

THE POST-WESTERN WESTERN

In the last few years, there has been much discussion among scholars and critics as to whether the Western is a moribund art form or is already dead. One can make an excellent case that the traditional Western is truly finished; on the other hand, one can present an equally strong argument that this genre is not dead at all, only transformed into the Post-Western Western. The nature of that change is the focus of this chapter.

Clearly, the version of history taught for many years in this country was warped and propagandistic. Beginning in the 1960s, the New Historicism was and is a movement designed to create a recounting of the American past, more accurate, inclusive, and less jingoistic than previous versions which focused primarily on the white male. The New Historicism reversed that pattern by exploring (and very often extolling) the experiences of minorities and women while simultaneously either devaluing the contributions of white males or in many cases, blaming them wholesale for the injustices and damage to the environment that are part of the American story. Often, the revisionists merely created a new kind of propaganda.

However, as so often happens, the rational, less ideological middle ground is where the truth is most likely to be found, and the Western has begun to reflect this notion by retaining the outward look of the genre while reshaping the hero and (now thankfully, I can say) the heroine. The mythology that presented us with larger-than-life heroes is being transformed, and the result is what Patricia Nelson Limerick calls the "sustainable hero" (212) in her essay "Believing in the American West." To Limerick, "sustainability in a hero means, very concretely, providing inspiration that sustains the spirit and the soul" (212). Instead of invincible heroes, we have real people who "[do] the right thing *some of the time*—people practicing heroism at a level that we actually aspire to match" (212).

Limerick also writes:

> The old heroes are a pretty battered and discredited lot. . . . The examples they provide often affirm the wrong faith entirely—the faith in guns or violence—or serve solely as individual examples of courage and determination, attached to no particular principle. Driven by . . . conquest and domination, or purely by the goal of personal fortune-seeking, the old heroes are looking pretty tired—depleted, exhausted, and ready for retirement. (212)

Limerick is largely correct. In retrospect, our old heroes did not always reflect the most admirable of values, and it is true that the parameters of American Heroic Mythology should be expanded to include women and minorities. The Western is not dead; it is simply finding a new voice with which to tell stories not shared before. It is, like all great art, concerned with an accurate reflection of human existence and national experience. Writing in the November/December issue of *True West*, Yardena Rand asserts in her essay "Stark Visions of Frontier History":

> The most controversial Westerns of 2005, *Deadwood, Into the West*, and *Brokeback Mountain*, may make some viewers uncomfortable, but they are pushing the edge of the genre, forcing audiences out of the comfort zone of a man on horseback sacrificing for the good of the community into the realm of true human existence that is never black and white, but always various shades of gray. (72)

This section of the text is dedicated to analyzing the Post-Western Western, seeking understanding of how the Western has adapted to a Post Viet Nam War and Post Watergate America in which John Wayne was an anachronism and replaced by the alienated man or the outsider. Today, the Post-Western Western reflects an emphasis on heroic individuals fighting not in defense of the community but very well in opposition to the corrupt institutions of civil life. Untraditional Westerns (which are rapidly becoming the norm) also acknowledge the increased participation of minorities and women in American Culture, making room in its version of American Heroic Mythology for people traditionally excluded. Finally, the Post-Western Western is more likely to be historically accurate and unwilling to whitewash its narrative; this welcome trend is especially obvious in the way the New Westerns treat Native American Culture.

These motifs are illuminated in "Variations on a Theme by Crèvecoeur" by Wallace Stegner and in "The American West and the Burden of Belief" by N. Scott Momaday. Stegner deconstructs the mythological cowboy as we have known him, and Momaday helps us to make sense of the past and to put it into today's context. Also included are two essays that delve into the movies *Unforgiven, Ride with the Devil, The Quick and the Dead, The Missing,* and *Lone Star.* These analyses will help us to evaluate the ways in which Westerns reflect changes in American Culture, especially when we compare these New Westerns with the more traditional ones discussed in the previous section. Study questions on *Unforgiven* will help us focus our examination of the Post-Western Western and give insight into how profoundly the Western genre has changed while retaining many of its traditional markings.

Variations on a Theme
by Crèvecoeur

W. Stegner

There are many kinds of wildernesses, Aldo Leopold wrote in *A Sand County Almanac,* and each kind forces on people a different set of adaptations and creates a different pattern of life, custom, and belief. These patterns we call cultures.

By that criterion, the West should have a different cultural look from other American regions, and within the regional culture there should be discernible a half dozen subcultures stemming from our adaptations to shortgrass plains, alpine mountains, slickrock canyons, volcanic scablands, and both high and low deserts.

But cultural differentiation takes a long time, and happens most completely in isolation and to homogeneous peoples, as it happened to the Paiutes. The West has had neither time nor isolation nor homogeneity of race and occupation. Change, both homegrown and imported, has overtaken time, time and again. We have to adapt not only to our changed physical environment but to our own adaptations, and sometimes we have to backtrack from our own mistakes.

Cultures evolving within heterogeneous populations do not grow steadily from definable quality to definable quality. Not only is their development complicated by class, caste, and social mobility, but they undergo simultaneous processes of erosion and deposition. They start from something, not from nothing. Habits and attitudes that have come to us embedded in our inherited culture, especially our inherited language, come incorporated in everything from nursery rhymes to laws and prayers, and they often have the durability of flint pebbles in puddingstone. No matter how completely their old matrix is dissolved, they remain intact, and are deposited almost unchanged in the strata of the new culture.

The population that for the eleven public lands, states and territories was four million in 1900 was forty-five million in 1984, with at least a couple of million more, and perhaps twice that many, who weren't counted and didn't want to be. Many of those forty-five or forty-seven or forty-nine million came yesterday, since the end of World War II. They have not adapted, in the cultural sense, very completely. Some of them are living anonymously in the Spanish-speaking barrios of San Diego, El Paso, Los Angeles, San Jose, where the Immigration Service can't find them. Some are experimenting with quick life-styles in the cultural confusion of western cities. Some are reading *Sunset Magazine* to find out what they should become. Some think they already know, from the movies and TV.

Being a Westerner is not simple. If you live, say, in Los Angeles, you live in the second-largest city in the nation, urban as far as the eye can see in every direction except west. There is, or was in 1980—the chances would be somewhat greater now—a 6.6 percent chance that you are Asian, a 16.7 percent chance that you are black, and a 27 percent chance that you are Hispanic. You have only a 48 percent chance of being a non-Hispanic white.

This means that instead of being suitable for casting in the cowboy and pioneer roles familiar from the mythic and movie West, you may be one of those "Chinks" or "Spics" or "Greasers" for whom the legendary West had a violent contempt. You'd like to be a hero, and you may adopt the costume and attitudes you admire, but your color or language or the slant of your eyes tells you that you are one of the kind once scheduled to be a villain or a victim, and your current status as second-class citizen confirms this view. You're part of a subculture envious of or hostile to the dominant one.

This ethic and cultural confusion exists not only in Lost Angeles but in varying proportions in every western city and many western towns. Much of the adaptation that is going on is adaptation to an uncertain reality or to a reality whose past and present do not match. The western culture and western character with which it is easiest to identify exist largely in the West of make-believe, where they can be kept simple.

———

As invaders, we were rarely, or only temporarily, dependent on the materials, foods, or ideas of the regions we pioneered. The champagne and oysters that cheered midnight suppers during San Francisco's Gold Rush period were not local, nor was the taste that demanded them. The dominant white culture was always aware of its origins; it brought its origins with it across the plains or around the Horn, and it kept in touch with them.

The Spanish of New Mexico, who also brought their origins with them, are in other ways an exception. Settled at the end of the sixteenth century, before Jamestown and Quebec and well before Massachusetts Bay Colony, New Mexico existed in isolation, dependent largely on itself, until the newer Americans forcibly took it over in 1846; and during those two and a half centuries it had a high Indian culture close at hand to teach it how to live with the country. Culturally, the Spanish Southwest is an island, adapted in its own ways, in many ways alien.

By contrast, the Anglo-American West, barely breached until the middle of the nineteenth century, was opened during a time of rapid communication. It was linked with the world by ship, rail, and telegraph before the end of the 1860s, and the isolation of even its brief, explosive outposts, its Alder Gulches and Cripple Creeks, was anything but total. Excited travelers reported the West in words to match its mountains; it was viewed in Currier and Ives prints drawn by enthusiasts who had never been there except in imagination. The outside never got over its heightened and romantic notion of the West. The West never got over its heightened and romantic notion of itself.

The pronounced differences that some people see between the West and other parts of America need to examined. Except as they involve Spanish or Indian cultures, they could be mainly illusory, the result of the tendency to see the West in its mythic enlargement rather than as it is, and of the corollary tendency to take our cures from myths in the effort to enhance our lives. Life does sometimes copy art. Not only drugstore cowboys and street-corner Kit Carsons succumb. Plenty of authentic ranch hands have read pulp Westerns in the shade of the bunkhouse and got up walking, talking, and thinking like Buck Duane or Hopalong Cassidy.

———

No matter what kind of wilderness it developed in, every part of the real West was a melting-pot mixture of people from everywhere, operating under the standard American drives of restlessness, aggressiveness, and great expectations, and with the standard American freedom that often crossed the line into violence. It was supposed to be a democracy, and at least in the sense that it was often every man for himself, it was. Though some of its phases—the fur trade, the gold rushes, the open range cattle industry—lasted hardly longer than the blink of an eye, other phases—logging, irrigation farming, the stock farm with cattle or sheep—have lasted by now for a century or more, and have formed the basis for a number of relatively stable communities with some of the attributes of the place, some identity as subcultures of the prevailing postfrontier culture of America. If Turner's thesis is applicable beyond the 98th meridian, then the West ought to be, with minor local variations, America only more so.

Actually it is and it isn't. It would take fast footwork to dance the society based on big reclamation projects into a democracy. Even the cattle kingdom from which we derive our most individualistic and independent folk hero was never a democracy as the Middle West, say, was a democracy. The real-life cattle baron was and is about as democratic as a feudal baron. The cowboy in practice was and is an overworked, underpaid hireling, almost as homeless and dispossessed as a modern crop worker, and his fabled independence was and is chiefly the privilege of quitting his job in order to go looking for another just as bad. Some went outside the law. There is a discrepancy between the real conditions of the West, which even among outlaws enforced cooperation and group effort, and the folklore of the West, which celebrated the dissidence of dissent, the most outrageous independence.

The dynamics of contemporary adaptation work ambiguously. The best imitators of frontier individualism these days are probably Silicon Valley and conglomerate executives, whose entrepreneurial attributes are not greatly different from those of an old-time cattle baron. Little people must salve with daydreams and fantasy the wounds of living. Some may imagine themselves becoming captains of industry, garage inventors whose inventions grow into Fortune 500 companies overnight; but I think that more of them are likely to cuddle up to a culture hero independent of the system and even opposed to it—a culture hero given them by Owen Wister, an eastern snob who saw in the common cowherd the lineaments of Lancelot. Chivalry, or the daydream of it, is at least as common among daydreamers as among entrepreneurs.

Physically, the West could only be itself. Its scale, its colors, its landforms, its plants and animals, tell a traveler what country he is in, and a native that he is at home. Even western cities own most of their distinctiveness to their physical setting. Albuquerque with its mud-colored houses spreading like clay banks along the valley of the Rio Grande could only be New Mexico. Denver's ringworm suburbs on the apron of the Front Range could only be boom-time Colorado. Salt Lake City bracing back against the Wasatch and looking out toward the dead sea and the barren ranges could only be the Great Basin.

But is anything except their setting distinctive? The people in them live on streets named Main and State, Elm and Poplar, First and Second, like Americans elsewhere. They eat the same Wheaties and Wonder Bread and Big Macs, watch the same ball games and soaps and suffer from the same domestic crises and industrial blights, join the same health clubs and neighborhood protective associations, and in general behave and misbehave much as they would in Omaha or Chicago or East Orange. The homogenizing media have certainly been at work on them, perhaps with more effect than the arid spaciousness of the region itself, and while making them more like everybody else have also given them misleading clues about who they are.

———

"Who is the American, this new man?" Crèvecoeur asked rhetorically in his *Letters from an American Farmer* more than two hundred years ago, and went on to idealize him as the American farmer—industrious, optimistic, upwardly mobile, family-oriented, socially responsible, a new man given new hope in the new world, a lover of both hearth and earth, a builder of communities. He defined him in the terms of a new freedom, emancipated from feudalism, oppression, and poverty, but with no wish to escape society or its responsibilities. Quite the contrary.

Crèvecoeur also sketched, with distaste, another kind of American, a kind he thought would fade away with the raw frontier that had created him. This kind lived alone or with a slattern woman and a litter of kids out in the woods. He had no fixed abode, tilled no ground or tilled it only fitfully, lived by killing, was footloose, uncouth, antisocial, impatient of responsibility and law. The eating of wild meat, Crèvecoeur said, made him ferocious and gloomy. Too much freedom promoted in him the coarse selfishness and readiness to violence.

The pioneer family as Crèvecoeur conceived him has a place in western history, and as the Jeffersonian yeoman he had a prominent place in the mistaken effort that oversettled the West, first by homestead and later by reclamation. Traces of him are to be found in western literature, art, and myth. Sculptors have liked his sturdy figure plodding beside the covered wagon on which ride his poke-bonneted wife and barefoot children. He strides through a lot of WPA murals. The Mormons, farmers in the beginning, idealize him. He has achieved more than life size in such novels of the migration as *The Covered Wagon* and *The Way West*.

But those, as I have already suggested, are novels more of motion than of place, and the emigrants in them are simply farmer-pioneers on their way to new farms. They have not adapted to the West in the slightest degree. They belong where the soul is deep, where the Homestead Act worked, where settlers planted potato peelings in their fireguards and adjourned to build a combination school-church-social hall almost before they had roofs on their shanties. The pioneer farmer is a mid-western, not a western, figure. He is a pedestrian, and in the West, horseman's country even for people who never got on a horse in their lives, pedestrians suffer from the horseman's contempt that seems as old as the Scythians. The farmer's very virtues as responsible husband, father, and home builder are against him as a figure of the imagination. To the fantasizing mind he is dull, the ancestor of the clodhopper, the hayseed, and the hick. I have heard Wyoming ranch hands jeer their relatives from Idaho, not because the relatives were Mormons—so were the ranch hands—but because they were farmers, potato diggers.

It was Crèvecoeur's wild man, the borderer emancipated into total freedom, first in eastern forests and then in the plains and mountains of the West, who really fired our imaginations and still does. We have sanitized him somewhat, but our principal folk hero, in all shapes, good and bad, is essentially antisocial.

In real life, as Boone, Bridger, Jed Smith, Kit Carson, he appeals to us as having lived a life of heroic courage, skill, and self-reliance. Some of his manifestations, such as Wild Bill Hickock and Buffalo Bill Cody, are tainted with outlawry or showmanship, but they remain more than life-size. Even psychopathic killers such as Billy the Kid and Tom Horn throw a long shadow, and some outlaws, such as Butch Cassidy and Harry Longabaugh, have all the engaging imitability of Robin Hood. What charms us in them is partly their daring, skill, and invulnerability, partly their chivalry; but not to be overlooked is their impatience with all restraint, their freedom from the social responsibility that Crèvecoeur admired in his citizen-farmer, and that on occasion bows the shoulders of every man born.

Why should I stand up for civilization? Thoreau asked a lecture audience. Any burgher or churchwarden would stand up for that. Thoreau chose instead to stand up for wildness and the savage heart.

We all know that impulse. When youths run away from home, they don't run away to become farmers. They run away to become romantic isolates, lone riders who slit their eyes against steely distance and loosen the carbine in its scabbard when they see law, or obligation, or even company, approaching.

Lawlessness, like wildness, is attractive, and we conceive the last remaining home of both to be the West. In a folklore predominantly masculine and macho, even women take on the look. Calamity Jane is more familiar to us than Dame Shirley, though Dame Shirley had it all over Jane in brains, and could have matched her in courage, and lived in mining camps every bit as rough as the cow towns and camps that Calamity Jane frequented. But then, Jane grew up in the short grass West, Dame Shirley in Massachusetts.

The attraction of lawlessness did not die with the frontier, either. Look as the survivalist Claude Dallas, who a few years ago killed two Idaho game wardens when they caught him poaching—shot them and then finished them off with a bullet in the back of the head. In that act of unchivalrous violence Dallas was expressing more than an unwillingness to pay a little fine. For months, until he was captured early in 1987, he hid out in the deserts of Idaho and Nevada, protected by people all over the area. Why did they protect him? Because his belated frontiersman style, his total self-reliance and physical competence, his repudiation of any control, appealed to them more than murder repelled them or law enlisted their support.

All this may seem remote from the life of the average Westerner, who lives in a city and is more immediately concerned with taxes, schools, his job, drugs, the World Series, or even disarmament, than with archetypal figures out of folklore. But it is not so remote as it seems. Habits persist. The hoodlums who come to San Francisco to beat up gays are vigilantes, enforcing their prejudices with violence, just as there were miners who used to hunt down Indians and hang Chinese in the Mother Lode, or the ranchers who rode out to exterminate the nesters in Wyoming's Johnson County War.

Habits persist. The hard, aggressive, single-minded energy that according to politicians made America great is demonstrated every day in resource raids and leveraged takeovers by entrepreneurs; and along with that competitive individualism and ruthlessness goes a rejection of any controlling past or tradition. What matters is here, now, the seizable opportunity. "We don't need any history," said one Silicon Valley executive when the Santa Clara Historical Society tried to bring the electronics industry together with the few remaining farmers to discuss what was happening to the valley that only a decade or two ago was the fruit bowl of the world. "What we need is more attention to our computers and the moves of the competition."

We are not so far from our models, real and fictional, as we think. As on a wild river, the water passes, the waves remain. A high degree of mobility, a degree of ruthlessness, a large component of both self-sufficiency and self-righteousness, mark the historical pioneer, the lone-riding folk hero, and the modern businessman intent on opening new industrial frontiers and getting his own in the process. The same qualities inform the extreme individualists who believe that they belong to nothing except what they choose to belong to, those who try on lifestyles as some try on clothes, whose only communal association is with what Robert Bellah calls "life-style enclaves," casual and temporary groupings of the like-minded. One reason why it is so difficult to isolate any definitely western culture is that so many Westerners, like other Americans only more so, shy away from commitment. Mobility of every sort—physical, familial, social, corporate, occupational, religious, sexual—confirms and reinforces the illusion of independence.

Back to the freedom-loving loner, whom we might call Leatherstocking's descendant, as Henry Nash Smith taught us to, if all that tribe were not childless as well as orphaned. In the West, this figure acquired an irresistible costume—the boots, spurs, chaps, and sombrero bequeathed to him by Mexican vaqueros, plus the copper-riveted canvas pants invented for California miners by a peddler named Levi Strauss—but he remained estranged from real time, real place, and any real society or occupation. In fact, it is often organized society, in the shape of a crooked sheriff and his cronies, that this loner confronts and confounds.

The notion of civilization's corruption, the notion that the conscience of an antisocial savage is less calloused than the conscience of society, is of course a bequest from Jean-Jacques Rousseau. The chivalry of the antisocial one, his protectiveness of the weak and oppressed, especially those whom James Fenimore Cooper customarily referred to as "females," is from Cooper, with reinforcement from two later romantics, Frederic Remington and Owen Wister, collaborators in the creation of the knight-errant in chaps.

The hero of Wister's 1902 novel *The Virginian* is gentle-seeming, easygoing, humorous, but when the wicked force him into action he is the very gun of God, better at violence than the wicked are. He is a daydream of glory made flesh. But note that the Virginian not only defeats Trampas in a gunfight as formalized as a fourteenth-century joust, the first of a thousand literary and movie walk-downs, but he also joins the vigilantes and in the name of law and order acts as jury, judge, and hangman for his friend Shorty, who has gone bad and become a rustler.

The Virginian feels sorry about Shorty, but he never questions that the stealing of a few mavericks should be punished by death, any more than Wister questioned the motives of his Wyoming rancher host who led the Johnson County vigilantes against the homesteaders they despised and called rustlers. This culture hero is himself law. Law is whatever he and his companions (and employers) believe (which means law is his and their self-interest). Whatever action he takes is law enforcement. Compare Larry McMurtry's two former Texas Rangers in *Lonesome Dove*. They kill more people than the outlaws in that book put together do, but their killings are *right*. Their lawlessness is justified by the lack of any competing socialized law, and by a supreme confidence in themselves, as if every judgment of theirs could be checked back to Coke and Blackstone, if not to Leviticus.

Critics have noted that in *The Virginian* (and for that matter in most of its successors, though not in *Lonesome Dove*) that are no scenes involving cattle. There is no manure, no punching of postholes or stringing of barbed wire, none of the branding, castrating, dehorning, dipping, and horseshoeing that real cowboys, hired men on horseback, spend their laborious and unromantic lives at. The physical universe is simplified like the moral one. Time is stopped.

The Virginian is the standard American orphan, dislocated from family, church, and place of origin, with an uncertain past identified only by his nickname. With his knightly sense of honor and his capacity to outviolence the violent, he remains an irresistible model for romantic adolescents of any age, and he transfers readily from the cowboy setting to more modern ones. It is only a step from his "when you call me that, smile" to the remark made famous by a recent mayor of Carmel and by the fortieth president of the United States: "Go ahead, make my day."

There are thousands more federal employees in the West than there are cowboys—more bookkeepers, aircraft and electronics workers, auto mechanics, printers, fry cooks. There may be more writers. Nevertheless, when most Americans east of the Missouri—most people in the world—hear the word "West" they think "cowboy." Recently a documentary filmmaker asked me to be a consultant on a film that would finally reveal the true West, without romanticizing or adornment. It was to be done by chronicling the life of a single real-life individual. Guess who he was. A cowboy, and a rodeo cowboy at that—a man who had run away from his home in Indiana at the age of seventeen, worked for a year on a Texas ranch, found the work hard, made his way onto the rodeo circuit, and finally retired with a lot of his vertebrae out of line to an Oklahoma town, where he made silver-mounted saddles and bridles suitable for the Sheriff's Posse in a Frontier Days parade and spun yarns for the wide-eyed local young.

Apart from the fantasy involved, which is absolutely authentic, that show business life is about as typically western as a bullfighter's is typically Spanish. The critics will probably praise the film for its realism.

———

I spend this much time on a mythic figure who has irritated me all my life because I would obviously like to bury him. But I know I can't. He is a faster gun than I am. He is too attractive to the daydreaming imagination. It gets me nowhere to object to the self-righteous, limited, violent code that governs him, or to disparage the novels of Louis L'Amour because they were mass produced with interchangeable parts. Mr. L'Amour sells in the millions, and at times has readers in the White House.

But what can one say, and be sure of, is that even while the cowboy myth romanticizes and falsifies western life, it says something true about western, and hence about American, character.

Western culture and character, hard to define in the first place because they are only half-formed and constantly changing, are further clouded by the mythic stereotype. Why hasn't the stereotype faded away as real cowboys become less and less typical of western life? Because we can't or won't do without it, obviously. But also there is the visible, pervasive fact of western space, which acts as a preservative. Space, itself the product of incorrigible aridity and hence more or less permanent, continues to suggest unrestricted freedom, unlimited opportunity for testings and hero-isms, a continuing need for self-reliance and physical competence. The untrammeled individualist persists partly as a residue of the real and romantic frontiers, but also partly because runaways from more restricted regions keep reimporting him. The stereotype continues to affect romantic Westerners and non-Westerners in romantic ways, but if I am right it also affects real Westerners in real ways.

In the West it is impossible to be unconscious of or indifferent to space. At every city's edge it confronts us as federal lands kept open by aridity and the custodial bureaus; out in the boondocks it engulfs us. And it does contribute to individualism, if only because in that much emptiness people have the dignity of rareness and must do much of what they do without help, and because self-reliance becomes a social imperative, part of a code. Witness the crudely violent code that governed a young Westerner like Norman Maclean, as he reported it in the stories of *A River Runs Through It*. Witness the way in which space haunts the poetry of such western poets as William Stafford, Richard Hugo, Gary Snyder. Witness the lonely, half-attached childhood of a writer such as Ivan Doig. I feel the childhood reported in his *This House of Sky* because it feels so much like my own.

Even in the cities, among the dispossessed migrants of the factories in the fields, space exerts a diluted influence as illusion and reprieve. Westerners live outdoors more than people elsewhere because outdoors is mainly what they've got. For clerks and students, factory workers and mechanics, the outdoors is freedom, just as surely as it is for the folkloric and mythic figures. They don't have to own the outdoors, or get permission, or cut fences, in order to use it. It is public land, partly theirs, and that space is continuing influence on their minds and senses. It encourages a fatal care-lessness and destructiveness because it seems so limitless and because what is every-body's is nobody's responsibility. It also encourages, in some, an impassioned protectiveness: the battlegrounds of the environmental movement lie in the western public lands. Finally, it promotes certain needs, tastes, attitudes, skills. It is those tastes, attitudes, and skills, as well as the prevailing destructiveness and its corrective, love of the land, that relate real Westerners to the myth.

David Rains Wallace, in *The Wilder Shore*, has traced the effect of the California landscape—the several California landscapes from the Pacific shore to the inner deserts—on California writers. From Dana to Didion, the influence has been varied and powerful. It is there in John Muir ecstatically riding a storm in the top of a two-hundred-foot sugar pine; in Mary Austin quietly absorbing wisdom from a Paiute bas-ketmaker; in Jack London's Nietzschean supermen pitting themselves not only against society but against the universe; in Frank Norris's atavistic McTeague, shackled to a corpse that he drags through the 130-degree heat of Death Valley; and in Robinson Jeffers on his stone platform between the stars and the sea, falling in love outward toward space. It is also there in the work of western photographers, notably Ansel Adams, whose grand, manless images are full of the awe men feel in the face of majestic nature. Awe is common in the California tradition. Humility is not.

Similar studies could be made, and undoubtedly will be, of the literature of other parts of the West, and of special groups of writers such as Native Americans who are mainly western. The country lives, still holy, in Scott Momaday's *Way to Rainy Mountain*. It is there like a half-forgotten promise in Leslie Marmon Silko's *Ceremony*, and like a homeland lost to invaders in James Welch's *Winter in the Blood* and Louise Erdrich's *Love Medicine*. It is a domineering presence, as I have already said, in the work of Northwest writers.

Western writing turns out, not surprisingly, to be largely about things that happen outdoors. It often involves characters who show a family resemblance of energetic individualism, great physical competence, stoicism, determination, recklessness, endurance, toughness, rebelliousness, resistance to control. It has, that is, residual qualities of the heroic, as the country in which it takes place has residual qualities of the wilderness frontier.

Those characteristics are not the self-conscious creation of regional patriotism, or the result of imitation of older by younger, or greater by lesser, writers. They are inescapable; western life and space generate them; they are what the faithful mirror shows. When I wrote *The Big Rock Candy Mountain* I was ignorant of almost everything except what I myself had lived, and I had no context for that. By the time I wrote *Wolf Willow*, a dozen years later, and dealt with some of the same experience from another stance, I began to realize that my Bo Mason was a character with relatives throughout western fiction. I could see in him resemblance to Ole Rölvaag's Per Hansa, to Mari Sandoz's Old Jules, to A. B. Guthrie's Boone Caudill, even to the hard-jawed and invulnerable heroes of the myth. But I had not been copying other writers. I had been trying to paint a portrait of my father, and it happened that my father, an observed and particular individual, was also a type—a very western type.

Nothing suggests the separateness of western experience so clearly as the response to it of critics nourished in the Europe-oriented, politicized, sophisticated, and anti-heroic tradition of between-the-wars and post war New York. Edmund Wilson, commenting on Hollywood writers, thought of them as wreathed in sunshine and bougainvillea, "spelling cat for the unlettered"; or as sentimental toughs, the boys in the back room; or as Easterners of talent (Scott Fitzgerald was his prime example) lost to significant achievement and drowning in the La Brea tar pits.

Leslie Fiedler, an exponent of the *Partisan Review* subculture, came west to teach in Missoula in the 1950s and discovered "the Montana face"—strong, grave, silent, bland, untroubled by thought, the face of a man playing a role invented for him two centuries earlier and a continent-and-ocean away by a French romantic philosopher.

Bernard Malamud, making a similar pilgrimage to teach at Oregon State University in Corvallis, found the life of that little college town intolerable, and retreated from it to write it up in the novel *A New Life*. His Gogolian antihero S. Levin, an intellectual, heir to a thousand years of caution, deviousness, spiritual subtlety, and airless city living, was never at home in Corvallis. The faculty he was thrown among were suspiciously open, overfriendly, overhearty, outdoorish. Instead of a commerce in abstract ideas, Levin found among his colleagues a devotion to fly-fishing that simply bewildered him. Grown men!

If he had waited to write his novel until Norman Maclean had written the stories of *A River Runs Through It*, Malamud would have discovered that fly-fishing is not simply an art but a religion, a code of conduct and a language, a way of telling the real from the phony. And if Ivan Doig had written before Leslie Fiedler shook up Missoula by the ears, Fiedler would have had another view of the Montana face. It looks different, depending on whether you encounter it as a bizarre cultural artifact on a Montana railroad platform, or whether you see it as young Ivan Doig saw the face of his dependable, skilled, likable, rootless sheepherder father. Whether, that is, you see it from outside the culture or from inside.

In spite of the testimony of Fiedler and Malamud, if I were advising a documentary filmmaker where he might get the most quintessential West in a fifty-six-minute can, I would steer him away from broken-down rodeo riders, away from the towns of the energy boom, away from the cities, and send him to just such a little city as Missoula or Corvallis, some settlement that has managed against difficulty to make itself into a place and is likely to remain one. It wouldn't hurt at all if this little city had a university in it to keep it in touch with its cultural origins and conscious of its changing cultural present. It would do no harm if an occasional Leslie Fiedler came through to stir up its provincialism and set it to some self-questioning. It wouldn't hurt if some native-born writer, some Doig or Hugo or Maclean or Welch or Kittredge or Raymond Carver, was around to serve as culture hero—the individual who transcends his culture without abandoning it, who leave for a while in search of opportunity and enlargement but never forgets where he left his heart.

It is in places like these, and through individuals like these, that the West will realize itself, if it ever does: these towns and cities still close to the earth, intimate and interdependent in their shared community, shared optimism, and shared memory. These are the seedbeds of an emergent western culture. They are likely to be there when the agribusiness fields have turned to alkali flats and the dams have silted up, when the waves of overpopulation that have been destroying the West have receded, leaving the stickers to get on with the business of adaptation.

The American West and the Burden of Belief

N. Scott Momaday

I

West of Jemez Pueblo there is a great red mesa, and in the folds of the earth at its base there is a canyon, the dark red walls of which are sheer and shadow stained; they rise vertically, to a remarkable height. You do not suspect that the canyon is there, but you turn a corner and the walls contain you; you look into a corridor of geologic time. When I went into that place I left my horse outside, for there was a strange light and quiet upon the walls, and the shadows closed upon me. I looked up, straight up, to the serpentine strip of the sky. It was clear and deep, like a river running across the top of the world. The sand in which I stood was deep, and I could feel the cold of it through the soles of my shoes. And when I walked out, the light and heat of the day struck me so hard that I nearly fell. On the side of a hill in the plain of the Hissar I saw my horse grazing among sheep. The land inclined into the distance, to the Pamirs, to the Fedchenko Glacier. The river which I had seen near the sun had run out into the endless ether above the Karakoram range and the Plateau of Tibet.

—The Names

When I wrote this passage, some years ago, it did not seem strange to me that two such landscapes as that of northern New Mexico and that of central Asia should become one in the mind's eye and in the confluence of image and imagination. Nor does it seem strange to me now. Even as we look back, the partitions of our experience open and close upon each other; disparate realities coalesce into a single, integrated appearance.

This transformation is perhaps the essence of art and literature. Certainly it is the soul of drama, and historically it is how we have seen the American West. Our human tendency is to concentrate the world upon a stage. We construct proscenium arches and frames in order to contain the thing that is larger than our comprehension, the plane of boundless possibility, that which reaches almost beyond wonder. Sometimes the process of concentration results in something like a burden of belief, a kind of ambiguous exaggeration, as in the paintings of Albert Bierstadt, say, or in the photographs of Ansel Adams, in which an artful grandeur seems superimposed upon a grandeur that is innate. Or music comes to mind, a music that seems to pervade the vast landscape and emanate from it, not the music of wind and rain and birds and beasts, but Virgil Thomson's "The Plow That Broke the Plains," or Aaron Copland's "Rodeo," or perhaps the sound track from *The Alamo* or *She Wore a Yellow Ribbon*. We are speaking of overlays, impositions, a kind of narcissism that locates us within our own field of vision. But if this is a distorted view of the West, it is nonetheless a view that fascinates us.

And more often than not the fascination consists in peril. In *My Life on the Plains*, George Armstrong Custer describes a strange sight:

> I have seen a train of government wagons with white canvas covers moving through a mirage which, by elevating the wagons to treble their height and magnifying the size of the covers, presented the appearance of a line of large sailing vessels under full sail, while the usual appearance of the mirage gave a correct likeness of an immense lake or sea. Sometimes the mirage has been the cause of frightful suffering and death by its deceptive appearance.

He goes on to tell of emigrants to California and Oregon who, suffering terrible thirst, were deflected from their route by a mirage, "like an *ignis fatuus*," and so perished. Their graves are strewn far and wide over the prairie.

This equation of wonder and peril is for Custer a kind of exhilaration, as indeed it is for most of those adventurers who journeyed westward, and even for those who did not, who escaped into the Wild West show or the dime novel.

For the European who came from a community of congestion and confinement, the West was beyond dreaming; it must have inspired him to formulate an idea of the infinite. There he could walk through geologic time; he could see into eternity. He was surely bewildered, wary, afraid. The landscape was anomalously beautiful and hostile. It was desolate and unforgiving, and yet it was a world of paradisal possibility. Above all, it was wild, definitively wild. And it was inhabited by a people who were to him altogether alien and inscrutable, who were essentially dangerous and deceptive, often invisible, who were savage and unholy—and who were perfectly at home.

This is a crucial point, then: the West was occupied. It was the home of peoples who had come upon the North American continent many thousands of years before, who had in the course of their habitation become the spirit and intelligence of the earth, who had died into the ground again and again and so made it sacred. Those Europeans who ventured into the West must have seen themselves in some wise as latecomers and intruders. In spite of their narcissism, some aspect of their intrusion must have occurred to them as sacrilege, for they were in the unfortunate position of robbing the native peoples of their homeland and the land of its spiritual resources.

By virtue of their culture and history—a culture of acquisition and a history of conquest—they were peculiarly prepared to commit sacrilege, the theft of the sacred.

Even the Indians succumbed to the kind of narcissism the Europeans brought to bear on the primeval landscape, the imposition of a belief—essentially alien to both the land and the peoples who inhabited it—that would locate them once again within their own field of vision. For the Indian, the mirage of the ghost dance—to which the concepts of a messiah and immortality, both foreign, European imports, were central—was surely, an *ignis fatuus,* and the cause of frightful suffering and death.

II

George Armstrong Custer had an eye to the country of the Great Plains, and especially, to those of its features that constituted a "deceptive appearance." As he stealthily approached Black Kettle's camp on the Washita River, where he was to win his principal acclaim as an Indian fighter, he and his men caught sight of a strange thing. At the first sign of dawn there appeared a bright light ascending slowly from the skyline. Custer describes it sharply, even eloquently:

> Slowly and majestically it continued to rise above the crest of the hill, first appearing as a small brilliant flaming globe of bright golden hue. As it ascended still higher it seemed to increase in size, to move more slowly, while its colors rapidly changed from one to the other, exhibiting in turn the most beautiful combinations of prismatic tints.

Custer and his men took it to be a rocket, some sort of signal, and they assumed that their presence had been detected by the Indians. Here again is the equation of fascination and peril. But at last the reality is discovered:

> Rising above the mystifying influences of the atmosphere, that which had appeared so suddenly before us and excited our greatest apprehensions developed into the brightest and most beautiful of morning stars.

In the ensuing raid upon Black Kettle's camp, Custer and his troopers, charging to the strains of "Garry Owen," killed 103 Cheyenne, including Black Kettle and his wife. Ninety-two of the slain Cheyenne were women, children, and old men. Fifty-three women and children were captured. Custer's casualties totaled one officer killed, one officer severely and two more slightly wounded, and eleven cavalrymen wounded. After the fighting, Custer ordered the herd of Indian ponies slain; the herd numbered 875 animals. "We did not need the ponies, while the Indians did," he wrote.

In the matter of killing women and children, Custer's exculpatory rhetoric seems lame, far beneath his poetic descriptions of mirages and the break of day:

Before engaging in the fight orders had been given to prevent the killing of any but the fighting strength of the village; but in a struggle of this character it is impossible at all times to discriminate, particularly when, in a hand-to-hand conflict such as the one the troops were then engaged in the squaws are as dangerous adversaries as the warriors, while Indian boys between ten and fifteen years of age were found as expert and determined in the use of the pistol and bow and arrow as the older warriors.

After the fighting, too, Black Kettle's sister, Mah-wis-sa, implored Custer to leave the Cheyenne in peace. Custer reports that she approached him with a young woman, perhaps seventeen years old, and placed the girl's hand in his. Then she proceeded to speak solemnly in her own language, words that Custer took to be a kind of benediction, with appropriate manners and gestures. When the formalities seemed to come to a close, Mah-wis-sa looked reverently to the skies and at the same time drew her hands slowly down over the faces of Custer and the girl. At this point Custer was moved to ask Romeo, his interpreter, what was going on. Romeo replied that Custer and the young woman had just been married to each other.

In one version of the story it is said that Mah-wis-sa told Custer that if he ever again made war on the Cheyenne, he would die. When he was killed at the Little Bighorn, Cheyenne women pierced his eardrums with awls, so that he might hear in the afterlife; he had failed to hear the warning given him at the Washita.

In the final paragraph of *My Life on the Plains,* Custer bids farewell to his readers and announces his intention "to visit a region of country as yet unseen by human eyes, except those of the Indian—a country described by the latter as abounding in game of all varieties, rich in scientific interest, and of surpassing beauty in natural scenery." After rumors of gold had made the Black Hills a name known throughout the country, General (then Lieutenant Colonel) George Armstrong Custer led an expedition from Fort Abraham Lincoln into the Black Hills in July and August 1874. The Custer expedition traveled six hundred miles in sixty days. Custer reported proof of gold, but he had an eye to other things as well. He wrote in his diary:

Every step of our march that day was amid flowers of the most exquisite colors and perfume. So luxuriant in growth were they that men plucked them without dismounting from the saddle. . . . It was a strange sight to glance back at the advancing columns of cavalry and behold the men with beautiful bouquets in their hands, while the headgear of the horses was decorated with wreaths of flowers fit to crown a queen of May. Deeming it a most fitting appellation, I named this Floral Valley.

In the evening of that same day, sitting at mess in a meadow, the officers competed to see how many different flowers could be picked by each man without leaving his seat. Seven varieties were gathered so. Some fifty different flowers were blooming in Floral Valley.

Imagine that Custer dreamed that night. In his dream he saw a man approaching on horseback, approaching slowly across a meadow full of wildflowers. The man drew very close and stopped, sitting straight up on the horse, holding Custer fast in his gaze. There could be no doubt that he was a warrior, and fearless, though he flourished no scalps and made no signs of fighting. His unbound hair hung below his waist. His body was painted with hail spots, and a white bolt of lightning ran down one of his cheeks, and on his head he wore the feathers of a red-backed hawk. Except for moccasins and breechcloth he was naked.

"I am George Armstrong Custer," Custer said, "called Yellowhair, called Son of the Morning Star."

"I am Curly," the man said, "called Crazy Horse."

And Custer wept for the nobility and dignity and greatness of the man facing him. And through his tears he perceived the brilliance of the meadow. The wildflowers were innumerable and more beautiful than anything he had ever seen or imagined. And when he thought his heart could bear no more, a thousand butterflies rose up, glancing and darting and floating around him, to spangle the sky, to become prisms of the sun. And he awoke serene and refreshed in his soul.

George Armstrong Custer sees the light upon the meadows of the Plains, but he does not see disaster lurking at the Little Bighorn. He hears the bugles and the band, but he does not hear or heed the warning of the Cheyenne women. All about there is deception; the West is other than it seems.

III

In 1872, William Frederick Cody was awarded the Medal of Honor for his valor in fighting Indians. In 1913, U.S. Army regulations specified that only enlisted men and officers were eligible to receive the Medal of Honor, and Cody's medal was therefore withdrawn and his name removed from the records. In 1916, after deliberation, the army decided to return the medal, having declared that Cody's service to his country was "above and beyond the call of duty."

Ambivalence and ambiguity, like deception, bear upon all definitions of the American West. The real issue of Cody's skill and accomplishment as an Indian fighter is not brought into question in this matter of the Medal of Honor, but it might be. Beyond the countless Indians he "killed" in the arena of the Wild West show, Cody's achievements as an Indian fighter are suspect. Indeed, much of Cody's life is clouded in ambiguity. He claimed that in 1859 he became a pony express rider, but the pony express did not come into being until 1860. Even the sobriquet "Buffalo Bill" belonged to William Mathewson before it belonged to William Frederick Cody.

Buffalo Bill Cody was an icon and an enigma, and he was in some sense his own invention. One of his biographers wrote that he was "a man who was so much more than a western myth." One must doubt it, for the mythic dimension of the American West is an equation much greater than the sum of its parts. It would be more accurate, in this case, to say that the one dissolved into the other, that the man and myth became indivisible. The great fascination and peril of Cody's life was the riddle of who he was. The thing that opposed him, and perhaps betrayed him, was above all else the mirage of his own identity.

If we are to understand the central irony of Buffalo Bill and the Wild West show, we must first understand that William Frederick Cody was an authentic western hero. As a scout, a guide, a marksman, and a buffalo hunter, he was second to none. At a time when horsemanship was at its highest level in America, he was a horseman nearly without peer. He defined the plainsman. The authority of his life on the Plains far surpassed Custer's.

But let us imagine that we are at Omaha. Nebraska, on May 17, 1883, in a crowd of 8,000 people. The spectacle of the "Wild West" unfolds before us. The opening parade is led by a twenty-piece band playing "Garry Owen," perhaps, or "The Girl I Left Behind Me." Then there comes an Indian in full regalia on a paint pony. Next are buffalo, three adults and a calf. Then there is Buffalo Bill, mounted on a fine white horse and resplendent in a great white hat, a fringed buckskin coat, and glossy thigh boots. He stands out in a company of cowboys, Indians, more buffalo, and the Deadwood Stage, drawn by six handsome mules, and the end is brought up by another band, playing "Annie Laurie" or "When Johnny Comes Marching Home." Then we see the acts—the racing of the pony express, exhibitions of shooting, the attack on the Deadwood Stagecoach, and the finale of the great buffalo chase. Buffalo Bill makes a stirring speech, and we are enthralled; the applause is thunderous. But this is only a modest beginning, a mere glimpse of things to come.

What we have in this explosion of color and fanfare is an epic transformation of the American West into a traveling circus and of an American hero into an imitation of himself. Here is a theme with which we have become more than familiar. We have seen the transformation take place numberless times on the stage, on television and movie screens, and on the pages of comic books, dime novels, and literary masterpieces. One function of the American imagination is to reduce the American landscape to size, to fit that great expanse to the confinement of the immigrant mind. It is a way to persist in our cultural being. We photograph ourselves on the rim of Monument Valley or against the wall of the Tetons, and we become our own frame of reference. As long as we can transform the landscape to accommodate our fragile presence, we can be saved. As long as we can see ourselves on the picture plane, we cannot be lost.

Arthur Kopit's play *Indians* is a remarkable treatise on this very subject of transformation. It can and ought to be seen as a tragedy, for its central story is that of Buffalo Bill's fatal passage into myth. He is constrained to translate his real heroism into a false and concentrated reflection of itself. The presence of the Indians is pervasive, but he cannot see them until they are called to his attention.

> BUFFALO BILL: Thank you, thank you! A great show lined up tonight! With all-time favorite Johnny Baker, Texas Jack and his twelve-string guitar, the Dancin' Cavanaughs, Sheriff Brad and the Deadwood Mail Coach, Harry Philamee's Trained Prairie Dogs, the Abilene County Girls' Trick Roping and Lasso Society, Pecos Pete and the—
> VOICE: *Bill.*
> BUFFALO BILL: (Startled.) Hm?
> VOICE: Bring on the Indians.
> BUFFALO BILL: What?
> VOICE: The *Indians.*
> BUFFALO BILL: Ah . . .

Solemnly the Indians appear. In effect they shame Buffalo Bill; they tread upon his conscience. They fascinate and imperil him. By degrees his desperation to justify himself—and by extension the white man's treatment of the Indians in general—grows and becomes a burden too great to bear. In the end he sits trembling while the stage goes completely black. Then all lights up, rodeo music, the glaring and blaring; enter the Rough Riders of the World! Buffalo Bill enters on his white stallion and tours the ring, doffing his hat to the invisible crowd. The Rough Riders exit, the Indians approach, and the lights fade to black again.

At five minutes past noon on January 10, 1917, Buffalo Bill died. Western Union ordered all lines cleared, and, in a state of war, the world was given the news at once. The old scout had passed by. Tributes and condolences came from every quarter, from children, from old soldiers, from heads of state.

In ambivalence and ambiguity, Cody died as he had lived. A week before his death, it was reported that Buffalo Bill had been baptized into the Roman Catholic Church. His wife, Louisa, was, however, said to be an Episcopalian, and his sister Julia, to whom he declared, "Your church suits me," was a Presbyterian. Following his death there was a controversy as to where Cody should be buried. He had often expressed the wish to be buried on Cedar Mountain, Wyoming. Notwithstanding, his final resting place is atop Mount Lookout, above Denver, Colorado, overlooking the urban sprawl.

IV

December 29, 1890

Wounded Knee Creek

In the shine of photographs
are the slain, frozen and black

on a simple field of snow.
They image ceremony:

women and children dancing
old men prancing, making fun.

In autumn there were songs, long
since muted in the blizzard.

In summer the wild buckwheat
shone like fox fur and quillwork,

and dusk guttered on the creek.
Now in serene attitudes

of dance, the dead in glossy
death are drawn in ancient light.

On December 15, 1890, the great Hunkpapa leader Sitting Bull, who had opposed Custer at the Little Bighorn and who had toured for a time with Buffalo Bill and the Wild West show, was killed on the Standing Rock reservation. In a dream he had foreseen his death at the hands of his own people.

Just two weeks later, on the morning of December 29, 1890, on Wounded Knee Creek near the Pine Ridge agency, the Seventh Cavalry of the U.S. Army opened fire on an encampment of Big Foot's band of Miniconjou Sioux. When the shooting ended, Big Foot and most of his people were dead or dying. It has been estimated that nearly 300 of the original 350 men, women, and children in the camp were slain. Twenty-five soldiers were killed and thirty-nine wounded. Sitting Bull is reported to have said, "I am the last Indian." In some sense he was right. During his lifetime the world of the Plains Indians had changed forever. The old roving life of the buffalo hunters was over. A terrible disintegration and demoralization had set in. If the death of Sitting Bull marked the end of an age, Wounded Knee marked the end of a culture.

I did not know then how much was ended. When I look back now from the high hill of my old age, I can still see the butchered women and children lying heaped and scattered all along the crooked gulch as plain as when I saw them with eyes

still young. And I can see that something else died there in the bloody mud, and
was buried in the blizzard. A people's dream died there. It was a beautiful dream.

—Black Elk

In the following days there were further developments. On January 7, 1891, nine
days after the massacre at Wounded Knee, a young Sioux warrior named Plenty
Horses shot and killed a popular army officer, Lieutenant Edward W. Casey, who
wanted to enter the Sioux village at No Water for the purpose of talking peace.
The killing appeared to be unprovoked. Plenty Horses shot Casey in the back at close
quarters.

On January 11, two Sioux families, returning to Pine Ridge from hunting near Bear
Butte, were ambushed by white ranchers, three brothers named Culbertson. Few Tails,
the head of one of the families, was killed, and his wife was severely wounded. Somehow
she made her way in the freezing cold a hundred miles to Pine Ridge. The other
family—a man, his wife, and two children, one an infant—managed to reach the
Rosebud agency two weeks later. This wife, too, was wounded and weak from the loss
of blood. She survived, but the infant child had died of starvation on the way.

On January 15 the Sioux leaders surrendered and established themselves at Pine
Ridge. The peace for which General Nelson A. Miles had worked so hard was achieved.
The Indians assumed that Plenty Horses would go free, and indeed General Miles
was reluctant to disturb the peace. But there were strong feelings among the soldiers.
Casey had been shot in cold blood while acting in the interest of peace. On February
19, Plenty Horses was quietly arrested and removed from the reservation to Fort
Meade, near Sturgis, South Dakota.

On March 27, General Miles ordered Plenty Horses released to stand trial in the
federal district court at Sioux Falls. Interest ran high, and the courtroom was filled
with onlookers of every description. The Plenty Horses trial was one of the most interesting and unlikely in the history of the West. Eventually the outcome turned upon
a question of perception, of whether or not a state of war existed between the Sioux
and the United States. If Plenty Horses and Casey were belligerents in a state of war,
the defense argued, then the killing could not be considered a criminal offense, subject
to trial in the civil courts.

General Nelson A. Miles was sensitive to this question for two reasons in particular.
First, his rationale for bringing troops upon the scene—and he had amassed the largest
concentration of troops since the Civil War—was predicated upon the existence of
a state of war. When the question was put to him directly he replied, "it was a war.
You do not suppose that I am going to reduce my campaign to a dress-parade affair?"
Second, Miles had to confront the logically related corollary to the defense argument,
that, if no state of war existed, all the soldiers who took part in the Wounded Knee
affair were guilty of murder under the law.

Miles sent a staff officer, Captain Frank D. Baldwin, to testify on behalf of Plenty Horses' defense. This testimony proved critical, and decisive. It is a notable irony that Baldwin and the slain Casey were close friends. Surely one of the principal ironies of American history is that Plenty Horses was very likely to have been the only Indian to benefit in any way from the slaughter at Wounded Knee. Plenty Horses was acquitted. So too—a final irony—were the Culbertson brothers; with Plenty Horses' acquittal, there was neither a logical basis for nor a practical possibility of holding them accountable for the ambush of Few Tails and his party.

We might ponder Plenty Horses at trial, a young man sitting silent under the scrutiny of curious onlookers, braving his fate with apparent indifference. Behind the mask of a warrior was a lost and agonized soul.

As a boy Plenty Horses had been sent to Carlisle Indian School in Pennsylvania, the boarding school founded by Richard Henry Pratt, whose obsession was to "kill the Indian and save the man." Carlisle was the model upon which an extensive system of boarding schools for Indians was based. The boarding schools were prisons in effect, where Indian children were exposed to brutalities, sometimes subtle, sometimes not, in the interest of converting them to the white man's way of life. It was a grand experiment in ethnic cleansing and psychological warfare, and it failed. But it exacted a terrible cost upon the mental, physical, and spiritual health of Indian children.

Plenty Horses was for five years a pupil at Carlisle. Of his experience there he said:

> I found that the education I had received was of no benefit to me. There was no chance to get employment, nothing for me to do whereby I could earn my board and clothes, no opportunity to learn more and remain with the whites. It disheartened me and I went back to live as I had before going to school.

But when Plenty Horses returned to his own people, they did not fully accept him. He had lost touch with the old ways; he had lived among whites, and the association had diminished him. He rejected the white world, but he had been exposed to it, and it had left its mark upon him. And in the process he had been dislodged, uprooted from the Indian world. He could not quite get back to it. His very being had become tentative; he lived in a kind of limbo, a state of confusion, depression, and desperation.

At the trial Plenty Horses was remarkably passive. He said nothing, nor did he give any sign of his feelings. It was as if he were not there. It came later to light that he was convinced beyond any question that he would be hanged. He could not understand what was happening around him. But in a strange way he could appreciate it. Indeed he must have been fascinated. Beneath his inscrutable expression, his heart must have been racing. He was the center of a ritual, a sacrificial victim; the white man must dispose of him according to some design in the white man's universe. This was perhaps a ritual of atonement. The whites would take his life, but in the proper way, according to their notion of propriety and the appropriate. Perhaps they were involving him in their very notion of the sacred. He could only accept what was happening, and only in their terms. With silence, patience, and respect he must await the inevitable.

Plenty Horses said later:

> I am an Indian. Five years I attended Carlisle and was educated in the ways of the white man. . . . I was lonely. I shot the lieutenant so I might make a place for myself among my people. Now I am one of them. I shall be hung and the Indians will bury me as a warrior. They will be proud of me. l am satisfied.

But Plenty Horses was not hanged, nor did he make an acceptable place for himself among his people. He was acquitted. Plenty Horses lived out his life between two worlds, without a place in either.

Perhaps the most tragic aspect of Plenty Horses' plight was his silence, the theft of his language and the theft of meaning itself from his ordeal. At Carlisle he had been made to speak English, and his native Lakota was forbidden, thrown away, to use a term that indicates particular misfortune in the Plains oral tradition, where to be "thrown away" is to be negated, excluded, eliminated. After five years Plenty Horses had not only failed to master the English language, he had lost some critical possession of his native tongue as well. He was therefore crippled in his speech, wounded in his intelligence. In him was a terrible urgency to express himself—his anger and hurt, his sorrow and loneliness. But his voice was broken. In terms of his culture and all it held most sacred, Plenty Horses himself was thrown away.

In order to understand the true nature of Plenty Horses' ordeal—and a central reality in the cultural conflict that has defined the way we historically see the American West—we must first understand something about the nature of words, about the way we live our daily lives in the element of language. For in a profound sense our language determines us; it shapes our most fundamental selves; it establishes our identity and confirms our existence, our human being. Without language we are lost, "thrown away." Without names—language is essentially a system of naming—we cannot truly claim to be.

To think is to talk to oneself. That is to say, language and thought are practically indivisible. But there is complexity in language, and there are many languages. Indeed, there are hundreds of Native American languages on the North American continent alone, many of them in the American West. As there are different languages, there are different ways of thinking. In terms of what we call "worldview," there are common denominators of experience that unify language communities to some extent. Although the Pueblo peoples of the Rio Grande valley speak different languages, their experience of the land in which they live, and have lived for thousands of years, is by and large the same. And their worldview is the same. There are common denominators that unify all Native Americans in certain ways. This much may be said of other peoples, Europeans, for example. But the difference between Native American and European worldviews is vast. And that difference is crucial to the story of the American West. We are talking about different ways of thinking, deeply different ways of looking at the world.

The oral tradition of the American Indian is a highly developed realization of language. In certain ways it is superior to the written tradition. In the oral tradition words are sacred; they are intrinsically powerful and beautiful. By means of words, by the exertion of language upon the unknown, the best of the possible—and indeed the seemingly impossible—is accomplished. Nothing exists beyond the influence of words. Words are the names of Creation. To give one's word is to give oneself, wholly, to place a name, than which nothing is more sacred, in the balance. One stands for his word; his word stands for him. The oral tradition demands the greatest clarity of speech and hearing, the whole strength of memory, and an absolute faith in the efficacy of language. Every word spoken, every word heard, is the utterance of prayer.

Thus, in the oral tradition, language bears the burden of the sacred, the burden of belief. In a written tradition, the place of language is not so certain.

Those European immigrants who ventured into the Wild West were of a written tradition, even the many who were illiterate. Their way of seeing and thinking was determined by the invention of an alphabet, the advent of the printed word, and the manufacture of books. These were great landmarks of civilization, to be sure, but they were also a radical departure from the oral tradition and an understanding of language that was inestimably older and closer to the origin of words. Although the first Europeans venturing into the continent took with them and held dear the Bible, Bunyan, and Shakespeare, their children ultimately could take words for granted, throw them away. Words, multiplied and diluted to inflation, would be preserved on shelves forever. But in this departure was also the dilution of the sacred, and the loss of a crucial connection with the real, that plane of possibility that is always larger than our comprehension. What follows such loss is overlay, imposition, the distorted view of the West of which we have been speaking.

V

My children, when at first I liked the whites,
My children, when at first I liked the whites,
I gave them fruits,
I gave them fruits.

—Arapaho

Restore my voice for me.

—Navajo

The landscape of the American West has to be seen to be believed. And perhaps, conversely, it has to be believed in order to be seen. Here is the confluence of image and imagination. I am a writer and a painter. I am therefore interested in what it is to see, how seeing is accomplished, how the physical eye and the mind's eye are related, how the act of seeing is or can be expressed in art and in language, and how these things are sacred in nature, as I believe them to be.

Belief is the burden of seeing. And language bears the burden of belief rightly. To see into the heart of something is to believe in it. In order to see to this extent, to see and to accomplish belief in the seeing, one must be prepared. The preparation is a spiritual exercise.

In order to be perceived in its true character, the landscape of the American West must be seen in terms of its sacred dimension. "Sacred" and "sacrifice" are related. Something is made sacred by means of sacrifice; that which is sacred is earned. I have a friend who wears on a string around his neck a little leather pouch. In the pouch is a pebble from the creek bed at Wounded Knee. Wounded Knee is sacred ground, for it was purchased with blood. It is the site of a terrible human sacrifice. It is appropriate that my friend should keep the pebble close to the center of his being, that he should see the pebble and beyond the pebble to the battlefield and beyond the battlefield to the living earth.

The history of the West, that is, the written story that begins with the record of European intervention, is informed by tensions that arise from a failure to see the West in terms of the sacred. The oral history, the oral tradition that came before the written chronicles, is all too often left out of the equation. Yet one of the essential realities of the West is centered in this still living past. When Europeans came into the West they encountered a people who had been there for untold millennia, for whom the landscape was a kind of cathedral of their spiritual life, the home of their deepest being. It had been earned by sacrifice forever. But the encounter was determined by a distortion of image and imagination and language, by a failure to see and believe.

George Armstrong Custer could see and articulate the beauty of the Plains, but he could not see the people who inhabited them. Or he could see them only as enemies, impediments to the glory for which he hungered. He could not understand the sacred ceremony, the significance of the marriage he was offered, and he could not hear the words of warning, nor comprehend their meaning.

Buffalo Bill was a plainsman, but the place he might have held on the picture plane of the West was severely compromised and ultimately lost to the theatrical pretensions of the Wild West show. Neither did he see the Indians. What he saw at last was a self-fabricated reflection of himself and of the landscape in which he had lived a former life.

The vision of Plenty Horses was that of reunion with his traditional world. He could not realize his vision, for his old way of seeing was stolen from him in the white man's school. Ironically, just like the European emigrants, Plenty Horses attempted by his wordless act of violence to persist in his cultural being, to transform the landscape to accommodate his presence once more, to save himself. He could not do so. I believe that he wanted more than anything to pray, to make a prayer in the old way to the old deities of the world to which he was born. But I believe too that he had lost the words, that without language he could no longer bear the burden of belief.

> The sun's beams are running out
> The sun's beams are running out
> The suns yellow rays are running out
> The sun's yellow rays are running out
> We shall live again
> We shall live again

—Comanche

> They will appear—may you behold them!
> They will appear—may you behold them!
> A horse nation will appear.
> A thunder-being nation will appear.
> They will appear, behold!
> They will appear, behold!

—Kiowa

The New West in John Sayles' *Lone Star*

Stephen Cook

When one examines a culture, one must always begin with geography, with *place*. For example, I suspect that California's uniqueness, its location "west of the west," as the poet Robinson Jeffers once wrote, is rooted in the isolation provided by the Great Basin and the Sierra Nevada. The Transcontinental Railroad, consummated in 1869 at Promontory Point, Utah was a jumping off place into the Age of Technology, but the Californio Society, even the remnants of it after the Treaty of Guadelupe Hidalgo and the Gold Rush, was still a world onto itself.

The Treaty of 1848 created a border between Mexico, California, Arizona, New Mexico, and Texas. However, it did not obviate the Native and Hispanic past anymore than contemporary proposals attempting to codify anti-immigrant fears, including the delusional notion that building a wall along the length of the border will somehow offer protection to those of us north of such a barrier. One of the themes in *Lone Star* is the xenophobia present in Border States although the movie focuses on southwest Texas, where the Rio Grande provides a natural separation. The river splits *Lone Star* in two as surely as it divides the land, but it is clear that most boundaries articulated by the script are imposed by the characters on themselves and others. A tragicomedic view of this mind-set occurs when the newly-unveiled plaque posthumously honoring the legendary Sheriff Buddy Deeds is tagged by vandals. Mayor Hollis Pogue looks at the damage and intones: "It happens again, we build a fence around it" (Sayles 34).

However, no obstacle will prevent the alluvial flow of power from the few to the many. Hollis and Fenton, two good ol' boys, know their run is about played-out, just as Sam Deeds, son of the acclaimed lawman and current sheriff, knows he is likely to be the last Anglo to hold that office in the town of Frontera. Sitting in a Mexican restaurant with Sam, Hollis and Fenton lament the power drain from their political machine:

FENTON: Every other damn thing is called after Martin Luther King, they can't let our side have one measly park [containing the plaque of Buddy Deeds set into a stone]?

HOLLIS: King wasn't Mexican, Fenton.

FENTON : Bad enough all the street names are in Spanish—

SAM: They were here first.

FENTON : Then name it after Big Chief Shitinabucket! Whoever that Tonkawa fella was. He had the Mexes beat by centuries—. (11)

Clearly, Sayles has a deft touch, but later in the script, he chooses a broad axe over a scalpel. Sam sips a bottle of beer in a country-western bar while a bartender named Cody euologizes a moribund society.

CODY: Now, I'm just as liberal as the next guy—

SAM: If the next guy's a redneck.

CODY:—but I gotta say I think there's something to this cold climate business. I mean, you go to the beach—what do you do? Drink a few beers, wait for a fish to flop up on the sand. Can't build no civilization that way. You got a hard winter coming, though, you got to plan ahead, and that gives your cerebral cortex a workout.

SAM: Good deal you were born down here, then.

CODY: You joke about it, Sam, but we are in a state of crisis. The lines of demarcation has gotten fuzzy—to run a successful civilization you got to have demarcations between right and wrong, between this one and that one—your daddy understood that. He was like the whatchamacallit—the referee for this damn *menudo* we got down here. He understood how most people don't want their sugar and salt in the same jar. (23–24)

Looking at characters like Cody and Fenton, one might question Sayles' seriousness as a social critic, but he also gives us Charley Wade, who represents the borderline mentality at its most primitive. Wade, living and dead in the script, was one of those "old-fashioned bribes or bullets kind of sheriffs" according to Hollis, who was a deputy under Wade, whom the script reveals as a racist thug and murderer. Wade is emblematic of the Old West, a link to a time when lynchings of Blacks or Mexicans or Chinese were commonplace and often conducted by law officers like the Texas Rangers, sworn to protect the very people they murdered.

Decency ultimately prevails, but in an Old West way, as Hollis shoots Wade in order to prevent him from murdering Otis Payne, a young Black man with the insolence to run an illegal gambling operation without cutting Wade in. Wade's body is buried in a location known only to three people, and the Old West gives way to the New West when Buddy Deeds takes over for Wade and builds a political machine incorporating the good ol' boy system yet actively making overtures to minorities.

Certainly, Deeds' actions are in keeping with demographic changes, which reveal the growing political power of those previously excluded from the good ol' boys club, in particular, the influence of Latinos. For example, in California, during the first quarter of this century, Latinos will achieve majority status. Texas will not be far behind, and *Lone Star* reflects this phenomenon in the characters of Ray Martinez and Jorge Guerra, who are next in line for sheriff and mayor, respectively. As Ray succinctly puts it, "We pretty much running things now. Our good day has *come*" (29).

The fictional town of Frontera is aptly named by Sayles, for here in the West, the geographical frontier is gone, but the social one lies ahead. Only since 1948, with Truman's desegregation of the armed forces, has this country made a sustained commitment to inclusion and legitimate representation, and the Border States, primarily Texas and California, are the main testing grounds for the development of social capital derived from a multicultural society. It is not an exaggeration to say the Republic is at stake. The only alternative is tribalism presided over by a vacuous popular culture, one exploited by demogogues.

It is also quite true that this factionalism is expressed not only in the Crips, Bloods, Mexican Mafia, or the Aryan Brotherhood, but also in the opulence of Lincoln Town Cars gliding past the guard outposts of gated communities. Frontera is a microcosm of the West, where the citizens live together, often uneasily, yet are beginning to agree on certain basic goals, for example the importance of education or the need to be safe from criminal activity. Groups seeking to achieve consensual ends often draw support from a variety of ethnicities, creating movement from an overweening loyalty to one's racial group to an identity largely rooted in ideas that express our hopes for ourselves, but especially our children.

Colonel Delmore Payne is an example of what I call the New American. Keenly aware of his roots, his boyhood of second-class status in Frontera, he is a proud man, a true war hero, who has accepted command of the local Army post. Payne is a contemporary Buffalo Soldier, adhering to a code of conduct and loyal to a country he believes is essentially just. However, he is no fool or an Uncle Tom, and this truth becomes clear in a scene when he confronts Athena, a private who has been nabbed in a surprise drug test. She is at a crossroads; she can stay in the Army under certain conditions, or she can slip into the Houston ghetto from which she came. Colonel Payne gently questions Athena about why she is in the Army at all. She answers honestly after a moment of hesitation, "Outside it's . . . such a mess . . . it's . . ." (40). Athena is stuck for a noun, so Delmore offers his own word choice, "Chaos" (40). Colonel Payne continues, asking Athena if she has been discriminated against on the post, and she replies, "No, sir. Not at all" (40). Delmore asks one more question, "Any serious problems with your sergeant or your fellow soldiers?" (40). Once more, Athena answers in the negative, and Payne is satisfied. He rises from the desk behind which he has been sitting and stands in front of Athena. "It works like this, private. Every soldier in a war doesn't have to believe in what he's fighting for. Most of them fight just to back up the soldiers in their squad. You try not to get them killed, try not to get them extra duty, try not to embarrass yourself in front of them" (40).

Colonel Payne dismisses Athena at this point, and both exit the encounter in a contemplative mood. Many citizens are like Delmore and Athena, who find daily life a chore, a struggle against negative assumptions expressed daily. The temptation is to retreat to the private, to a group language, to make group-view a self-view, even when it means imposing stereotypes articulated by the group on the self. The Border States, especially the diverse societies of California and Texas, are settings for these personal struggles. The growing numbers of bi-racial and multi-racial children, in particular, are at the center of the dilemma over the need to be true to one's "family" while practicing principles of equality and inclusion. Athena's venture into a larger society is tentative and unsure, but sincere nonetheless. Del has seen more, achieved more, and envisions a place for himself in this country even as he admits to the personal cost of his promotion. A tense conversation between Del and his estranged father Otis reveals that Otis has come to a similar understanding about society as Del considers settling a private score, mulling over the possibility of revenge for his father's abandonment of Del and his mother by making Otis's bar off-limits to the soldiers from the base.

> OTIS: Over the years, this is the one place that's always been there. I loan a little money out, settle some arguments. Got a cot in the back—people get afraid to go home, they can spend the night. There's not enough of us to run anything in this town—the white people are mostly out on the lake now, and the Mexicans hire each other. There's the Holiness Church, and there's Big O's place.
> DEL: And people make their choice—
> OTIS (*Smiles*): A lot of 'em choose both. There's not like a borderline between the good people and the bad people—you're not either on one side or the other—

Del is unconvinced.

> OTIS (*Softly*): I gonna meet that family of yours?
> DEL: Why would you want to do that?
> OTIS: Because I'm your father.

Del is furious and moves to the door.

> DEL: You'll get official notification when I make my decision. (25)

"A lot of 'em choose both," Otis tells Del (and us); it is a range of choices that allows for the building of a many-sided person reflective of a dynamic society predicated on equality and justice. Education is the primary tool for social architects. When it is not in the hands of pedagogues, it is a powerful antidote to separatism and the mendacious mythologies that support its various forms. Above all, curriculum must be honest and inclusive. Battles over textbooks are one hallmark of this search for a mirror that reflects truthfully. Sayles offers yet another tragicomedic scene as we view one such school board meeting in which Pilar Cruz, a teacher at Frontera's high school, defends her class content.

Anglo parents, unaware of the shortcomings of the history they have been taught, accuse her of teaching propaganda containing a pro-Mexican bias, but Pilar is resolute. She says, "There's no reason to be so threatened by this. . . . I've only been trying to get across some of the complexity of our situation down here—cultures coming together in both positive and negative ways. . . ."

An Anglo mother replies, "If you mean like music and food and all, I have no problem with that . . . but when you start changing who did what to who. . . ."

Here another teacher interrupts, "We're not *changing* anything, we're presenting a more complete picture. . . ."

The Anglo mother interrupts the teacher who interrupted her, "And that's what's got to stop!" (14).

Education should eventually set the historical record straight, and it may also bring us to the bedrock truth that we are family, not just metaphorically, but by blood. This biological reality underlies *Lone Star* the way the soundtrack flows from *Tejano* to Rhythm and Blues to Gospel to Country and back again without any clear boundaries between musical genres. This is because *there are no such boundaries*, and the social analogue becomes the nightmare realization for separatists who must find ways to argue for the impossible and to justify the indefensible.

The character of Mercedes Cruz shows us the emotional and logical disconnect that must occur when one seeks to maintain strict boundaries. When Pilar asks her mother about taking a trip to Mexico, Mercedes replies, "You want to see Mexicans, open your eyes and look around you. We're up to our ears in *them* [my italics]" (23). As she sips a cool drink out on the patio of her expensive home, a group of *mojados* runs across her well-tended lawn, and she immediately calls the Border Patrol. Mercedes appears to have forgotten her heritage and her personal history of having come across the Rio Grande illegally. Perhaps bitterness over the death of her husband Eladio at the hands of Charley Wade for acting as a *coyote* without giving Wade a piece of the action has caused denial to cloud her vision. Mercedes is very successful and powerful in Frontera, but she has paid a terrible psychic price.

Sayles makes family, nuclear and social, the underpinning of his screenplay. Mercedes and Pilar are at odds; Sam has lived his entire life in the shadow of his legendary father (Minnie Bledsoe refers to Sam as Sheriff *Junior*); Del simmers with resentment over Otis's long-ago abandonment of him and his mother; Del and his son Chet struggle over Chet's plans for the future; Pilar, a widow, is mystified by the behavior of her adolescent son Amado. The ebb and flow of these relationships mirror the larger society that often seeks to maintain stratification, but to no avail. The Paynes are Afro-American yet Seminole Indian as well and apparently are descendents of Issac and Adam Payne, two Medal of Honor winners while serving with the Seminole-Negro Indian Scouts in the 1870s. Cliff and Priscilla, who serve together as sergeants on the Army post and who are White and Black respectively, are likely to marry. Finally, in a plot twist at the end of the movie, we discover that lovers Sam and Pilar are half-brother and half-sister. An irony flowing from this situation is that Amado, who despises Anglos, is himself one-quarter Anglo.

Society in Frontera is not unlike a forest whose roots have overlapped and grafted. One may not tear out any tree without damaging the others. The Old West is as dead as Charley Wade. Our mythology need not be buried with him, however; it needs only to be broadened to reflect the West as it was and is. In California and Texas and the Border States, we must acknowledge our Native and Hispanic roots and teach history inclusive and truthful. We must be done with anything that encourages separatism, for it is socially unworkable and morally wrong. The final words of the screenplay are "Forget the Alamo," an admonishment from Sayles delivered through the character of Pilar to begin work on the New West, a place where the past is studied, but not perpetually replayed with its attendant shame, grief, pain, recriminations, or moral superiority attained by virtue of victimization. We can and must visit the past, but we do not have to live there, no, not anymore.

WORKS CITED

Lone Star. Dir. John Sayles. Perf. Chris Cooper, Kris Kristofferson, Matthew McConaughey, Frances McDormand, Joe Morton, and Elizabeth Pena. Castle Rock Entertainment, 1996.

Sayles, John. *Lone Star.* Screenplay reprinted in *Scenario Magazine* Vol. 2, #2, Summer, 1996: 6–49.

West of the Western

Stephen Cook

What exactly is a Post-Western Western? What movies are examples of this new kind of art form? Does it matter that Westerns are changing? Are these changes cause for grief or for celebration?

In general, what the viewer sees on the screen has the physical earmarks of a Western; for example, the setting is the United States west of the Mississippi, or it might be southwestern Canada (primarily Alberta), or the location could well be northern Mexico. The scenery will be harsh yet extraordinarily beautiful, and it will be vast. The openness of the land emphasizes traditional themes in Westerns of mobility (room to move) as well as transformation (the resources necessary for a fresh start and the ability to lose one's personal history), and the landscape provides a grand stage upon which the hero does the work that only he can do.

Traditional themes also remain. Death is present as is struggle. Westerns celebrate masculine strength. Phallic symbols and references to virility are plentiful. The hero's transformation in response to a duty to protect those who cannot fend for themselves still provides the heart of the narrative. The genre continues to preach adherence to a heroic code that supersedes law and social conventions.

However, American culture has undergone enormous changes in the last fifty to sixty years, and the radically different cultural context demands that art stay relevant. Baby Boomers, particularly men, grew up watching television westerns when they provided a large degree of prime time entertainment and the Saturday shows catering to children. Boomers absorbed from shows like *Have Gun Will Travel*, *Wagon Train*, *Cheyenne*, *Bonanza*, and *Gunsmoke* earnest messages about how we conduct ourselves as men and as women, and we learned a moral code that had no gray areas.

However, coming of age during the Viet Nam War and watching Watergate unfold left Boomers suspicious of authority and contemptuous of a heroic mythology that seemed empty at its best and destructive or evil at its worst. Many young Americans felt alienated from social conventions that for so long had provided the underpinning to American culture. The Civil Rights Movement and the rise of Feminism discredited American Heroic Mythology because its central icon had traditionally been the white male. Finally, the rural and pastoral world so often depicted in Westerns seemed at odds with a culture more and more in love with technology.

What has become increasingly clear is, the Western had to change or die. While retaining certain physical trademarks and themes, the genre also began to reflect certain contemporary ideas. The hero has become less cocksure; death is no longer glorious; women and minorities have started appearing and in some instances are taking on leading roles; Native Americans are more accurately and sympathetically shown; finally, historical truth often wins out over a mythology so overblown as to be painful to observe. Certain recent movies demonstrate this analysis particularly well. *Dances with Wolves* is an obvious choice although its role reversals are oh-so-politically correct, causing the movie to sometimes discard logic for genuflection.

However, other Westerns exist that are less a reaction against a discredited mythology and are more a reflection of reality. The preeminent example is the 1992 classic *Unforgiven*. Winner of the Best Picture Oscar, it thoroughly deconstructs the traditional Western. Although it is bloody, the picture does not sanitize violence or justify it through the evocation of a moral code. Death is not glorified. Rather, it haunts the film. A Black actor, Morgan Freeman, plays a central role, yet not once is his skin color alluded to in *Unforgiven*. This refreshing "omission" is a nod to the true American cowboy, who was often Mexican, Indian, Black, or a mixture thereof. The women in *Unforgiven* are whores, true enough, but it is they who ultimately reshape the town of Big Whiskey by putting out contracts on two drovers, one of whom badly disfigures the face of one of the prostitutes with a hunting knife.

Still, it is the character of Will Munny, one of four men who come to town looking to claim the reward, who reveals the greatest reshaping of the traditional hero in Westerns. Munny, once a blind drunk and merciless killer, has reformed because of the influence of his late wife. However, he and his two children have fallen on hard times, and the money calls to him as well as the chance to once again be horseback and free in the company of his old companion Ned Logan (Morgan Freeman). Munny is no heroic figure. His motivations are mercenary although *Unforgiven* implies that he acts out of some concern for the welfare of his children. Still, he is a terrible shot with his pistol, and his horse throws him time after time. He is unshaven, burnt raw by the sun, and nearly dies from fever. While he is ill, nightmares torment him.

Any viewer who believes that Munny and Logan and their third companion the Scholfield Kid are acting heroically and as avengers for the harm done to the cut-up whore is deluded, for the three of them are assassins, nothing more. In fact, the Kid, who is so near-sighted as to be virtually blind, spends much of the first hour of the film puffing up his reputation as a killer and denying that he needs spectacles. However, near the end, he really does claim a victim, actually his first, the cowboy Quick Mike, who is sitting in an outhouse. Quick Mike, the one who wielded the knife against the prostitute and a man as full of bluster as the Kid, dies with his pants around his ankles and begging for his life. The Kid, sickened by what he has done, renounces any claim to the "whores' gold" and leaves a badly-chastened man. Logan, unable to take the life of Davey, who is the second marked cowboy, had already left for home the day before, mystified yet relieved by his inability to kill anymore.

However, Logan is apprehended and dies under the hand of Little Bill Daggett, a brutal sheriff who whips Ned until his heart simply stops under the punishment. Munny rides into Big Whiskey when he gets the news and exacts a terrible revenge for the death of his friend. All of this mayhem takes place in front of W.W. Beauchamp, a hack writer with very romantic notions of the American West. Beauchamp is a brilliant stroke by the screenwriter David Webb Peoples and represents an earlier version of American history, one first captured by Buffalo Bill's Wild West Show and the dime novels. Beauchamp's gullibility is thoroughly obviated by the brutality he witnesses. It is in the character of Beauchamp that viewers most see how *Unforgiven* deconstructs the traditional Western, replacing hero-worship and an uncritical eye with the horror of truth and actual experience.

Other movies since *Unforgiven* have continued transforming the Western, particularly in the ways that minorities and women have begun to be present, often in leading roles, and even more notably in heroic roles. For example, *Ride with the Devil* is a film directed by Ang Lee (who also recently directed *Brokeback Mountain*) showing the savagery during the Civil War between paramilitary groups supporting the South and regular Army troops in Missouri and Kansas, including the infamous butchery of Lawrence, Kansas. The movie is notable for its realism, yet even more telling is its portrait of Daniel Holt, a freedman who stays by the side of his emancipator George Clyde even though doing so requires that Holt fight as a Confederate. Jeffrey Wright offers a remarkable portrait of a man within a historical context who must make difficult moral choices concerning loyalty and still stay alive. One thing is clear: as George Clyde says, Holt is "one nigger I wouldn't try to hitch behind a plow." Not knowing if his mother, whom Clyde did not have enough money to purchase and set free, is alive or dead, he sets out to discover whether she is in "Kansas or Kingdom." One of the final shots of *Ride with the Devil* is of Holt riding off into the horizon, and while this kind of scene is a cliché, it is rare that the figure at the center of the camera's eye is a Black man.

Similarly remarkable is the appearance of women in leading roles. Sharon Stone manages to be sexy and androgynous at the same time in *The Quick and the Dead*. As the character Ellen, she enters a gunslingers' contest so that she may confront John Herod, a man who caused Ellen as a child to inadvertently shoot and kill her father. Herod now rules cruelly over the town in which the contest is being held, and as the duels ensue and as the bodies are carried off, a showdown arrives in which Ellen finds personal redemption and liberates a town in the process. *The Quick and the Dead* uses many of the standard motifs of a Western, but Sam Raimi's baroque directorial style, special effects, and female protagonist give an old genre a new spin.

More recently, *The Missing*, directed by Ron Howard, offers the viewers Cate Blanchett as Magdalena Gilkeson, a tough woman who teams up with her estranged father Samuel Jones, played by Tommy Lee Jones, to reclaim her teenaged daughter from slavers intending to sell the young woman into prostitution in Mexico. Magdalena in some ways is very unlike Ellen, for Magdalena's earthy beauty and homespun clothing are a contrast to Ellen's leather pants, duster, and cleavage-revealing shirt. In fact, the opening scene of *The Missing* is of Magdalena in an outhouse, surely Howard's way of emphasizing that she is a tough frontier woman but not necessarily a heroine of any note. However, circumstances demand that she ride and shoot and kill in defense of her family. An especially brilliant scene is of Maggie encountering and chasing away a coyote that has come into the house and is on the kitchen table. The wild has invaded her domestic life, and she must respond by entreating her father, a man she initially despises, to help her recover her daughter Lily and to engage in a form of spiritual warfare against a brujo, a black magician who means to prevent her from doing just that and to kill them for even trying. Ultimately, it is the brujo who dies as does Samuel, and the closing shot reveals that as Maggie begins the journey home with Lily and with Dot, her younger daughter who has also demonstrated considerable courage, she has traded her more feminine hat with a bow for her father's well-used Stetson.

That image holds more meaning than simply being a personal gesture of making one's peace; the trading of hats signals a change. American women soldiers fight, die and win medals for bravery in Iraq these days, and there is utterly no justification for American Heroic Mythology to exclude women any longer. One who observes American culture might argue that few heroic models exist in this country for women. One might ask, "What does a female hero look like?" Students struggle to describe and to define, but they are working too hard, it seems. Rather, a female hero is a woman doing heroic things, however she may appear and whatever that brave action may be. At the same time, the Western and by extension any other form of American Heroic Mythology must make room for ethnic heroes. This country is too diverse for our art to be limited, and while some traditionalists bemoan the changes in the Western, other more forward-looking fans and artists understand that a new array of images and a vast reservoir of untold stories await those willing to expand the borders of a genre not dead, only in need of change.

THE POST-WESTERN WESTERN

STUDY QUESTIONS

1. How does Wallace Stegner differentiate between the farmer and the cowboy in "Variations on a Theme by Crevecoeur"?
2. Do Americans have a fascination with lawlessness, outlaws, and gangster (or gangsta) culture? Why or why not?
3. How does Stegner regard the mythological Cowboy figure?
4. What does N. Scott Momaday mean when he uses the term "the burden of belief" in "The American West and the Burden of Belief"?
5. Does mythology hinder or help Americans in discovering the truth about this country?
6. Consider two opposing forces in American history, the Native Americans and the settlers who resolutely moved west. What role did dreams and aspirations play in this conflict?
7. What are some similarities and differences between oral and written narratives? What are the advantages and disadvantages of both forms of communication? Which one is more group or community oriented?
8. What are some differences between the Old West and the New West according to the author of "The New West in John Sayles' *Lone Star*"?
9. What is the "New American"? Is Barack Obama an example of the "new American"?
10. When Pilar Cruz says, "Forget the Alamo," what does she mean?
11. What attitude toward boundaries and lines of demarcation does Sayles reveal in *Lone Star*?
12. How did traditional Westerns fall out of step with American culture after the 1950s, according to the author of "West of the Western"?
13. How do recent Westerns reflect changes in American culture?

STUDY QUESTIONS—*UNFORGIVEN* (1992)

1. Focus on Will Munny, and evaluate his character. What admirable qualities does he possess? What despicable qualities does he reveal? Does the movie show Munny as being heroic?
2. How does *Unforgiven* regard death?

3. How does the movie treat women? How are viewers likely to see them?
4. Consider the character of W.W. Beauchamp. Look at the way in which he represents the romantic mythology of the West. How do his views change as the movie progresses?
5. Also, consider the character of English Bob. What are his views of American culture, and why does the writer of the movie have him come to Big Whiskey on July the Fourth? Does *Unforgiven,* in this regard, describe the differences between the Old World of Europe and the New World of America? Why does English Bob use the phrase "infernal distances"? Why does he pronounce Americans as being "savages"? (Think back to Crevecoeur's reference to frontier people as "barbarous.")
6. Describe the character of Ned Logan. Why does the movie never point out that Logan is African-American?
7. What is *Unforgiven*'s view of guilt? Why does Munny say, "We've all got it coming"?
8. Describe the character of Little Bill. How does his portrayal fly in the face of the Western cliché of the brave town marshal?
9. Consider the Scholfield Kid. How does his character change? Why does the screenwriter have the Kid's first (and only) victim be sitting in an outhouse with his pants around his ankles when he meets his end?

SUGGESTED ESSAY TOPICS

1. Watch *Shane*, and compare the characters of Shane and Joe. How are they similar, and how are they different? What are the ways in which *Shane* examines the tension between the communal instincts of the farmer and the individualistic nature of the gunfighter? How do Shane and Joe complement each other?
2. Write a research paper on Claude Dallas. Who is he? Why did he murder two game wardens, and why did so many residents of rural Idaho and Nevada shelter him when he was on the run from the FBI and from local law enforcement?
3. Write a paper on Plenty Horses, the Lakota warrior who killed Lt. Edward Casey shortly after the Wounded Knee Massacre. What were the motivations of Plenty Horses? How does the story of Plenty Horses represent the dilemma of Native Americans since the advent of Europeans?
4. Compare Trinity in *The Matrix* and Maggie in *The Missing*. How are they similar, and how are they different? What attitudes/emotions/ideas are evoked by images of women as warriors and killers?
5. Working individually, in small groups, or as a class, write a plot summary for a Western featuring minority and/or women characters. The movie treatment you write can be a modern Western or can be set in the Old West. Also, keep

in mind that many obscure historical accounts exist that can be dramatized and fleshed out. The key thing is to tell the stories that have been ignored for much too long.

6. Does Ellen, the central protagonist of *The Quick and the Dead* seem torn between being a woman and acting like a man? Are women in the political arena caught in the same dilemma? For help with this question, read Gail Sheehy's article "Hillaryland at War" in the August 2008 issue of *Vanity Fair.* Another article that may be of some help is "Should Women Govern?" by Sandra Tsing Loh in the November 2008 issue of *The Atlantic.* Is Ellen's androgeny similar to Hillary Clinton's situation with some of her advisors insisting she show "testicular fortitude" (Sheehy 77) and others asking her to model the traditional female qualities of kindness, compassion, and emotionality?

The 21st Century Cowboy: From Owen Wister and Teddy Roosevelt to Barack Obama and a Contemporary Progressive Movement

Stephen Cook

"That Damned Cowboy is President of the United States"
—Mark Hanna

One may think that Mark Hanna is speaking about George W. Bush, yet in reality, Hanna, the Karl Rove of his time, was referring to Teddy Roosevelt becoming president after the assassination of William McKinley. Still, Teddy Roosevelt did a better job than Hanna anticipated, so much so that in the recent presidential campaign, John McCain consciously evoked Roosevelt's legacy while McCain's running mate Sarah Palin seemed to be channeling the spirit of another cowboy president, Ronald Reagan, in her populist appeal, frontier ethos, and patriotic fervor.

In this final section of *Realizing Westward*, we examine two connected ideas: Teddy Roosevelt was the first president to link cowboy values to middle class America (and by extension, the country), and those values have traditionally been expressed in the doctrine of American Exceptionalism, a belief in America's unique status, a "city on a hill" as Reagan was fond of saying. Heather Cox Richardson writes of Roosevelt and his muse Owen Wister, author of *The Virginian*, in an excerpt from her book *West of Appomattox: The Reconstruction of America after the Civil War*, while the author/editor of this text analyzes American Exceptionalism.

Both selections are meant to convince even the most skeptical of readers that cowboy values are American ones for better and for worse, even for those readers who hate westerns or say they despise the principles westerns espouse. However, at the heart of the western and at the core of America's national life is a belief in individualism so strong as to be a secular religion, among its adherents even those who disdain American values, for, in the end, Americans are classic liberals in that we are suspicious of the state and its tentacles into our lives. We certainly want government help, but to play off a Stewart Brand idea, it must be *appropriate* support improving the quality of our lives but not telling us how to live them.

As a corollary, Barack Obama must not usher in a European-style, Socialist "Golden Age." As Reagan dismissed the Christian Right, so Obama should ignore the ideologues of the Left to forge a centrist coalition bent on solutions rather than redistribution or retribution visited on members of the Bush Administration. The changes Obama is likely to propose should use as a foundation the middle-class/cowboy values Richardson discusses in her essay. His new progressive movement should be more Teddy Roosevelt than Franklin Roosevelt. Certainly, like FDR, Obama must rebuild infrastructure and create a new economy (featuring green technology), but the overarching imperative is, like TR, to strengthen the middle-class, but *unlike* TR, make this category more available to those excluded as special interests during the more-xenophobic early Twentieth Century. Still, the commonality between TR and Obama must be a belief that what's good for the middle-class is good for the country.

During the recent presidential campaign, Obama supporters were dismayed to discover that their candidate had actually praised Reagan, but as usual, the Left missed the point. What Obama saw in Reagan were not policies to be resurrected but an ethos built of core American qualities: optimism, faith, personal responsibility, work, and patriotism. To the list, let me add fairness, enterprise, self-reliance, individualism, democracy, and a love of freedom—egalitarian values advanced by Jefferson, Jackson, and Lincoln, ones central to a frontier cosmology codified by Frederick Jackson Turner, Buffalo Bill and Owen Wister, principles consciously invoked by Teddy Roosevelt, Ronald Reagan, and unfortunately, George W. Bush. (A difference between the latter and the previous two may be that Roosevelt and Reagan actually rode horses, which makes a point not as much about equitation as authenticity.)

This is not to say that the values enumerated are the exclusive property of the middle class, nor would I argue that the American figures alluded to are sole representatives of such a value system. In addition, I would never assert that the positive qualities mentioned are the only ones America has demonstrated. I can list others: greed, imperialism, arrogance, a need to control, racism, misogyny, and involvement in wars of dubious merit, to name only some.

Still, qualifiers made, I will reiterate: cowboy values are middle class values, and we Americans are centrists. However, I will amend my argument to allow for the imperatives of the time, which require Americans to combine pragmatism, sharpened moral sensibilities, and a raised social and fiscal consciousness, thus creating a true progressive movement with a broad reach and support neither Left nor Right can ever hope to muster. The hope is that Obama will be above politics and apply his considerable intellect to making government actually work, fostering non-partisan coalitions, and modeling a mainstream morality—the center of which will be corporate and personal responsibility—rather than a divisive appeal to the doctrinal codes of religion.

Conversely, the fear is that Obama will simply grow government to an untenable degree, the true third rail of politics, for Americans will always favor the individual over a collective that impoverishes those whom it ought to serve so that it may simply go its bloated way.

So, is Barack Obama a cowboy? To answer this query, I will only suggest that the reader google a picture of Obama in Austin, Texas on 2/23/07 as he put on a cowboy hat handed to him by a supporter. It fits beautifully—but the fear is that the image is but an apparition, smoke and mirrors, a photo-op.

THE COWBOY AS SYMBOL OF THE AMERICAN MIDDLE CLASS

Heather Cox Richardson

The late nineteenth century defined modern America. Fewer than forty years separated the presidency of Roosevelt from the Abraham Lincoln, but it is impossible to imagine the two men exchanging eras. Lincoln took the country into the Civil War to protect the idea that opportunity should be open to any man—no matter his race or background. By the time Roosevelt moved into the White House in 1901, the nation had reunited, but its principles were no longer inclusive. Instead of offering a hand to the poor and disfranchised, government dedicated itself to advancing the interests of a new, economically powerful middle class, one that was largely white and unwilling to include in its ranks people of color, the needy, or other "special interests." As their enthusiastic support for the Spanish-American War demonstrated, Americans entered the twentieth century so secure in the values of middle-class individualism that united them that they believed it was their duty to impose those values beyond their borders. From 1865 to 1901, Lincoln's widespread egalitarian vision evolved into a middle-class American dream.

Postwar struggles over the role of government in society drove the transformation of Lincoln's midcentury vision of opportunity for all into the middle-class imperialism of Roosevelt's era. In Lincoln's time, most northerners believed that the establishment of free labor across the nation would enable every individual to achieve prosperity, so long as government avoided disrupting perceived natural economic laws. The example of men like Andrew Carnegie convinced most northerners that hard work guaranteed success. Tremendous postwar technological innovation and economic growth dramatically improved the standard of living for upwardly mobile Americans, cementing their conviction that the free labor system offered universal prosperity. Electric bulbs lit up cities; ready-made clothing filled new chain stores; refrigerated meats and canned foods were widely distributed; cigarettes became a national fad. Economically secure and increasingly comfortable, rising Americans based their ideal image of national life on the traditional idea of an economically self-sufficient father. To this image they added an ideal domestic wife, whose homebound motherhood could erase the war's profound disruption of family life.

But this ideal image of American society immediately came under siege by advocates for government action to protect interests that were threatened, rather than fostered, by the new economy. Industrialists worried by the booms and busts of the market called for beneficial tariffs and tax laws to protect their businesses. Workers earning between $1.25 and $1.50 for ten hours of work in a factory—$2.30 to $2.80 an hour in today's money—demanded that government establish minimum wages and maximum hours. Poor ex-slaves forced into tenant farming and kept there by white supremacists demanded that the government give them land and protect their civil rights. Women agitated for the right to vote; and western farmers, who felt their economic and cultural power slipping away, called for government to regulate railroads and grain companies. To adherents of a free labor ideal, these calls for government support sounded perilously like an admission that certain groups of Americans did not have the initiative to make their own way in the world.

These pleas had the opposite of the desired effect. Rather than responding to them, mainstream Americans—those vocal and powerful men and women who prospered in the dynamic postwar economy—turned against special interest legislation for those on both ends of the economic spectrum, coming to believe that those who could not succeed on their own were not entitled to measures that would protect their access to economic success. Even worse, they seemed to threaten American society. The special interest legislation they coveted would destroy America's system of individual enterprise by inducing the poor to scurry after government handouts while the taxation necessary to pay for government programs would remove the financial incentive for individual effort. By the time Roosevelt gained the White House, middle-class Americans had found means to silence those they saw as special interests. In the North, new suffrage restrictions kept poor workers from the polls. In the South, new state constitutions took the vote away from African Americans, and white southerners increasingly let lynching provide final solution to the problem of "dangerous" voters. At the same time, national laws sought to break the power of business trusts and their ties to the government.

During the late nineteenth century, opponents of special interest legislation self-consciously coalesced into a middle class, setting aside the idea of opportunity for all in favor of the concept of individualism, personified by the mythologized "self-made man," who pulled himself up by his own bootstraps. This self-made man opposed labor organization, business lobbying, black rights activism, and other special interest agitation. He was independent, hardworking, and opposed to government activism and the taxes that funded it. Regardless of the size of their wallets, Americans who believed they could succeed on their own rallied around this image. Critically, they identified their interests with those of the nation. They believed that what was good for them was good for the country.

Because members of this middle class identified their values with the interests of the country at large, the government could—and did—advance their interests, creating the paradox of a middle class that benefited mightily from government protection while its members espoused self-help and government inaction. At the same time that members of the middle class celebrated individual enterprise, self-reliance, and small government, they promoted certain forms of government action. The need to create taxable property during the war had made them willing to use the government to promote the individual enterprise that lay at the heart of their vision of American life. With fewer and fewer misgivings about government action, they passed a series of laws designed to foster economic growth. After the war, this government activism gradually expanded to government prohibitions on a range of business practices—price fixing, kickbacks, and so on—which threatened the economic security of a developing middle class. In the two decades after 1880, this willingness to use the government to defend middle-class values stretched further to embrace social welfare legislation demanded by women who insisted that they could not fulfill their roles in the home and community without government oversight of the industrial world. In the belief that it nurtured an ideal individualist society, men who would not tolerate the idea of what they saw as redistributive legislation were willing to back the Progressive movement, in which reformers led by middle-class women supported legislation to regulate business and ameliorate the abuses of industrial capitalism.

Even as government's influence expanded, however, mainstream Americans managed to preserve a myth of individual self-reliance and success that was fueled by the rise of a romantic vision of the American West. In the postwar years, southerners and westerners infuriated by the actions of the federal government in their regions began to celebrate the West as the antithesis of the East. Westerners were portrayed as autonomous and even heroic individuals living in a pristine land. Romantic tales of cowboys and of men like Jesse James and Billy the Kid, who, in spite of their outlaw status, represented loyalty, fairness, antimonopoly, and self-government, permitted mainstream Americans to relocate American individualism to the Far West as it disappeared in the East. In this idealized world, independent individuals rose through their own hard—but often enviable—work in a world unfettered by big government.

By 1898, the powerful image of western individualism had come to define the reuniting nation. When Americans launched the terrifically popular Spanish-American War, they were attempting both to bring the country together and to export economic opportunity and free labor society to Cuba. Popular with neither businessmen nor government leaders, the conflict appealed to the American middle class, which saw it as an opportunity to promote individualism abroad while strengthening it at home. Highlighting the role of the heroic westerner in this overseas crusade, newspaper reporters named the troops that easterner-turned-cowboy Theodore Roosevelt led up San Juan Hill the Rough Riders, after the horsemen in Buffalo Bill's Wild West Show. Emerging victorious from the war, America had won an international identity as a land of rugged individualism. By 1901, when Owen Wister's epic western *The Virginian* described the ideal nation, Americans could accept thoroughgoing government intervention in the economy while still embracing the myth of American individualism. When Theodore Roosevelt—to whom *The Virginian* was dedicated—assumed the presidency in 1901, he could use the government to address the inequities of corporate capitalism feeling confident that socialism could never displace individualism.

The broader patterns of reconstruction echo down to our own time. The wrenching conflicts of the years from 1865 to 1901 forged a new national identity that was based on the needs and expectations of a new middle class, and America entered the twentieth century united around a distinctive ideology of individualism. This ideology made no room for those laborers, African Americans, or advocates for other special interests who organized to demand that government protect their access to economic success. Instead, this American worldview promised economic opportunity for upwardly mobile members of the middle class—professionals, farmers, businessmen, shopkeepers, and those on the make—who rejected the idea of collective action for economic success and instead embraced values of hard work and self-reliance. Even today, taxes and how they are spent define the way we approach political questions as Americans struggle to defend the "middle class" that they see as the heart of the nation. Those who support government programs to address the systematic inequities in American society are much less likely to win popular support than those who speak in the language of mainstream individualism, and those who profess concern for the middle class often garner support even when their programs benefit only a particular group.

Americans' dislike of "special interests" controlling government has meant that twentieth-century politics have swung between, on one hand, opposition to businessmen controlling government and, on the other, a dislike of those laborers, immigrants, advocates for women's rights, and minority activists who call for government protection. During the Progressive Era, the Depression, and the sixties and seventies, Americans protested the businessmen who unfairly stacked the economic deck in their own favor through ties to the government. In these eras, Americans created legislation to protect individuals, disdained business leaders, emphasized government corruption, and worked to curb the power of the wealthy. In the twenties, the fifties, and the conservative revolution of the late twentieth century, the pendulum swung the other way, as middle-class Americans argued that the poor refused to work, that calls for women's rights threatened the fabric of society, and that "liberals" calling for legislation to address racial, economic, and gender inequalities were attacking the individualism that made America great.

In the late nineteenth century, the American cowboy came to represent middle-class individualism, and Theodore Roosevelt brought the cowboy image to the White House. Since then, the cowboy has been a powerful talisman for those trying to invoke the idea that they would defend the American individual, especially in the years after the outbreak of the post–World War II cold war between the United States and the USSR. As the United States sought to distinguish its ideology from communism,

Americans turned to the western. In the fifties and sixties westerns ruled the television; it was the era of *The Lone Ranger, Gunsmoke*, and *Bonanza*. By the 1970s, western clothing was worn across the nation; 75 million pairs of Levis sold in 1974. Cowboy hats and boots represented America. Elected president in 1980, Ronald Reagan rose to power with a careful evocation of the western image to represent the American mainstream. Shedding jodhpurs for Levis, Reagan continually invoked the western image and declared his California ranch the heart of his inspiration. "I have always believed that this land was placed here between the two great oceans by some divine plan," he told voters. "It was placed here to be found by a special kind of people—people who have a special love for freedom and who had the courage to uproot themselves and leave hearth and homeland and come to what in the beginning was the most undeveloped wilderness possible." He claimed to be a cowboy president who would reduce the size of the federal government to accomplish the will of true Americans. The cowboy image was an irresistible representation of American freedom, equality, and opportunity.

But the upbeat image of the cowboy obscures the systematic inequality and aggressive foreign policies of American society. Cold war westerns shored up the unpopular Vietnam War, and western antigovernment symbols were deployed in the 1970s to protest racial integration of schools and accommodations. Reagan's promises of fairness and small government meant cuts to social programs, but his administration poured federal money into defense contracts offered to favored businessmen. In addition, much like Wister's Virginian, or like the Wyoming cattlemen on whom the Virginian was patterned, Reagan skirted the law to do what he thought was right. Congressional legislation prohibiting aid to the Nicaraguan Contras fighting the leftist Sandinista government in that country did not stop Reagan's men from making a Wild West decision to spread "American values" overseas.

The western image of the American individualist was the key to the map of the 2004 presidential election. George W. Bush promised to be a cowboy president. He vowed to cut through government red tape, cut taxes, slash budgets, take government out of the hands of special interests, and retain America's standing as God's chosen land, even as he spread liberty and humanity abroad. All of these promises had been the rallying cries of first southerners and westerners, and then mainstream Americans in general in the late nineteenth century. Like those invoking the cowboy image before him, Bush carefully painted a picture of his opponents as a godless band of lazy ne'er-do-wells controlling government to garner tax dollars, while he promised to protect morality, the individual, and the American family. Supporters cheered Bush's rhetoric, but opponents recognized that the positive cowboy imagery obscured administration policies that favored the wealthy, challenged racial gains, and threatened women's rights. The western image also obscured important realities of the Iraq War. Saddam Hussein had no significant connection to the terrorists of 9/11, there were no weapons of mass destruction, and the conflict would pour billions of dollars into the pockets of the businessmen who supported the administration. Opponents greeted with skepticism the idea that America was fighting for freedom in Iraq. In 2004, red state voters who championed American individualism and blue state voters who recognized the limitations of that vision both reflected patterns established over a century ago.

At the turn of the twentieth century, Theodore Roosevelt exploded into national prominence as a man who would bring mainstream equality back to America, endorsing western values of individualism and sweeping away special interests at both ends of the economic spectrum that sucked up taxes from those doing the real work of the country. With Roosevelt, the cowboy came to maturity as the symbol of the nation. But the image of the American cowboy has always had two sides. It contains the great hope of American equality of opportunity, of a world where anyone can rise and where no one has special privileges. But it also contains the deliberate repression of anyone identifying racial, gender, or economic inequalities in society, as well as a dangerously self-righteous expansionism. Both sides of the cowboy represent America; both define our nation.

The story of reconstruction is not simply about the rebuilding of the South after the Civil War. This pivotal era defined modern America as southerners, northerners, and westerners gradually hammered out a national identity that united three regions into a country that could become a world power. Ultimately, the story of reconstruction is about how a middle class formed in America and how its members defined what the nation would stand for, both at home and abroad, for the next century and beyond.

American Exceptionalism

Stephen Cook

American exceptionalism is not a myth, but the meaning of that singularity is certainly open to interpretation. For some, it is reason to celebrate; for others, it is reason to despair and to denigrate the culture we Americans inhabit, a milieu most of us simply live within while not fully understanding it. Still, the simple recognition of the existence of Cowboy Mythology is a strong start to gaining an understanding.

We can begin by considering two epic events that occurred in America in 2003: The United States invaded Iraq, and the Space Shuttle Columbia destructed upon re-entry into the earth's atmosphere. Both occurrences offer us profound truths about this country. In the aftermath of the shuttle tragedy, a handful of scientists and journalists advanced the idea of future spacecraft outfitted with robots rather than people—a perfectly reasonable and workable proposition according to these experts and yet a notion quickly discarded in favor of emotional and poetic arguments for hurling human astronauts into space. Dogs and monkeys didn't cut it in the last century; robots won't in this one. We Americans are a frontier people. Our history makes this point, and our mythology reinforces it by equating astronauts with cowboys or explorers. In our space shuttle crews, we see a talented ensemble blending technological expertise with human sensibilities and frailties, people paradoxically shaped by a collective philosophy emphasizing the individual. Apparently, a goal of NASA is development of the Orion Project, which aims to send a space shuttle mission to the moon. Of course, there are other space programs in the world, but the nation that built the transcontinental railroad only sixty-five years after Lewis and Clark first took measure of that country's vast expanse is most likely to accomplish it. Even those who would pronounce these words jingoistic must acknowledge their truth. Our experience with physical space and more recently our ventures into cyberspace have confirmed Americans as pathfinders. Even the diverse make up of the shuttle crews reflects our willingness to cross over into a social frontier.

Some will argue that the space program is a waste of money better spent on social programs, and other critics will see space exploration as another example of American colonialism, the most currently evident example of which is our disastrous takeover of Iraq. While it may be true the Kurds will benefit (as will Iran and Syria), we Americans are very likely to spend the next generation recouping our loss of diplomatic capital and repaying the staggering debt incurred in fighting the war. I have no doubt the U.S. will repair itself; Iraq's future is much more questionable. I cannot assert that our leaders' motives were pure, but I am willing to make the claim that rank and file supporters of the war believed the evidence offered by the administration and bore the Iraqi people no malice. Certainly, improved access to 14% of the world's oil was part of the ethical calculus, but the Iraqi people would be winners, too, or so the rationalization went. Iraq would be free of Saddam Hussein and his psychotic sons, and a free, democratic Iraq would rise from the ashes. Our client state would be a bulwark against Iran and Syria, and Israel would be safer since Saddam's financial support of the Palestinians would end.

The plan seemed like a win-win, and the incursion would follow the script of our principal folk-drama, the Western. Lack of support around the world did not matter; its absence would only add to the glory attained by the boss cowboy and his faithful sidekick, two heroic figures possessing deadly skills, resolute will, and uncompromising virtue, who would ride into town, take out the corrupt sheriff, and return the town to its grateful citizens. Clearly, formulating foreign policy based on mythology is unwise and dangerous, but the White House got the intelligence *and* the mythology wrong, for the truly virtuous cowboy is *reluctant* to fight and does the work that he alone can do *after the citizens of the town make their desperate pleas.* Finally, there is usually no recompense, no financial reward, not even the possibility of remaining with the ones the cowboy has saved because to accept anything other than an intangible reward compromises the cowboy's motives.

The examples of the space shuttle and the Iraqi War reveal two sides of American exceptionalism, of which our most iconic figure's singularity is emblematic.

Americans can act with autonomy and heroic selflessness, and we can be obstinate and pathetically wrong-headed. Like Hector St. John de Crevecoeur, other nations in the world look at us in wonderment and ask, "Who are these Americans?" and it is a worthwhile question. As this text has made clear, it is a query we Americans must certainly make to ourselves.

Thus, to observers, I would say that we Americans are pragmatic centrists, leaning toward conservatism, but not the discredited ideology of the Neo-Conservatives. Of course, there are bastions of liberalism like the Northeast or the West Coast, hence the Blue States—Red States dichotomy and the so-called cultural warfare accompanying that division. Still, this supposed separation of believers from non-believers (that distinction made according to one's ideology) is only a rough indicator of who we are. To understand American character, look to history and to geography. Look to Manifest Destiny and the values called out by a vast frontier. Americans still revere self-reliance, an expression of which is the prevalence of gun ownership, and individual endeavor (even as we look to increased governmental services). A corollary to this paradox is that as a rule Americans distrust government and believe its primary role is not to provide for the needy as much as it is to guarantee that individuals are free to live their lives with as few restrictions as possible. The kind of socialism we see in Europe is anathema here because of our belief that the acquisition of wealth and prosperity is largely a private matter reflective of a person's character. We may hate the rich, but we also know that they really are different from you and me (and perhaps better). The sheer size of the United States as well as its wealth of natural resources were and still are the foundation upon which rests the gospel of self-advancement. Space allows for mobility and the chance for regeneration. The possibility of re-creation gives rise to optimism, and a material base provides the wherewithal to build an empire if one only has the necessary vision and determination. Of course, many a dreamer has had to settle for an average life, yet anyone reading these words can also probably conjure up the image of someone who began poor or oppressed and succeeded beyond his or her wildest imaginings.

Wealth allows the acquisition of material goods, but there is a cost beyond mere numbers on a sticker, for the pursuit of mammon requires a religious devotion, and in America, while there is something of a wall between church and state, the Good News is that there is no prohibition against the commingling of religion and living large. America is a very religious country, which reinforces the work ethic required to become wealthy (unless one hits it big on the lottery, but that's another kind of American story about luck and opportunity and dreams). The benediction religion offers to advancement on a material plane has as a flip side a willingness to disregard or even punish those who break stride. Not only is there a general neglect of the poor but a willingness to severely punish criminals. According to John Micklethwait, co-author with Adrian Wooldridge of *The Right Nation*, half of Americans believe in Satan, which leads me to conclude Americans are less likely to turn to socio-economic analyses to explain criminal behavior. Rather, crime is seen as a choice (and certainly, to some degree it is), a conscious turning to evil rather than to work and the utilization of opportunity. Long periods of incarceration and capital punishment seem much more appropriate within the framework of this cosmology.

Similarly, Americans tend to regard our international conflicts as contests between good and evil. There should be little doubt that after 9/11, President Bush put our encounter with Islamic terrorism in moral terms rather than secular, and in so doing, articulated a message that resonated with Americans. The surge of post 9/11 patriotism was a product of our grief and shock, yet the outpouring of patriotic fervor was also an offshoot of the ever present hum of nationalism. Micklethwait writes that 80 to 90% of the citizens of this country are proud of being Americans and that this sentiment cuts across the political spectrum. Micklethwait's numbers stand in stark contrast with a general European fear or distrust of nationalism, and they are further indicators of American exceptionalism even among those on the Left who would decry a perception of singularity as jingoistic.

As this anthology points out, American Heroic Mythology has codified American character through its protagonist—a leader and a redeemer, yes, but still a self-reliant loner, possessing a keen moral sense, yet not especially introspective. He (and sometimes she) has a commitment to justice; however, that reckoning usually comes violently at the hands of the cowboy-figure, who will show mercy to the defenseless but nobody else. Finally, there is no room for moral ambiguity—our mythological hero is righteous (in some cases answering a summons from God), and while he or she is likely to say little, what is uttered is never equivocal.

Cowboy mythology is a superb microscope through which one may view American character and see our values and aspirations. I predict that in coming decades we will continue to see ourselves as singular because *we are*, a point Tom Wolfe emphasizes in "Pell-Mell," an essay in the November 2007 issue of *The Atlantic:*

> America remains, as it has been from the very beginning, the freest, most open country in the world, encouraging one and all to compete pell-mell for any great goal that exists and to try any sort of innovation, no matter how far-fetched it may seem, in order to achieve it. It is largely this open invitation to ambition that accounts for America's military and economic supremacy and absolute dominance in science, medicine, technology, and every other intellectual pursuit that can be measured objectively. And it *is* absolute. (62)

However, the ways in which we choose to express our exceptionalism will determine whether we are world leaders capable of finding the balance between mercy and muscle or corrupt, self-righteous, arrogant bullies who must ultimately face a deserved backlash. Fareed Zakaria, writing in the May 12, 2008 issue of *Newsweek* echoes Wolfe's assessment yet also cautions Americans to heed the better angels of our nature:

> . . . America's great—and potentially insurmountable—strength [is that] it remains the most open and flexible society in the world, able to absorb other people, cultures, ideas, goods, and services. The country thrives on the hunger and energy of poor immigrants. Faced with the new technologies of foreign countries, or growing markets overseas, it adapts and adjusts. When you compare this dynamism with the closed and hierarchical nations that were once superpowers, you sense that the United States may not fall into the trap of becoming rich, fat, and lazy. (31)

Zakaria argues that we Americans must remain true to values formed during the American experience, ones transforming the world, a phenomenon he calls "the rise of the rest" (24) as others outside our borders "become consumers, producers, inventors, thinkers, dreamers, and doers" (31). The elevation of others is "because of American ideas and actions" (31) and because "the United States has pushed countries to open their markets, free up their politics, and embrace trade and technology" (31). Still,

Zakaria cautions us against inclinations toward "parochialism" (31) and asks Americans to accept that "America's unimpeded influence will decline" (31) as "other countries grow" (31).

Zakaria offers a reasonable argument that makes a resonant point: America's founding ideas are exceptional indeed, yet they have often been imperfectly applied, and any rational student of American history would most likely affirm the truth of Zakaria's balanced position. The challenge of today (and the great hope) is to find a fresh approach, one that weighs nationalism against internationalism. However, the caveat I must raise is that as we move to a multilateral approach, we do not lose faith in or negotiate away out of guilt our identity and legacy as Americans.

The 21ˢᵗ Century Cowboy: From Owen Wister and Teddy Roosevelt to Barack Obama and a Contemporary Progressive Movement

Study Questions

1. Heather Cox Richardson writes: "The late nineteenth century defined modern America." How so?
2. How would you define "special interests" after reading Richardson's historical overview? Is the term still in use today?
3. What does Richardson mean by "middle-class imperialism"?
4. How did and does a "romantic vision of the American West" reinforce the notion of self-reliance and preach an anti-totalitarian message?
5. What are the social obligations of those who see themselves as self-reliant?
6. What is a proper balance between self-reliance and government help? This is a big question, so try to find a few key generalizations.
7. How would you define "American Exceptionalism"?
8. What do Tom Wolfe and Fareed Zakaria identify as American ideological strengths?
9. Are Americans "pragmatic centrists" as the author of "American Exceptionalism"asserts? If you disagree, how would you define the core philosophy of Americans?
10. What portrait of American character do Mickelthwait and Wooldridge draw? What do you think of their depiction of the American psyche?
11. What proclivities must Americans guard against as we engage in geopolitics? What is a suitable set of criteria for intervention in the affairs of other nations?
12. Does Barack Obama want to strengthen the middle class while making it more inclusive? Or does he want to tax it and redistribute the proceeds to those who have been traditionally excluded? Does he believe that government alone can achieve the latter?

13. The cover of the March 16, 2009 issue of *Fortune* shows Meg Whitman, candidate for governor of California in 2010 posing with her horse. The centerpiece of the magazine is also a photo of Whitman and her horse, with the Pacific Ocean as a backdrop. The portraits are obviously well thought out and designed with an eye to "branding" Whitman. What emotions/ideas/historical allusions are the pictures designed to evoke?

Suggested Essay Questions

1. Write a paper in which you explore the relationship between Owen Wister and Teddy Roosevelt. How did *The Virginian* influence TR's cosmology?

2. How does Heather Cox Richardson show the ideological linkage between Teddy Roosevelt, Ronald Reagan, and George W. Bush? How did they interpret American ideology and its role in geopolitics?

3. What was the role of cowboy mythology in American culture during the Cold War?

4. Americans have a strong sense of national pride—we love our flag, for example, and we often join together to sing the national anthem. Is our overt nationalism a concern? Under what conditions might nationalism devolve into fascism?

5. Some historians argue that a strong historical analogy to the war in Iraq is *not* Viet Nam but the long war in the Philippines, which had as its roots the Spanish American War, begun in 1898. Do a research paper in which you examine the status of the Philippines. Was the war inherited and pursued by Teddy Roosevelt against Filipino insurrectionists ultimately a success, in spite of casualties, allegations of torture, and the disruption of Filipino domestic life? Conversely, was the war in the Philippines a mistake, an immoral exercise in imperial hubris? Finally, speculate on the ultimate success or failure of George W. Bush's cowboy diplomacy/adventurism in Iraq, using your conclusions about the Philippines as a basis for the analysis.